COGNITIVE-BEHAVIOURAL THERAPY

Research, practice and philosophy

Brian Sheldon

ROUTLEDGE

London and New York

First published 1995
by Routledge
11 New Fetter Lane, London EC4P 4EE

Transferred to Digital Printing 2003

Simultaneously published in the USA and Canada
by Routledge
29 West 35th Street, New York, NY 10001

© 1995 Brian Sheldon

Typeset in Garamond by
Michael Mepham, Frome, Somerset.

British Library Cataloguing in Publication Data
A catalogue record for this book is available from the British Library

Library of Congress Cataloging in Publication Data
A catalogue record for this book has been requested

ISBN 0–415–09373–2 (hbk)
ISBN 0–415–09374–0 (pbk)

Printed and bound by Antony Rowe Ltd, Eastbourne

Equal with colleagues in a ring
I sit on each calm evening,
    Enchanted as the flowers
The opening light draws out of hiding
From leaves with all its dove-like pleading
    Its logic and its powers.

That later we, though parted then
May still recall these evenings when
    Fear gave his watch no look;
The lion griefs loped from the shade
And on our knees their muzzles laid,
    And Death put down his book.

W. H. Auden, 'A Summer Night'
(To Geoffrey Hoyland)

To Hugh and Florence Millington
and to my dear Kate,
with love

CONTENTS

FIGURES AND TABLES

FIGURES

TABLES

FIGURES AND TABLES

PREFACE

This new edition of *Behaviour Modification*, with its new title, has been substantially revised and updated. The fact that this is a second edition may set off some inhibiting, cost–benefit calculations among the potential readership who already own *Behaviour Modification* (1982), so I had better explain the changes. Behaviour therapy and applied behavioural psychology have undergone a 'cognitive revolution' during the past decade. Accordingly I felt it necessary to include accounts of the research on which these changes in practice are (largely) based. Here is an authoritative statement of the new position:

> Most of the people who used to consider themselves behavioural therapists now identify themselves as cognitive-behavioural. Also, most people who once considered themselves strictly cognitive practitioners now are willing to take on the cognitive-behavioural label as well. Although many influences have produced these changes, it is pleasing to note that the effect of research has been substantial.
> (Bergin and Garfield 1994:824)

Effectiveness research in social work, and probation too, has shown that the use of cognitive-behavioural methods is strongly associated with positive outcomes. Therefore this new volume has been cautiously adapted to these new trends – 'cautiously' because traditional behavioural methods, despite the 'antibody reactions' they have triggered from time to time in parts of the social work profession, have always worked well. The evidence that the addition of a formal, cognitive component improves results is, as yet, no more than moderately encouraging – but this is a difficult field and we need all the help we can get. *Cognitive-Behavioural Therapy* has been written with the particular challenges of social work in mind but could be read with profit by any member of the helping professions.

The second major set of changes to be accommodated concerns both the way in which, for better or worse, for richer for poorer, social work is now organized, and the new legislation which governs its activities. These developments have been driven largely by political ideology, viz., by a belief that the adoption of commercial principles would do much to improve the efficiency and effectiveness of the personal social services. Despite the fact that some of these 'purchaser–provider' schemes more closely resemble the reinvention of the East German economy, they are a fact of life. Those of us with a concern for developing effective practice by giving attention to the *content* of what is done rather than concentrating exclusively on narrow, quantitative factors have little choice but to accommodate ourselves to these changes and make the most of them. Cognitive-behavioural methods, as we shall see, contain many features which should endear them to case-managers, and so 'catastrophic thinking' about the future of therapeutic social work is arguably more than usually maladaptive and unnecessary.

The last decade has seen a considerable change in our professional fortunes in respect of the amount and the quality of outcome research conducted on social work services. The position is now substantially more optimistic than it was in the early 1980s – not that one would know it from the depressed morale of staff having to cope with regular 'cultural revolutions'. This new volume seeks to focus the attention of practitioners on this a priori question: does social work work? And, if so, what factors are most strongly associated with effectiveness and efficiency?

So much is new, but I have decided to retain certain features of the first edition, I hope for good, rational reasons.

Despite a growing appetite for gladhanding, 'checklist' publications – 'Ten positive steps to effective case-management', etc. – this book still treats its readers as intelligent, critical beings, who are capable of responding to a case – indeed, who *require* a case to be argued with them if they are to consider making demanding changes to their practice in these rather unpropitious circumstances. Thus, although the text retains a concentration on 'how to' issues, and provides many authentic, mainstream case examples, a considerable portion of it is still taken up with 'why' questions derived from philosophy, from psychological theory, and from ethics. This is so because, despite the fact that we shall be reviewing many technical matters together, it is not my intention to persuade social workers to become mere technicians.

As to the level of this text, I would say that it is now rather more intellectually demanding – but then given the challenging nature of our present responsibilities, so is the job.

Nothing in this book is intended to divert the attention of staff away from their practical responsibilities, my long-held belief being that it is this combination of concerns for financial security, adequate housing, access to medical care, social support for vulnerable people, *and* the problems that stem from the person and his or her history, which gives this profession its distinct identity.

I have retained the use of the term *client* throughout this book in preference to faddish alternatives such as 'service user' or 'customer', since I think it better describes the ethical relationship that should exist between ourselves and those we seek to help. Are children in our care, or the people from whom they have been removed, our 'customers'? Can anyone read the phrase 'child care business' without hearing echoes of Dickens's Fagin? Are people who have to be admitted to psychiatric hospital against their will 'using our services' in any meaningful sense? Service users and customers have charters; clients have the right to professional and ethical treatment.

ACKNOWLEDGEMENTS

Heartfelt thanks are due to Geraldine Macdonald, colleague, co-researcher and regular source of inspiration, for her help in the preparation of this book. Thanks also to Sheila Sweet for her permissions-chasing work. Gratitude is hereby generally extended to the various authors and publishers who have kindly allowed me to use their material – individual thanks are recorded beneath each item. Finally, it has been my privilege over the years to work alongside a number of gifted students, some of whose labour is contained in the case examples used throughout the book, and without whom many of these clients would have received little more than routine 'support'.

1

BEHAVIOUR THERAPY IN A COLD CLIMATE

During twenty years as a behaviour therapist and teacher of behavioural psychology, the prospect that this well-researched and broadly applicable approach might leap to prominence among the therapeutic methods employed by social workers has always seemed tantalizingly close. However, the plain fact is that although each generation of students produces a handful of enthusiasts, and the journals and publication lists now contain much more of this work than hitherto, these methods are still not as widely used as empirical research suggests that they should be. This said, proponents have had another, more general influence on the profession. For example, it is now taken for granted that social workers should plan their interventions, look at contemporary behaviour and what influences it as well as at the historical origins of their clients' difficulties, that they should set clear and specific goals for themselves, and that they should evaluate their influence as objectively as possible. Behaviour therapy has not been the only source of such ideas, but it has undoubtedly been the major one (Reid and Hanrahan 1980). This is not to be sneezed at, but the more specific aims of equipping all social workers with the knowledge and skills necessary for effective behavioural practice, and for this work to become routine in appropriate cases – as it is to a much greater degree in the United States – have not been achieved. We are still a school. This is regrettable, not least because where social workers do make use of these approaches they tend to do so in an attractively broad and pragmatic way, usually in the context of a range of other practical help and against a backdrop of social deprivation. Social work has, therefore, provided an interesting test-bed for behaviour therapy and cognitive-behavioural therapy in 'least propitious' conditions. The results have been convincing (see Macdonald and Sheldon 1992; Scott 1989), but there remains the problem of extending their application. Several difficulties stand in the way of this and these are the concerns of this first chapter. It has four aims:

(i) To take a critical look at the disciplinary context; the occupational world in which cognitive-behavioural therapy is struggling to make its contribution.

1

(ii) To examine the a priori issue of the kind of relationship that exists between theory, research and practice in our field and which frustrates the rational selection of helping approaches for specific problems.

(iii) To review the empirical research evidence on the comparative effectiveness of cognitive-behavioural methods.

(iv) To identify the problems and opportunities which arise from the use of cognitive-behavioural approaches in mainstream social work, taking account of recent legislative and organizational changes.

All this requires an anthropological foray into social work country, to examine some of the interesting tribal customs to be found there.

THE DISCIPLINARY CONTEXT

With a name like yours, you might be any shape almost.

(Lewis Carroll 1872:192)

If social work were a person rather than an occupation then its symptoms – lack of stable identity; chronic self-doubt; depression punctuated by bouts of mania and self-destructiveness – would qualify it as a suitable case for treatment within any of the therapeutic traditions represented on our training courses. One can even have fun with the different diagnoses that would be advanced. One group of adherents might indict 'the never fully-resolved oedipal relationship with the State'. Another set would portray us as 'the scapegoated younger child of the professions who knows what is really going on at home and so must be silenced by ridicule'. Another, as the bashed-about embodiment of the female principle of condemning less and understanding more; while acolytes of the latest managerial cult might simply prescribe a dose of 'business training', pausing briefly afterwards to ask what the problem was.

If by now you think I am about to propose a course of cognitive-behavioural therapy as the real solution to all our ills, you are mistaken. This is a book about certain aspects of the therapeutic role of the social worker, and has been written in full knowledge that we have others. As I write, I have students on placement giving advice on welfare benefits to discharged psychiatric patients; trying to organize reliable patterns of care for frail elderly people at home, and helping a community association in the East End of London to get something done about neglected housing repairs. I can think of one or two behavioural principles that might apply to these situations but I would be surprised to receive case studies written entirely from this perspective. However, I also have students struggling to keep truanting schoolchildren within the normal educational provision; helping people with alcohol problems to moderate their drinking; and trying to teach inexperienced parents how to control their children without resorting to physical force. In these cases, and many more like them, I would be very surprised, given the available research, *not* to see a substantial cognitive-behavioural element in their practice. The point is that both sets of students are doing social work. Indeed, social workers in Britain now appear to be responsible for anything that does not fall clearly into the ambit of the police, the army or the fire service, hence the continual reappearance throughout our literature of the 'what *is* social work?' debate. This is a question that the general public might well expect us to have well behind us, but the reason why no catchy, one-sentence definition springs to mind (though plenty of long, turgid ones do) is that social work is really a series of interrelated jobs ranging from care, support and case management, through the various recipes for changing problematic behaviour, thoughts and feelings which concern us here, to overlapping approaches which seek to change circumstances rather than people (though by this we usually mean the behaviour of *other* people). This unprecedented range and diversity creates serious problems. For depending on what kind of social work you do, your perspective on the whole, and your sense of priorities, will be different. Thus, social services staff often look askance at what they see as the mollycoddling working conditions of child guidance units. People who do youth and community work often see social services more as part of the problem than as part of the solution. Probation officers are not sure whether they belong to the same species though they do rather similar things. In the professional literature, to paraphrase Shaw, it is impossible for one social worker to open his mouth (or pick up his pen) without making another social worker despise him.

For all its other faults, the medical profession solved this problem of the 'one true faith' some time ago. They have heart surgeons *and* public health specialists. Occasionally the latter claim that the former soak up a disproportionate share of available resources, or that drains rather than scalpels are the key to good health, but by and large they accept that the term 'medical practitioner' covers all sorts of different functions within the health field.

These points out of the way, I am free to argue that cognitive-behavioural therapy – that is, that branch of applied psychology which seeks to change problematic behaviour by (i) modifying the environmental contingencies that surround it; (ii) weakening previous conditioned associations which have resulted in maladaptive emotional reactions; (iii) offering clients more effective models of problem-solving and interpersonal behaviour; and (iv) which seeks to change the ways in which stimuli are recognized and interpreted in the first place – offers an objectively superior basis for the therapeutic, counselling or casework roles of the social worker.

This tough statement, which I shall defend later, contains some implicit premises which need examining. First, that choosing an *approach* to someone else's problems (a recipe, if you like) ought, as far as possible, to be a rational act. That is, it should be based on defensible notions of case-appropriateness, likely effectiveness and tolerable efficiency. This is, after all, what we expect from our doctors, dentists, plumbers and garage mechanics. They may occasionally try to get away with 'doing what works for them' but if we catch them at it we make trouble. Certainly, as citizens, we are usually extremely resistant

3

to any occupation attempting to elevate professional comfort to the level of a principle. We rightly cluck our tongues at the tranquilliser-happy GP ('Watch out, they're addictive, but I don't have time to talk'), or the ECT-happy psychiatrist ('I know this works best, I've been doing it for years') but how many social workers fall into the same pattern of reflexive practice in less visible ways? Nor is this awkward matter resolved by managers declaring that in future all services will be 'needs-led' because this obviously begs the question: who decides what is a need?

This argument for the considered rather than the purely reactive deployment of social workers has never been better put than in the following quotation:

> The personal social services are large-scale experiments in helping those in need. It is both wasteful and irresponsible to set experiments in motion and to omit to record and analyse what happens. It makes no sense in terms of administrative efficiency, and however little intended, indicates a careless attitude towards human welfare.
>
> (Seebohm Report 1968:142)

These telling observations were made about the lack of evaluation in social services in general. But what of the many 'small-scale experiments' in helping carried out (whether they know it or not) by individual members of staff? Do they make informed choices among approaches in the face of given problems and observe the effects that they have? 'Sometimes' is the fairest answer – but certainly not as a matter of course. There are several reasons for this. First, they are still trained to believe that the various theories about how best to provide help are, in the right hands, created equal. Therefore, like religious or political affiliations, the professional beliefs of staff (that mental illness is caused by family tensions; that satanic abuse is widespread throughout Britain) are no one's business but their own, and are largely matters of conviction and commitment, less so of evidence and debate. This can lead to some unlikely courses of action which go unchallenged because they are seen to be individually 'creative' (a word easily confused with 'unusual'). Here is an example:

> In the constant search for 'tools' which aid the therapeutic process with abused children and adults, we have found a new medium which seems in many ways ideal for post-disclosure therapy. The medium is ice. It can be very cheaply made in large amounts, and sustains the child's interest, especially in large quantities. If the room and the child are hot, and the child is asked to touch the ice quickly, the experience is refreshing, exciting and meets the needs of the hot child.
>
> (Zelickman and Martin 1991:16)

The questions 'why?' 'does it?' and 'how do you know?' are not addressed in the article in which the aforementioned extract appears alongside many, equally dubious assertions. Moreover, although this magazine could find space for this nonsense, it could not for a palatable review of 95 empirical studies on the effectiveness of social work, including results from 13 child protection projects.

Second comes the idea that there are better and worse ways of finding things out. Over the years most social work courses have tended to favour congeniality of outcome or the professional implications of results, independently of the methodological rigour employed. For just these reasons, social workers were the first to gulp down the vague but professionally flattering proposals of Gregory Bateson *et al.* (1956), R. D. Laing (1960), and Michel Foucault (1965) that schizophrenia was (respectively) the product of 'double-bind' communication, 'the power politics of the nuclear family', or due to fall-out from the collapse of capitalism. Despite the weight of evidence in other, less immediately reassuring biological and social directions (see Gottesman 1991; Brown and Birley 1968; Brown *et al.* 1972), we look like being the last professional group concerned with the mentally ill to regurgitate them.

In case any reader is thinking (like CCETSW[1]), that all this theoretical talk is arcane, and that what we should be concentrating on are skills, values and services, then my reply is: which ones? Much of the work done by psychiatric social workers in pursuit of double binds was 'skilful' in the sense that one had to be trained to work around the 'defensiveness' of families who stubbornly continued to see themselves as victims rather than unwitting perpetrators. It was value-laden in the sense that great weight was given to the coded, special insights of the martyred patient, and great stress laid on the importance of protecting him or her from further oppression at the hands of the medical establishment. As for a concentration on service issues, remember that the entire psychiatric provision of Italy was (and, to an extent, still is) based upon these ideas, with many calamitous effects.

Consider also that services are always predicated upon ideology-laden assumptions about what has gone wrong and how problems should therefore be addressed. Our present community care policies are riddled with implicit pessimism about the possibility of remission in chronic schizophrenia and the poor cost-effectiveness of prevention which, paradoxically, is strongly contradicted by empirical research in this field (Birchwood *et al.* 1988; Goldberg and Huxley 1992; Sheldon 1994a). Thus, in this sevice context, we are charged with what in another economic debate has been called 'the management of decline'. Therefore the progress of our clients up the medical ladder and down the social services snake is only occasionally interrupted by effective combinations of therapeutic and practical services which address what is known from research about these afflictions. Choice of approach matters. Theory and research matter – in our field as in others. These factors make a tangible difference, for better or worse, to the lives of clients.

THEORY AND PRACTICE IN SOCIAL WORK

Social work's field of operation is the poor, troubled, marginalized, outcast individual in his or her social circumstances. With such a remit it must always remain an eclectic discipline. Yet while the benefits of being able to call up potentially useful ideas, concepts and findings from a wide range of other fields (social policy, psychology, sociology, literature and so forth) have been widely celebrated, the pitfalls of this diversity of intellectual sources are much less well documented (see Sheldon 1978a). The greatest danger is that in the face of such an embarrassment of riches we get careless about the terms and conditions of our borrowings, moving on to the next source when we get bored, when the political climate changes, or when we just feel like something new. Others have been here before us. Here is the problem expressed in the terms of eighteenth-century physical science:

> Being able to take no common body of belief for granted, each writer on physical optics felt forced to build his field anew from its foundations. In doing so, his choice of supporting observation and experiment was relatively free, for there was no standard set of methods or of phenomena that every optical writer felt forced to employ and explain. Under these circumstances, the dialogue of the resulting books was often directed as much to the members of other schools as it was to nature.
>
> (Kuhn 1970:13)

If we continue in this pre-paradigmatic state then, unlike other professions (psychology, psychiatry and, increasingly, nursing) which also have to cope with the formidable methodological problems inherent in attempts to understand human behaviour, our store of reliable intellectual assets will not steadily accumulate, with the result that we shall end up with something closer to a 'knowledge pile' than a 'knowledge base'.

A further danger is that as other subjects expand, and our functions are extended, we are forced to teach more on the basis of less and to pile up pre-prepared, 'shrink-wrapped' ideas from everywhere in our curricula. The 'supermarket principle' could easily take over, where choice is left to the browsing consumer, but a consumer without benefit of an Advertising Standards Authority or a Trades Descriptions Act, and no *Which?* guide to consult.

Worrying over this problem for twenty-odd years, first as a student exasperated not so much by the many contradictory views presented to me, but by the fact that these differences of view created so little intellectual tension within or between the proposers (think again, Festinger); then as a social worker held closely to account over trivial administrative matters, but free as a bird over what to do about clients' problems; then as an academic, watching fads and fashions sweep the profession every five years or so with the force of viral epidemics – my conclusion was, and still is, that science (without the little inverted commas) offers the best chance of developing a *cumulative* knowledge base for the profession. One within which ideas are positively selected, reinforced and if necessary abandoned in favour of something better.

This may seem an arrogant position to take, but only if the reader has retained an old-fashioned sense of science as grand certainty built upon grand certainty. Science is rather a set of rules to rein in the human perceptual and cognitive tendency to jump to conclusions and stick to them; to 'join up the dots' of observations and turn them into large theories (ignoring the spaces between); to see things that closer investigation reveals not to have been there at all; and not to see things which later evidence shows were always there. If readers think such concerns far removed from practical social work, let them apply this list of factors to the field of child abuse, in which such false negatives and false positives abound (see Sheldon 1987a).

The other fallacy regarding scientific activity which appears to rule out its application to social work is that austere emotional detachment is required to make it work. This stereotype, propagated by media images of steely-eyed, physical scientists peering inductively at their data as if to make them confess all, serves to remove this form of evaluating evidence from the everyday sphere. Yet we all do something similar every day via the little experiments we conduct with the behaviour and motives of ourselves and others, and we all have clients whom we suspect of over- or under-responding to evidence from their experience. At the outset, science is a matter of insight, creativity, unsupported 'knight's move' speculations, and luck. Consider this reassuring statement:

> Induction based on many observations is a myth. It is neither a psychological fact, nor a fact of ordinary life, nor one of scientific procedure . . .
> The actual procedure of science is to operate with conjectures: to jump to conclusions – often after one single observation . . . Repeated observation and experiments function in science as tests of our conjectures or hypotheses, i.e. as attempted refutations.
>
> (Popper 1963:53)

Finding out is therefore a two-stage activity. Having the good idea, and then devising tests of its veracity. Social workers are encouraged by their training to give their main attention to stage one. Note the popularity of so-called 'brainstorming' sessions – but ask yourself what happens afterwards? Often nothing does, since there are no rules for deciding on the plausibility of different propositions, or deciding which should be more rigorously looked into. There is also the desire to avoid committing the heinous crime of 'devaluing' the contributions of some by suggesting that they may have less face validity. Therefore, the flip charts are kept for a while, not usually as a plan to guide further work, but as trophies testifying to the collective nature of creativity and the value of catharsis:

> Alice laughed. 'There's no use trying,' she said: 'One can't believe impossible things.' 'I dare say you haven't had much practice,' said the

Queen. 'When I was your age, I always did it for half an hour a day. Why sometimes I've believed as many as six impossible things before breakfast.'

(Lewis Carroll 1872:184)

It is as if Archimedes, having had his bright idea, were to have settled back contentedly into the warm bath water. But yes, I do know that human behaviour is a more complicated phenomenon than the displacement of water, but then this is exactly why our need for rules of evidence to try to live up to is more not less urgent.

Let us now examine the implications of all this, beginning with the way we should relate to available theories about the nature of personal and social problems and what can be done about them.

1   My first proposal is that it is psychologically impossible *not* to have theories about things. It is impossible at a basic perceptual level, at a cognitive and at an emotional level. The search for meaning, as a basis for predicting behavioural success and avoiding danger, appears to have been 'wired' into our brains by evolution (see Chapter 2). Families, groups, and organisations too, develop theories about priorities, and 'antibody responses' to views and evidence which appear to threaten them. The disasters at Pearl Harbor, Arnhem and Singapore provide good military examples of this process at work, where substantial and threatening evidence of impending catastrophe was ignored or reinterpreted (see Dixon 1976; Sheldon 1987a). The collective mindsets revealed by inquiries into the Cleveland and Orkney child abuse scandals (Butler-Sloss Report 1988; Clyde 1992) provide examples closer to home.

    If you think all this far-fetched, then try asking at your next management-liaison meeting whether anyone thinks that the application of business practices to social work might not do more harm than good, and observe carefully what happens in response to this perfectly reasonable question.

2   There are certain qualities possessed by theories in different measure. First among them is *potential refutability*. This constitutes Popper's line of demarcation as to what is or could ever be scientific knowledge (Popper 1963; see also Gillies 1993). Thus, theories that contain built-in defences against disbelief or refutation (e.g. much of Freud's and Marx's work and the propositions of certain American writers on allegedly repressed memories of sexual abuse in childhood) must occupy the lowest position in any hierarchy stressing validity and reliability.

    It is my habit near the beginning of my developmental psychology course to ask the male students whether any of them ever experienced anxiety regarding castration at the hands of their fathers. I ask the women students if they had ever worried that the operation might already have been performed? No hands ever go up, but of course this makes no

8

difference. Indeed, were we randomly to sample, say, two million respondents and only 1 per cent answered in the affirmative, this too would make no difference. For according to Freud's theory, it happened to us all, but we have all repressed it. Sometimes we have interesting debates on what castration anxiety really means, though the author of the theory was clear enough. Were we to call it 'castration anxiety'[2] instead, and allow evidence of fathers tripping up their sons at beach football, then the affected sample would grow, but the concept would fade, and we might as well substitute 'juvenile competitiveness', or 'showing off', instead.

Currently fashionable feminist theories (I have nothing against the stance, only the methods) on the extraordinary prevalence of child sexual abuse depend upon the proposition that the enormous numbers of children alleged to have suffered it have repressed the fact. The corollary being that ten thousand persistent denials that this was ever so count for nothing. Indeed, mounting exasperation in the face of this interpretation might itself be 'interesting'.

> 'Then you should say what you mean,' the March Hare went on. 'I do,' Alice hastily replied; 'at least – at least I mean what I say – that's the same thing, you know.'
>
> (Lewis Carroll 1872:66)

3   Popper's second criterion of scientific worth is that of *riskiness of prediction*. The preferable theory or proposition is that which prohibits the most. This somewhat counter-intuitive point means that we should learn to prefer those explanations which place themselves at greatest risk of potential refutation by stating clearly what ought *not* to occur. The psychoanalytic concept of 'insight' runs no such risks since if the right degree or direction of behavioural change does not follow from the client's rehearsal of his new understanding, then he is deemed, retrospectively, not to have attained true insight, but to be employing 'defensive intellectualization'.

4   The next point concerns *testability*. The preferable theory or model is that which yields the widest range of testable *hypotheses*. Many quite elaborate social work theories produce low yields of these operational statements. Virtually any statement about potential improvement can be rendered testable providing that the proposer is willing to specify types of observable outcome which could reasonably be connected with the implementation of the theory. Predicted outcomes add in this way to the reliability of concepts. Where this is not done, it is usually because the originators or users of theories feel that 'something' is lost in the process. Yet surely, if we were to advance the (entirely plausible) proposition that many women suffering from anorexia nervosa are in that condition because of undealt-with feelings about their bodies and their identities following sexual abuse in childhood, then three things would be required:

9

(a) convincing evidence of over-representation of sexual abuse in the case histories of anorectics, and *vice versa*; (b) an operational definition of what 'dealt with' looks like when it happens; (c) weight gain in those who have attained this state, and less of this in those who have not (perhaps backed up by other standardized assessments of changes in self-esteem and self-perceived body image) (see Garner and Bemis 1982). Without these developments, or steady progress towards them, the theory remains interesting, logically consistent, but speculative. Further, none of this has anything to do with the sympathy which we naturally feel towards people caught up in this problem.

5   *Logical consistency* is the next point of evaluation. This sub-divides into (a) internal consistency: is what the theory proposes in all its cases logical? For example, Freud's adaptation of the Oedipus complex to cover little girls – the Electra complex (important since he implicates it in the formation of conscience) produces many problems of internal consistency. What is proposed in the first part of the theory is at odds with the second (see Brown 1969); (b) external consistency: if a theory, as yet untested empirically, contains propositions which contradict a body of findings from elsewhere, then it *may* still be worth pursuing, but only on a very 'experimental' basis. It could also be argued that the theory should be made to account for any reliability in the predictions of its competitors. For example, the developmental theories of Melanie Klein (1975), still popular in child guidance and child psychiatric centres, imply pre-linguistic, cognitive capacities in the infant which are substantially at odds with studies of the intellectual development of children from Piaget onwards (see Donaldson 1978). Therefore the latter explanations are preferable for now, though they may not be the last word on the subject. 'Clinical evidence' (optimistic opinions from vested interests) cannot be allowed to stand against such considerations.

Some things cannot be true unless other things are false, since they purport to offer causal explanations for the same phenomena. Klein, Freud and Piaget rule each other out in the matter of moral development – the ages and the sequencing are all at odds, to say nothing of the mechanisms of acquisition.

6   *Clarity of expression* is our next concern. The less ambiguous the presentation of a theory, the better. This is not simply a reference to literary style, but to the quality of the *prescription* contained within a statement. It is often surprising how little definitional work has gone into concepts which are in everyday use in social work. For example, 'family homeostasis', or the operation of the 'family system'. How exactly shall we recognize these when we see them and distinguish them from states somewhat similar?

7   *Applicability* comes next. Convincing theories or concepts may be available which it would be inappropriate to implement. Opposition may follow from ethical grounds, or may stem from considerations of feasi-

bility, cost, or level of contact required. This point is of particular importance in social work where 'knowledge for use' must have a high priority. Thus, some forms of 'regression therapy' may have logical consistency within their theoretical origins, as does aversion therapy, but, questions of effectiveness aside, the 'medium' (treating people like dependent children – or punishing people for their own good) can easily become the 'message' and we may decide to have nothing to do with the ideas on moral grounds.

8 The next point concerns the degree of *simplicity* of a given theory. This test is called, variously, 'Occam's razor' or 'the law of parsimony'. It proposes that the more economical the explanation of a given set of events, the more preferable. Thus, attribution theory (Bem 1967) covers the propositions of Festinger's 'cognitive dissonance' theory of attitude change (1957) without recourse to hypothetical internal states and has a superior claim on our attentions when we are involved in such work.

9 Within this framework, great store must be set by findings from the history of any attempts to test the propositions of a given theory. However, not only do approaches which have very little backing from research continue to be used, but promising trends are often neglected or undermined for no rational reasons. For example, certain types of group and individual work (based on social learning theory) which combat the causes of offending behaviour at a cognitive, social and behavioural level have been shown to be effective with juvenile delinquents at a time when the emphasis is swinging back towards 'short sharp shock' approaches that have already been shown to be ineffective (Gendreau and Ross 1987; Sheldon 1994b). Parent-training programmes to prevent accelerating patterns of child abuse are now showing up well in the research (see Macdonald and Sheldon 1992) at a time when the family centres, where such measures are typically employed, are under threat of closure on economic grounds.

10 What of the circumstances in which there is no convincing explanation available? Popper's advice is that we should set about developing *criteria of relative potential satisfactoriness*. This is quite a mouthful, but it simply means that we should try to construct the best 'template' of what a good theory would look like, and what it would have to explain. Social workers do this all the time at a microlevel when, struggling with a complex case, they and their supervisors try to imagine what a comprehensive assessment would look like had they the information necessary to construct one: important things not yet known.

Cognitive-behavioural theories fit the evaluative framework developed over the last few pages rather well, but that is the wrong starting point. It is more important to be discerning in one's selection of methods than to join a school and then justify membership. To change one's mind and professional behaviour in the light of research trends; to have a friendly, limited-liability relationship with theories and research findings, rather than falling in love with them – being unwilling to listen to anything untoward about them, sulking when they are criticized in your presence – are all signs of professional maturity. This book has a new title and has been substantially rewritten for just these reasons. Accommodating new material from cognitive research has not been comfortable; indeed, some misgivings remain; but it is *necessary* in the light of empirical findings.

STUDIES OF THE EFFECTIVENESS OF THERAPEUTIC METHODS

I have a favourite daydream in which I am invited on to a chat show to defend the reputation of social work. In response to a battery of hostile questions I fix Jeremy Paxman with my special Clint Eastwood stare (perfected on the Second Years) and say: *'Social work is demonstrably worthwhile since, aside from any moral questions, the distinctive methods and patterns of organisation of the profession have been shown by empirical research to have had a measurable and significant impact on the problems which fall within its scope.'* Then I wake up.

If we are not yet in a position to say such things confidently, hand on heart, then arguably it is not for want of trying. For social work, particularly social work in the United States, began to submit its working practices to the very strictest kinds of scientific test as early as did any of the would-be helping professions (see Lehrman 1949; Powers and Witmer 1951). Let us take the time now to see whether there is still anything to learn from these brave attempts to apply scientific principles to good intentions.

Early studies

The 1950s and 1960s saw the publication of a series of random-allocation controlled studies (see Fischer 1973, 1976; Mullen and Dumpson 1972; Sheldon 1986) directed mainly but not exclusively at juvenile delinquency prevention, featuring well-trained social workers making use of psychoanalytically-flavoured casework techniques, deployed at a level of intensity and over periods sufficient to turn modern social workers green with envy. For example, the Miller (1962) 'Midcity Total Community Project' (n=377) involved counselling for delinquent children and their families, a community work programme, group work, street-based youth work, liaison schemes with recreation centres, schools, and the police. Each subject was exposed to an average of 3.5 hours per week professional contact over the three-year study period. A comprehensive battery of quantitative and qualitative outcome indicators (including official statistics) was used. Here is the stark result:

The researcher and project workers are not aware of any measurable inhibition of law-violating morally-disapproved behavior as a consequence of project efforts.

(Miller 1962:187)

Worse was to come, in some later studies, for example, the 'Seattle Delinquency Prevention Project' (Berleman *et al.* 1972) – a similar study with a similarly extensive menu of approaches and an average professional contact time of 313 hours per subject. Results revealed worrying signs of deterioration in the experimental group, with two-thirds of comparisons with untreated controls favouring the latter.

Remember that this was a time of rising fortunes for the profession. Social work journals were read openly on public transport and employment levels were climbing steeply. Yet virtually every experiment showed negative results. Here are the conclusions of two noted reviewers of this early material:

The researchers for many reasons were rarely able to conclude that a program had even modest success in achieving its major goals.

(Mullen and Dumpson 1972:42)

The available controlled research strongly suggests that at present lack of evidence of the effectiveness of professional casework is the rule rather than the exception. A technical research corollary to this conclusion and a comment frequently appearing in the social work literature, is that we also lack good scientific proof of ineffectiveness. This assertion, however, taken alone, would appear to be rather insubstantial grounds on which to support a profession.

(Fischer 1973:19)

It is hard at this distance to recapture the sense of defeat and disillusion among the *cognoscenti* which greeted the publication of these reviews. In a series of letters and articles the bruised and the angry wrote to complain that scientific methodology was much too blunt an instrument with which to poke about in the necessarily mysterious dynamics of what passes between would-be helper and might-be-helped. Given what we *now* know about the intractability of offending behaviour (see Folkard *et al.* 1976 for a British example), these accounts do bring to mind an image of cavalry charging tanks. But this is not quite the case, because few of the subjects of these early studies were hard-core offenders. Most were troubled young people with family and school problems who in Britain might have ended up in a child guidance clinic. Moreover, some well-organized methods do make a difference in the face of such problems, and with persistent offenders to boot (see Gendreau and Ross 1987; Sheldon 1994). The point is that *these* methods did not, though a generation of textbook writers never, ever conceived that they would not, and a generation of social workers always felt that they were getting somewhere with them. Jones and Borgatta (1972) confront this problem of rampant subjectivity in the following quotation:

13

These qualities cannot reside in the mind of someone in the agency who knows what he thinks is important but cannot express it because it is too subtle to be communicated or because it is a relationship so fragile that any attempt to measure it would destroy it.

(Jones and Borgatta 1972:41)

More recent reviews have not brought forward complaints that something helpful may be happening inside clients though batteries of indicators checking for changes in behaviour and circumstances are not able to detect it. Criticism has broadened and softened. Queries are raised as to what 'effectiveness' really is. Many social workers approach this question as if the concept presupposed some predetermined and universal state of epistemological grace – rather like 'truth' – in which all aspirations are satisfied, all possible points of view accommodated and all possible objections dealt with. It quickly becomes apparent that little or nothing of what we do, and none of our measures of it, exist in such a form. Effectiveness for whom? Assessed in relation to what, and why? All fair questions, but the idea of effectiveness that I have in mind is a less ambitious affair. It implies describing carefully the nature, extent and implications of a problem prior to intervention; saying, as far as possible in consultation with clients, what it is that you might do to alter things or to stop them getting worse; why what is proposed looks like a good bet; describing how this change is to be brought about; saying in advance what public tests might be applied to support the views that something worthwhile has been achieved; designing a methodology to minimize the risk that any beneficial change might be due to some collateral influence; pursuing a solution; and defending the results against criticism from peers. It is that simple, and that difficult.

Another criticism that often appears in this country is that since the majority of these studies are American the results cannot simply be transferred to British practice. Not automatically, no, but then we have many British studies illustrating the difference between intention and outcome (see Gibbons et al. 1978; Goldberg, E.M. 1970; Folkard et al. 1976). A better way to approach this question is to ask whether what is done in another context is similar to what is, or has been, or easily could be, done here. Whether the problems are similar, the clients roughly comparable in socio-economic terms, the periods of contact not too out of step, the methodological quality acceptable and so forth. On all such comparisons, even allowing for one or two procedural inconsistencies (Powers and Witmer 1951; Meyer et al. 1965) the result from my own close reading of every study (Sheldon 1989) is that they *are* applicable. Had the recipes in use (which, remember, had always made up beautifully when no one was watching) been at all suitable for the purposes in hand, then positive results should have shone forth. After we stopped being defensive, and stopped engaging in what cognitive therapists call 'catastrophizing', it was realized by a few that clear, negative results have something to teach us regarding what ingredients we might emphasize less in future. Here is a list of likely factors: long-term, generalized, historically-focused, psychoanalytically-flavoured, relationship-dependent, verbal counselling methods, which do little to bridge the gap between any insight that may accrue, and behaviour and circumstances. The 1970s saw these principles turned on their head and so we can conduct a kind of experiment between two groups of experiments with different independent variables.

Later studies

We are dealing here with some 28 studies (Reid and Hanrahan 1980) conducted between 1972 and 1979. They are, again, predominantly American, but an interesting scatter of British studies can be added to the sample (see Goldberg and Connolly 1981; Sheldon 1986). This work differs from what went before in a number of respects: -

(i) It features a broader range of client groups, e.g. child abuse, psychiatric problems, sick children and their families, school social work, elderly people. Also, a wider range of approaches were applied, e.g. behaviour therapy, task-centred casework, social skills training, family therapy.

(ii) With two or three exceptions (Jones, J. A. *et al.* 1976; Stein and Gambrill 1977), samples are smaller in this work (and remember that small is not necessarily beautiful in social research – it depends on what is being claimed).

(iii) The participating clients are a much more highly selected group than their predecessors. Here the social workers seem to have taken a leaf out of the book of psychologists who have long looked askance at our willingness to take on all-comers in big 'win or lose' experimental prize fights. There are dangers in this new realism, however. Two or three of the studies deal with straightforward, rather 'manageable' problems which, in Britain, would never get past reception. Prevention is one thing (see Rose and Marshall 1975); selecting easy targets and achieving statistical significance at the expense of professional significance, quite another.

(iv) Best of all, these authors paid greater attention to the issue of defining, describing and, as far as possible, standardizing the approaches employed, with a view to replication.

Turning now to the results of this work, the majority of studies produced positive outcomes. That is, those subjects receiving the services improved against the study-specific outcome criteria – though it must be admitted *some* studies lacked longer-term follow-up arrangements, and so some questions about the staying power of these interventions remained for later research. Having reviewed these studies in the original the claims made appear justified in terms of the methodologies employed, and represent a considerable change in our prospects – providing, of course, that we learn to favour the approaches used. Reid and Hanrahan capture the service-input differences of this work in the following quotation:

> In brief, one is struck by the dominance of structured forms of practice in these experiments – that is, of practice that takes the form of well-explicated, well-organized procedures usually carried out in a step-wise manner and designed to achieve relatively specific goals. The influence of the behavioral movement is quite apparent and pervasive.
>
> (Reid and Hanrahan 1980:11–12)

These findings mirror results in psychotherapy and clinical psychology, but the issue has been raised as to whether it is the behavioural techniques and their various adaptations *per se* that were responsible for improved results, or the way in which the therapeutic encounters were *organized*? Such a question has limited meaning for behaviour therapists, who regard the structure of their intensive, focused and closely-monitored programmes as being as much derived from knowledge of how people learn or 'unlearn' a sequence of behaviour as are the techniques themselves. Indeed, work by Stein and Gambrill (1976 – contracts to prevent reception into care or to speed rehabilitation) and Reid (1968 – task-centred casework) have these factors as their main independent variables – on the grounds that no sensible person takes driving lessons lasting 30 minutes every three weeks for two years.

Such questions are important issues for research and practice (see Reid and Shyne 1968; Rachman and Wilson 1980; Bergin and Garfield 1986), and those studies which have directly addressed this question of the relative impact of medium and message suggest the following:

(i) Short-term, intensive exposure to therapeutic help where the likely length of contact is known to all parties is, where specific changes are being sought, just as effective as (and possibly more so than) long-term help. Certainly it is more efficient. Figure 1.1 illustrates this phenomenon of 'decreasing marginal utility' in psychotherapy and clinical psychology.

Findings for social work effectiveness research match the pattern in Figure 1.1, which is not to argue that *all* work can be short-term and focused as it is in most cognitive-behavioural programmes. Children in long-term care, for example, or psychiatric patients discharged into the community, may require years of regular contact. The point is that most long-term care is supportive in intent, the social worker acting as a kind of 'buoyancy aid'. It is intended also to forestall crises; however, when crises or relapses occur, research suggests that the intensity of contact needs to be stepped up considerably – as in the period before discharge from care, or when a discharged patient begins to experience acute stress and a return of florid symptoms. Problems arise when we expect our administratively convenient 'drip-feed' patterns of contact somehow to deal with sudden manifestations of extra need; or where we spread contact

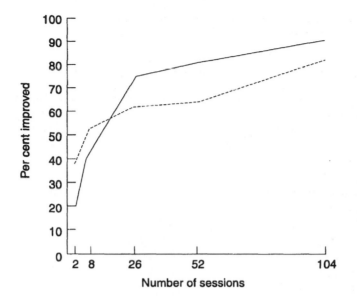

Figure 1.1 Decreasing marginal utility in helping

equally throughout a period of statutorily defined contact (as in a two-year probation order) and let this largely dictate frequency and intensity rather than what is happening, or about to happen, in the lives of clients.

(ii) With one or two exceptions the staff in these 'second wave' studies intervene more *directly* in problems than their predecessors. That is, there was less of an expectation that if an easy-to-target variable (usually verbal behaviour) is changed in one setting, this will necessarily affect harder-to-get-at factors elsewhere. The relationship between the two – even where there is a substantial cognitive-reappraisal component – is *managed*, this through rehearsal and graded exposure to real-life contingencies.

(iii) Open negotiation with clients regarding ends and means appears also to be an influential factor, as is a contractual style or the use of written agreements. Ends–means confusions are rife in therapeutic work (revealed particularly in social work by client-opinion research) and regular reviews of progress against pre-negotiated objectives appear to be our best means for keeping them at bay.

Whether regarded as collateral or intrinsic, such case-management factors undoubtedly make a substantial contribution to the outcomes achieved in effectiveness research and are probably best thought of as necessary but not sufficient conditions for change (see Macdonald and Sheldon 1992).

Let us now consider those studies of social work effectiveness conducted over the last decade or so.

Contemporary studies

Conscious of the criticism that given social work's level of disciplinary development, it is premature for us to attempt the 'quick fix' that (if all goes well) controlled experiments can provide, Macdonald and Sheldon (1992) reviewed all empirical studies of social work effectiveness (including multi-disciplinary work) produced in a trawl of English language journals published between 1979 and 1991, and screened them within their different conventions for methodological adequacy. Table 1.1 summarizes the methodologies employed and the client groups covered:

Table 1.1 Distribution of client groups across research methodology

	Experimental	Quasi-experimental	Pre-experimental	Client-opinion	
Families	4	0	11	10	25
Child protection	2	3	7	1	13
Offender	2	5	6	6	19
Mental disorder	4	4	6	3	17
Other	3	2	2	3	10
'Ordinary'	8	0	2	1	11
TOTALS	23	14	34	24	95

It will be seen that the client groups covered in this research are typical of those featured on caseloads in mainstream social work here and in the United States. There is little question here (apart from the minor problems contained in the 'ordinary' category, above) of researching the 'easily researchable'.

Let us turn next to the question of which methods of intervention were used in the research studies. Figure 1.2 is a diagram of the methods employed in these studies.

The first finding to report is that the predominance of behavioural and cognitive-behavioural approaches noted by Reid and Hanrahan (1980) continues in our later sample (for example, Ross and Scott 1985; Bentley 1990). Such approaches are distinguishable by their concentration on the rehearsal and reinforcement of new behaviour rather than reliance on purely verbal reviews of the options available, and are based on the common-sense principle that no one learns to swim by attending seminars on it. Further, these

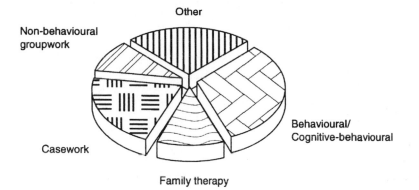

Figure 1.2 Distribution of therapeutic methods in effectiveness research

Table 1.2 Distribution of interventions across client groups

	Behavioural /cognitive- behavioural	Family therapy	Casework	Group- work	Other	
Families and children	4	3	14	1	3	25
Children at risk	7	0	2	2	2	13
Offenders	3	1	2	6	7	19
Mental disorder	7	3	3	0	3	16
Other	1	0	4	0	5	10
'Ordinary'	9	0	1	1	0	11
TOTALS	31	7	26	10	20	94

approaches are used across a wide range of problems (Table 1.2), contradicting the view (common in Britain) that they are useful only with phobics and bedwetters.

As will be seen more clearly when we look at the strong correlation between such methods and positive outcomes, this trend places British social work in a vulnerable position in that 80 per cent of studies featuring these approaches are American, yet the problems being dealt with are typical of those on caseloads here. Compare the position of behavioural and cognitive-behavioural approaches with that of family therapy which accounts for only 8 per cent of studies and yet is widely popular in the curriculum and in practice.

Table 1.3 Results of intervention (excluding client-opinion data)

	Positive	Mixed	Negative	
Behavioural/Cognitive-behavioural	25	2	3	30
Family therapy	5	1	0	6
Casework	5	0	5	10
Non-behavioural groupwork	3	1	2	6
Other	10	0	1	11
TOTAL	48	4	11	63

When looking at the overall distribution of results (Table 1.3) we used three categories: *1: Positive.* Included here are studies whose results are wholly or predominantly positive, within a secure methodological framework. *2: Mixed.* In addition to pre-experimental and client-opinion studies whose results contained both positive and negative outcomes, this category includes experimental and quasi-experimental studies where some treatment goals were attained and others not. *3: Negative.* This included studies where the control group subjects did better than their experimental counterparts (or where a no-treatment control did equally well); studies in which both experimental and control subjects deteriorated or failed to improve; studies where results were mixed but generally negative or where there were more positive findings in favour of a control group, if used.

Table 1.3 gives results by method of intervention and contains some good news for the profession in that 75 per cent of studies contained clearly-positive results in respect of the objectives set and within methodologies containing no major confounding difficulties. If we add in those studies where *some* worthwhile effects were produced then the overall percentage rises to 82 per cent – a considerable improvement in our fortunes when compared with the early findings. Adding in evidence of well-exemplified gains reported by clients in 'softer' client opinion studies brightens the picture still further. Let us now examine the features associated with these positive results:

(i) Cognitive-behavioural methods produced the largest cluster of positive outcomes and were (a) more likely to have been subject to experimental test (17 examples) and evaluated against 'hard' outcome indicators; and (b) if pre–post tests or comparison groups methods were used, identical or very similar methods are likely to have received this treatment in other research outside the scope of this review (e.g. at the hands of clinical psychologists). Moreover, these gains were not achieved at the expense of relevance, since the problems featured are all of a challenging nature, e.g. child abuse prevention, young offenders or relapse-prevention in cases of mental ill-health.

(ii) Many of these cognitive-behavioural methods were employed with groups of clients – adding to their cost-effectiveness (see Ross and Scott 1985).

(iii) The great majority of positive studies reveal that other kinds of practitioner have adopted the protocols discussed on p. 16, in that they operate with clear, tangible objectives, in a pre-prescribed, predominantly short-term and intensive way.

(iv) In these studies, social work is no longer 'what social workers do'; the methods in use are carefully described and, more importantly, were for the most part selected on the basis of what is known from empirical research about the aetiology of the problems in view. In other words, the problems and methods have a 'logical fit', the straightforwardness of which correlates well with positive outcome.

Thus, as far as social work effectiveness research is concerned, the case is made. There are good empirical reasons for considering the use of behavioural and cognitive-behavioural methods alongside our other work. They are not the 'only game in town', but it appears that the effectiveness of other methods is enhanced the closer they come to resemble cognitive-behavioural approaches. Indeed, if present patterns continue, deciding *not* to make use of these methods where conditions permit will become as much an ethical issue as a technical one.

However, we need not rest the case here. The members of other professions also undertake research of the kind discussed above (indeed, in much greater volume) and much of this is relevant to aspects of social work. Let us now review this material from clinical psychology and psychotherapy.

FINDINGS FROM CLINICAL PSYCHOLOGY AND PSYCHOTHERAPY

The cognitive-behavioural therapies are made up of a series of hybrid combinations and this makes for difficulties in deciding which strains are the relevant and important ones. The problem is compounded by the fact that practitioners in the main constituent disciplines (behaviour therapy, cognitive therapy) tend each to claim that they have been incorporating the essential principles of the other for years. It is true that behaviour therapists were often concerned with interpretations and attributions – how could they not be since language is inevitably the medium of communication about problems and what might be done about them? Similarly, cognitive therapists often give their clients homework assignments and use behavioural indicators alongside thinking-style changes to evaluate outcomes. The test for inclusion used here is whether treatment protocols give due recognition to the dual emphasis of thought and affect on behaviour, and of behaviour on thought and affect, in other than a background, facilitative way. This still leaves a very substantial body of experimental and other research – so much so that space permits only an identification of main trends in the literature:[3]

   (i) Cognitive-behavioural therapies are now employed in a wide range of clinical and field settings against a broad range of problems, including depression (Beck *et al.* 1985; Blackburn *et al.* 1981; Dobson 1989); child behaviour problems (particularly self-instructional training used in cases of aggressiveness and impulsivity) (Kazdin *et al.* 1992; Herbert 1978); phobias and anxiety disorders (Beck and Emery 1985; Ost 1987); schizophrenia (BABCP 1993); pain control and medical conditions (Salkovskis 1989; Blanchard 1994).

  (ii) The literature on the treatment of depression based on scheduling pleasant events, self-reinforcement, confronting dysfunctional attributions, is probably the most robust in respect of methodology and observance of treatment protocols (see Blackburn *et al.* 1981). Major controlled studies have shown that cognitive-behavioural therapy is at least the equal of pharmacological approaches (but note that this finding can be stated the other way around) and shows more durable results at long term follow-up.

 (iii) Studies comparing cognitive therapy alone with cognitive-behavioural alternatives show mildly superior results for the latter combination approaches (Hollon and Beck 1994; Emmelkamp and Mersch 1982). Studies comparing traditional behavioural techniques with cognitive-behavioural alternatives show (with the exception of depression, where no well-developed non-cognitive approaches exist) that while both are superior to no-treatment controls, there are few really significant differences in outcome.

 (iv) Various types of cognitive-behavioural approach have now demonstrated their efficacy across a wide range of problems: self-instruction, self-control and self-management approaches, rational restructuring, stress-inoculation, covert sensitization, Rational-Emotive Therapy (see p. 220).

Given that outcome differences between cognitive-behavioural and traditional behavioural methods are small, why all this fuss about the incorporation of a cognitive element? Here are some reasons which find support in the research and professional literatures:

   (i) Since developing or having a problem always involves cognitive components, and therapeutic approaches likewise, it is better that we should deal with these elements systematically and look to see whether facilitative treatment effects result from their incorporation into our assessment and treatment practices.

  (ii) A scatter of studies (see Beck *et al.* 1985; Hollon *et al.* 1991) suggest that a cognitive component carries advantages for longer-term relapse prevention via a generalized 'immunization effect', or a 'portable' set of prompts and cues which trigger more adaptive responses to the re-emergence of stressors (for a good review of this research, see Ludgate 1994).

(iii) Cognitive-behavioural configurations appear to be effective across a *wider range* of problems than can be claimed for unadorned behavioural methods, e.g. child sexual abuse (Jehu 1989), eating disorders (Mitchell *et al.* 1990), obsessive-compulsive disorders (Salkovskis and Westbrook 1987).

(iv) Research into the nature of psychological and emotional problems regularly implicates strong cognitive components. For example, in cases of long-delayed recovery following sexual abuse, in cases of impulsive violence, persistent offending behaviour, child molestation, drink dependency, sexual problems, depression and so forth. This is not to say that these elements are necessarily causative (because cognitions readily come into line with mood and experience), rather that they may provide therapeutic opportunities for influence in reverse – in line with the fact that headache is not caused by lack of aspirin. Consider these results from an epidemiological study:

> Prior to becoming depressed, these future depressives did not subscribe to irrational beliefs, they did not have lower expectancies for positive outcomes, or higher expectations for negative outcomes, they did not attribute success experiences to external causes and failure experiences to internal causes, nor did they perceive themselves as having less control over the events in their lives.
>
> (Lewinsohn *et al.* 1981:218)

Thus, for many problems, irrational or misdirected beliefs appear to play a part in cueing and maintaining problematic behaviour though they do not necessarily constitute the origins of such difficulties.

(v) Where client reactions to the therapeutic *medium* are gathered in studies, cognitive-behavioural approaches emerge as a 'user-friendly' approach compared to alternatives, and drop-out rates are often lower (see Salkovskis and Warwick 1986; Warwick and Marks 1988).

This developing discipline thus continues to show promise across a wide range of problems, and in the hands of a range of different professionals. What evidence there was of doctrinaire, 'my therapy right or wrong' behaviour appears now to be dying away, and therapists are using the continuum from cognitive therapy with background rehearsal of appropriate behaviour, to behaviour therapy with discussion of cognitive coping mechanisms. There is, however, one discordant note sounding in the chorus of mutual congratulation. High drop-out rates are still strongly associated with class position and, overall, the evidence is that psychological therapies do not attract, or are not readily offered to, socially disadvantaged people or culturally diverse groups (Garfield 1986; Sue *et al.* 1994). It would be a good thing for the reputation of behaviour therapy for 'classlessness' to be extended to new cognitive-behavioural formulations, through the adaptation of practice to the needs of all troubled people, not just those with isolated problems and the highest levels of motivation. With all their experience of such matters, social workers are in a good position to help correct this imbalance.

INDIVIDUAL FACTORS IN HELPING

The case made thus far relies heavily (though not exclusively) upon group-controlled experiments. These provide us with our securest results but are essentially contests of averages – averages of influences and of outcomes. The language of science, developed in other more controllable and less reactive settings, can easily mislead us, encouraging us to forget that in our field we are dealing with processes, not substances. Calling the actions of ten or so social workers or other therapists allegedly using the same approach 'the independent variable' can lead to unwitting acceptance of the 'therapist uniformity myth' (see Bergin and Garfield 1986). Any one of us asked whether our school or university department was a good one would probably start with a global judgement, but then immediately start to think of a small number of gifted teachers, another group of 'good enough' individuals, and then grimace at the memory of a hopeless case or two. The picture would probably be more complicated in that some staff might have been outstanding at some things and not good at others, some friendly but intellectually challenged, still others cleverer but unapproachable. The same is true of social workers, and indeed of all types of helper. Therefore, buried in the data of controlled experiments are potentially reinforceable clusters of effective practice and potentially avoidable deterioration effects; and in many control samples, clusters of unaided im-provement – or 'most remarkable providences', as they are termed by Rachman and Wilson (1980, ch. 4). Therefore two issues for future research arise: (a) the need to examine the individual results of therapists and tease out how these might reflect differences in professional behaviour; (b) the need to record and analyse how different helpers interpret the protocols of the methods or ap-proaches under test. This is happening increasingly, but more often in psychological research than in studies of social work effectiveness.

It is a common mistake to regard such therapist variables and 'placebo' effects (that is unintentional influences) as magically indeterminate and unde-finable. Considerable research has been undertaken to pin down these factors – all on the principle that clients and helpers transmit verbal and non-verbal behaviour to each other, not mysterious 'essences and atmospheres'. Certainly, human interaction is complex, subtle and often rapid. It is strewn with cultural and subcultural signals and replete with distortions and misattributions. Nevertheless, respondents in client-opinion studies give surprisingly pointed and detailed testimony as to what it is they find encouraging and discouraging in interviews (see Macdonald and Sheldon 1994). Indeed it is often difficult to move them from discussions of the style and content of these to considerations of methods, goals and outcomes.

We have a number of studies employing tough-minded empirical measures and a number of scales against which to assess therapist behaviour (see Carkhuff 1968; Maluccio 1979; Bergin and Garfield 1986). Probably the most influential work in this field is that of Truax and Carkhuff (1967) – a substantial research compilation based on the concepts developed by Carl Rogers (1951) with many clinical examples and much direct advice. This research, though plagued by some problems of construct validity, has stood the test of time and has given rise to other empirical work showing that helpers who regularly demonstrate the main features of effective interpersonal behaviour identified in analogue studies produce superior results in practice. The authors identified three major therapist variables and a range of other significant factors.

The three main items are *warmth*, *genuineness* and *accurate empathy*, and the important point is that Truax and Carkhuff have so refined these concepts that they are identifiable on videotape and can be scaled to a high degree of reliability. Let us now look at each of these in a little more detail.

Non-possessive warmth. This consists of (i) getting across to clients feelings of respect, liking, caring, acceptance and concern; (ii) managing to do this in a non-threatening way, so that there is no question of the client feeling managed or taken over, and no question that his or her standing in the eyes of the therapist depends on the production of approved-of responses to questions. Such a contingency is similar to Rogers's (1951) 'unconditional positive regard'. This obviously poses problems for behaviourists – indeed for any therapist. The first problem is that it may be that few of us can live up to it. This may be especially true of behaviourists, because of our interest in deliberately produced and manifest change. A key principle of behaviour modification is that behaviourists expect change to occur through the rewarding contingencies they produce. However, the approval and the disapproval of the therapist must be counted as a significant shaping influence – whether the therapist is aware of the process, or not (Rogers and Skinner 1956). Indeed, the literature is full of evidence of the unwanted shaping of clients by therapists of all persuasions (Heine 1953). Presumably these findings apply to behaviour therapists too. Perhaps Truax and Carkhuff are warning us of the dangers of the deliberate and easily visible presentation and withdrawal of approval – in a highly mechanical way? There is evidence to suggest that to the degree that clients feel coerced and manipulated, they will feel free to abandon discussions made in this context whenever the going gets rough (Festinger 1957). But this poses ethical problems, because does it not suggest that effective shaping equals covert shaping (see Chapter 8)?

The second problem is that even if we could do it, it may not be a good idea. Here are Bandura's forthright views on the matter:

Even if unconditional social approval and acceptance were possible, it would be no more meaningful as a precondition for change than non-contingent reinforcement in modifying any form of behavior. If this principle were applied in child rearing, parents would respond approvingly and affectionately when their children appeared with stolen goods, behaved unmanageably in school, physically injured their siblings and peers, refused to follow any household routines etc. 'Unconditional love' would make children directionless, impossible and completely unpredictable.

(Bandura 1969:79)

The traditional solution to this difference is to argue for the possibility of 'loving the sinner and hating the sin' – a very powerful set of contingencies but not easy to manage! The idea of separating out 'the behaviour' from 'the person' is a difficult one for a discipline that has always argued that 'the person *is* the behaviour'. My own solution is to argue first that a recognition of the power of external forces on behaviour, and second that a recognition of the enormous potential for change that exists in human beings, help considerably with the development of that other prerequisite for good therapists – a liking for people of all shapes and sizes. Further assistance comes from the idea of a cognitive-behavioural *programme* – note the word. To succeed, behavioural schemes have to be 'packaged' in some way. In my view they are best used as a special therapeutic device within a broader therapeutic relationship.

Therefore it is possible to conceive of applying Truax and Carkhuff's principle overall, partly as an ethical stance, partly as a supportive device; but within this context there should also exist an agreed course of action wherein different behaviours will produce different consequences. Failure to meet these special therapeutic contingencies will not and should not threaten the status of the client as a person of worth, but differential reinforcement of responses has to occur at certain points in the interests of producing worthwhile change. This suggestion is similar to that found in Hollis (1964), who argues for a distinction between 'sustaining procedures' and 'procedures of direct influence' in social casework. The implication is that, in complex cases, behaviour therapy *per se* would exist as a 'module' within a less distinctively technical approach based on relationship-maintaining attributes. Moving from one set of concerns to the other would then involve a noticeable 'change of gear' signalling to the client that now there are more closely prescribed tasks to be attempted.

Genuineness. Truax and Carkhuff (1967) have given us the best definition of this therapist attribute by telling us what it is not. To be 'genuine' in this sense is not to be 'phoney', not to hide behind a professional façade or 'image', not to be defensive in the face of criticism or challenge, and not to be unpredictable in the type of responses made to the client. Genuineness is to do with confidence, being yourself, not acting a part, appearing relaxed and at ease with yourself. The only (extra) problem here for behaviour therapists stems from the somewhat technical nature of our discipline. Many social workers and some clients reject behavioural approaches because of this aura of 'treating people like machines' – the *Clockwork Orange*-type of imagery that surrounds it. It is no good just dismissing this as ignorance; better to think of ways of presenting behaviour therapy in such a way that it does not sound so artificial and does not put up a barrier between client and helper. Behaviour therapy contains rather more 'headwork' than other, more gushing approaches, and this can be problematic if it produces an excessively businesslike 'Mr Fix-It' style: 'What have we got here? Tantrums? Right, do this three times a day for a week and . . .'. There is no necessity for a mechanical approach to behavioural methods. Indeed, the Sloane *et al.* study (1975) found that clients rated the behavioural workers higher than other groups on friendliness and empathy.

Accurate empathy. This is also a particular category of *behaviour* shown by the therapist. Positive feelings that the therapist has inside are of little practical use unless their presence is communicated to the client. Similarly, any detailed knowledge that the therapist achieves of the client's problem is likely to affect the client only to the extent that it can be accurately communicated to him. There are three key elements in this behaviour: (i) accuracy of understanding – letting the client know that you have a pointed grasp of his or her problems and dilemmas; (ii) showing the client that you are really trying to see things from his or her vantage point; (iii) letting the client see that your own mood and feelings are in tune with his. This ability is at least as much an attribute as a skill capable of being taught. It is the ability to imagine just how it must be to stand in the shoes of another person and to be able to experience feelings similar to those of the other person, and to demonstrate, in a tentative way, that this is the case.

Other influential factors include high *activity*: clients are reassured by helpers who are manifestly busy on their behalf – a finding which contradicts the principles of much psychoanalytical counselling. From a psychological, let alone a practical point of view, this makes sense. We all expend considerable amounts of time conducting little experiments on the differences between what people *say* and how they actually *behave* towards us. Cognitive-behavioural therapy fits easily with this injunction.

Another surprising factor is *self-disclosure*. Occasional references to commonalities of experience can have an encouraging and destigmatizing effect – provided that they are occasional and appropriate, and so do not degenerate into 'so you think you've got problems' exchanges.

A further factor is willingness to confront important discrepancies in clients' responses or examples of illogical or 'catastrophic' inferences. There is solid evidence for the potency of this variable, which is a key element in certain cognitive approaches (see Greenberg and Dompiere 1986).

Many social workers have neglected behavioural approaches in the past because they seemed to them too 'mechanical'. In reality, any understanding of reinforcement principles shows immediately that distant, automaton-like behaviour is unlikely to sustain co-operation. Social reinforcement – being listened to and understood, in a kindly, professional, manner – is among the most powerful of influences. Client-opinion studies over the last twenty years have shown that social workers are rather good at this. Our difficulties have traditionally lain in different directions, viz. striking up good relationships but not pursuing solutions; having an excellent settee-side manner, but being uneasy about giving the direct advice based on expertise – which clients in these studies were quite obviously looking for, but only occasionally getting.

Comparison studies of behavioural and cognitive approaches versus more traditional approaches do not in any case support this view that the former either attract the stiff and the stern, or that something in the technicalities of these methods shapes people into this style. Indeed, there are studies showing that clients prefer to work with behaviour therapists on just the grounds that they appear more genuine and sympathetic (see Bergin and Garfield 1986, ch. 7). This finding could be accounted for by the fact that cognitive-behavioural therapists have a substantial body of research grounding both their assessment and intervention skills. This gives confidence, which may well transmit itself to clients. Such factors are known to be important in studies of social influence and attitude change (see Cohen 1964). Moreover, practitioners in this field are not relying solely upon verbal influence, which emphasis regularly shows up in client-opinion research as a source of frustration.

On the evidence then, and from practical experience, there is nothing contained in cognitive-behavioural principles that threatens the core values of social work.

ORGANIZATIONAL FACTORS

What social workers do and do not do is probably more closely influenced by legislation, agency policy and political climate than is the case for any of the other helping professions. At the time of writing we are having to accommodate ourselves to the Children Act 1989; the far-reaching operational changes laid down in the National Health Service and Community Care Act 1990 – including the creation of an 'internal market' for welfare services. These legislative changes have been accompanied by a decade's worth of cost-conscious managerial and organizational change, somewhat akin to the application of Mao Tse Tung's policy of 'continuous revolution' to the public services. The result is *some* improvements in service delivery (Le Grand and Bartlett 1993; Davis 1992) but a state close to 'learned helplessness' (see p. 61) among professional staff. What chance that the none-too-well-rooted plant of cognitive-behavioural therapy can survive in a soil where fertilizer is in limited supply and everything is regularly dug up to see how well it is doing? Here are some reasons for qualified optimism:

(i) In those local authorities where the protocols of the 'internal market', including the separation of purchasing and providing functions, were piloted prior to April 1993 one has the impression of a growing awareness that due concern for issues of service quality requires attention to the content of what is supplied as well as who gets it, for how long and at what cost. There are parallels here with education, where despite the introduction of 'business principles' the key issues of teaching quality, teaching methods, and how validly to measure outcomes, refuse to go away. Pre-packaged services have their place. They can be effective and efficient in the face of well-understood, predictably recurring and relatively straightforward problems. I buy them myself when I need a new car tyre or battery, or where I know that a plastic bag of 4mm screws will do the job. However, for anything more complicated I want a diagnostician, not a technician. Much in the world of social services is *very* complicated.

(ii) A major objective of the introduction of business practices into the social services was the prevention of waste caused by the aimless provision of unfocused, long-term contact with expensive-to-deploy staff to no discernible effect. The principles of cognitive-behavioural work: clear assessments; closely-defined objectives; rigorous monitoring of progress; research-based methods of intervention and the pursuit of tangible outcomes within an agreed period of time, match these concerns almost exactly. Indeed, they predate them. Therefore, apart from ignorance and unfamiliarity, there are no reasons to suggest that this approach cannot be accommodated within purchasing and providing systems where something over and above basic care is required – as in child abuse prevention, or acute mental health work.

(iii) What happens, however, if cash limitations prohibit purchasing decisions above this statutory bottom line? My view is that simply to monitor risk or social decline, stepping in at the last moment to prevent collapse or scandal, will come to be seen for what it is – the most expensive form of service delivery available to us. Reception into care, long-term hospital treatment, secure accommodation are, apart from their known anti-social side effects, the least cost-effective disposals. To admit the possibility that the social services will be forced inevitably into this worst-case scenario, where no preventive therapeutic work is commissioned, is to accept that rationality has been permanently displaced by ideology in the public services. The history of social policy contains passing examples of irrationality (e.g. ineffective 'short sharp shock' treatment for delinquents) but also reminds us that the sieve of history has large holes.

(iv) Social services departments are currently required to spend 80 per cent of their purchasing power for community care in the voluntary and private sectors, the statutory authority being charged with monitoring contract compliance. It is very likely then that relevant but non-statutory functions will be farmed out – ultimately both, perhaps. This separation of functions within cases carries dangers yet to be realized. Indeed the risks and inefficiencies of providing different, overlapping services from different organizations were the main target of an earlier generation of reformers (Seebohm 1968). My prediction is that the general principle will not be extended to all sectors since it will be foreseen to be ineffective and dangerous. However, given that a large-scale transfer of therapeutic and other work to the voluntary sector will inevitably take place, what does the profession have to fear from it? Very little, I think. Social work thrives in the United States under a very similar system. It pioneered the development of effective approaches (admittedly with a high chaff–wheat ratio) and it undertakes most of the world's effectiveness research. A greater danger lies in the abandonment of public welfare principles by the profession.

(v) Next, imagine two equal-sized balls of plasticine representing the resources available for given cases. Note that, analogously, patterns of service provision can also be 'rolled out' either long and thin, short and fat or knobbly, or in 'knobbly' fashion. Long and thin allows for priorities to be switched rapidly between cases (since contact is infrequent in any event). Short and fat models of intervention, as usually required in cognitive-behavioural therapy, though they cost no more and are more likely to be effective, are administratively inconvenient in this regard. They demand attention to case-resolution indicators, not to caseload numbers. Here is a challenge for case managers worthy of the name.

(vi) Success and failure in cognitive-behavioural approaches is a more public affair than in others. It is not impossible to imagine a team in which a number of clear and readily apparent failures of influence (which can be learnt from) is regarded as better practice than a mass of poorly formulated, unconvincingly vague and subjective claims. However, 'smokescreen recording' can carry short-term 'benefits' for all concerned. The only reasonable counter-case is that effective organizations depend upon good 'intelligence'. Reliable, though occasionally uncomfortable, feedback on performance *must* carry advantages in the longer term.

(vii) The provision of social services has always been riddled with distortions. Now, again, we have a new set opportunities and problems. What stands in the way of the rational accommodation of new policies is the lack of a strong professional voice and, at the time of writing, an independent platform from which it can be heard to speak.[4] We would do well to consider the costs of this, and model our future behaviour on the good cognitive-behavioural principle that unless you have plans for yourself you run the risk of being swallowed up in someone else's.

CONCLUSIONS

This chapter has set out to review the professional and disciplinary circumstances in which cognitive-behavioural methods are being used, but could be used more by social workers. I have attempted to make a case for this by drawing together trends in social work effectiveness research and outcome research from related disciplines. Where obstacles exist to the selection of methods of helping on rational, empirical grounds, I have identified these and argued why I think they should be pushed aside or circumvented. Nevertheless, I am conscious that, whatever their merits, many social workers turn away from these approaches on vague philosophical grounds – aesthetic grounds might be a better phrase, since objections are rarely accompanied by the disciplined logical analysis that real philosophy requires. In short, they just don't like the look and sound of anything 'behavioural' because of what they think it implies about the nature of human existence. Accordingly, since friendly persuasion is the aim of this book, the next chapter presents a counter-case to these misgivings.

2

PHILOSOPHICAL IMPLICATIONS

Although the greater part of this book is devoted to technical matters, it is not, as I have said, my intention to persuade social workers to become mere technicians. Given the complex and controversial nature of the problems confronting them, it is vital that they should be able to think for themselves and make clear judgements about what their actions – even allegedly common-sensical and non-theoretical actions – assume about the person needing their help, and about the most effective way of providing it. Therefore, they cannot afford to be philosophically naive.

The first set of questions concerns the processes by which behaviour is instigated, influenced and controlled.

MIND AND BEHAVIOUR

The common view held of behaviour in our culture, and most others, is that it is a surface manifestation of a much more complex and interesting process going on somewhere inside our heads. Further, that (except in the case of a few bodily reflexes) a non-material, non-detectable 'something', obeying none of the known physical laws, manages, nevertheless, to control, via its host organ the brain, the sum total of our behaviour. I refer, of course, to the concept of mind. So much is obvious, you might think. But however natural-seeming and taken-for-granted such notions are, they raise a number of awkward logical problems. How, for example, *can* a non-physical, quasi-spiritual entity give rise to something as tangible as behaviour? Speaking metaphorically: what kind of cerebral 'clutch mechanism' connects and disconnects mental activity and physical activity? How can an event of any kind, even a thought, arise spontaneously out of nothing as an *uncaused* happening? Certainly such things are not within our everyday experience of the rest of the material world. So why do we suppose that we are not bound by the same laws that appear to forbid this elsewhere? Part of the answer is that given the anticipated complex-ity of having to account scientifically, that is materially, for something so enormously divergent as human behaviour, there is an almost irresistible temptation to assign the whole question of causality to the action of some magical 'black box' phenomenon within, thereby short-circuiting the whole vexing issue, or at least moving the discussion to a metaphysical plane. This done, we are left to contemplate only whether 'the mind' is a unity, or how it is different from 'the soul'; whether it has 'compartments' and 'faculties' or an unconscious bit; how it can get 'diseased' or 'unbalanced', and so forth. In the same way, it is easier to explain the origins and development of life by inventing another supreme being, a marvellous version of ourselves, who fortunately views us as His favourite creation. Then we can assign to Him the responsibility for everything. Similarly, many prefer to account for their daily fortunes by the movements of the stars and planets. We do it because, despite appearances, it is easier. The baffling alternative is to try to work out the complex interrelationship between our actions and the forces of the environment to which we respond – and which responds to us.

The notion of man as a physical shell, piloted from within by another kind of influence, is amusingly caricatured in the children's comic strip shown in Figure 2.1 on p. 34. The trick is to try to imagine what these *homunculi* have inside *their* heads, controlling their actions.

An early advocate of this idea of man as some kind of complicated machine, driven from within, was the seventeenth-century philosopher René Descartes. In trying to square his interest in materialism and his orthodox Christian beliefs, he invented the doctrine of dualism. Here is the first half of it: 'I desire, I say, that you consider that these functions (respiration, sight, hearing, ideas) occur naturally in this machine solely by the disposition of its organs, not less than the movements of a clock'(Descartes 1664).

As to the other half of this duality which so mysteriously influences the 'clockwork' at every click and turn, no knowledge was claimed of it beyond the certainty of its existence. Descartes saw thinking as the main evidence for it, and a surer guide to his own existence than the inferred sensations of his physical body. He expressed this view in the famous dictum: *cogito ergo sum* – 'I think, therefore I am'.

Descartes made his analogy with the most complex machine available to him – the clock. Today behaviour is more likely to be seen as resulting from the operation of some cerebral super-computer – the most complex machine available to us. But even in this contemporary version, 'the computer' is usually said to be controlled from within by the magic of mind, by a 'ghost in the machine' (Ryle 1949). Gilbert Ryle argued with great clarity that this problem of the mind–body relationship is less a scientific conundrum than a philosophical one. It is an error of attribution, or in his terms a 'category mistake' and a 'philosopher's myth'. He offers the following illustration of this view:

A foreigner visiting Oxford for the first time is shown a number of colleges, libraries, playing fields, museums, scientific departments and administrative offices. He then asks 'But where is the University? I have seen where the members of the colleges live, where the Registrar works,

Figure 2.1 'The Numskulls'
Source: The Beezer Book, 1980, © D.C. Thomson & Co. Ltd.

where the scientists experiment and the rest. But I have not yet seen the University in which reside and work the members of your University.' It has then to be explained to him that the University is just another collateral institution, some ulterior counterpart to the colleges, laboratories, and offices which he has seen. The University is just the way in which all that he has already seen is organised. He was mistakenly allocating the University to the same category as that to which the other institutions belong.

(Ryle 1949:17–18)

Accepting that attempts to define mind as an independent entity with self-generating causative properties have fallen into this 'category mistake', it is possible to see how much more logical it is to infer mind from observable behaviour. This is the view of behaviourism, which, proponents suggest, can best be thought of as the philosophy of the science of human behaviour (Skinner 1974), and which is seen by detractors as a philosophical and metho-dological dead-end.

Traditional behaviourism further suggests that since behaviour occurs as a phenomenon within the physical universe it must therefore obey the same laws of cause and effect. Behaviour is seen in this philosophy as an organic adapta-tion to an ambivalent physical and social environment. In turn, human behaviour acts upon this environment, changes it, and so provides a source of stimulation for others and of feedback for the individual.

Behaviourism further proposes that, contrary to the established view, the cognitive processes which we call consciousness are an interesting by-product of this relationship between body and environment, if you like: *ago ergo sum* – 'I act, therefore I am'.

The experience that we have learned to categorize as 'mind' is the experience of our brains at work, processing sensory stimuli, and, through the use of language, encoding, classifying, manipulating and storing in symbolic form information about the contingencies in our environment and the likely effects of our future behaviour upon these. Given that this organ, a wondrous super-computer made of meat, has upwards of thirteen thousand million nerve cells, we really have no need to resort to 'ghosts in machines'. A 'machine' of this incredible complexity is likely to have some pretty ghostly propensities of its own:

> Each cubic inch of the cerebral cortex probably contains more than ten thousand miles of nerve fibres, connecting the cell together. If the cells and fibres in one human brain were all stretched out end to end they would certainly reach to the moon and back. Yet the fact that they are not arranged end to end enabled man to go there himself. The astonishing tangle within our head makes us what we are. Every cell in the cortex receives on its surface an average of several thousand terminals from the fibres of other cells. The richness of interconnection makes each neuron a Cartesian soul.

(Blakemore 1977:85)

Popper and Eccles (1977) – a philosopher collaborating with a neurologist – have described the effects of the almost unimaginably complex development hinted at here as 'materialism transcending itself'. Their view is that a quantitative extension of function to this seemingly near-infinite degree results 'without any violating of the laws of physics' in *qualitatively* different effects.

Behaviourism does not seek to deny the subjective importance of consciousness, rather to challenge views of this phenomenon which represent it as some sort of disconnected entity, impervious, when it chooses, to environmental influence:

> The objection to inner states is not that they do not exist, but that they are not relevant in a functional analysis. We cannot account for the behaviour of any system while staying wholly inside it; eventually we must turn to forces operating upon the organism from without.
>
> (Skinner 1953:55)

The point is that while I can have direct access to my own conscious processes, I cannot have ready access to yours. What you may tell me about the goings-on inside your head is subject to all sort of internal and external pressures and distortions before it reaches me. A genuinely scientific account of the relationship between thinking and doing must therefore, it was/is argued, concentrate as fully as it can on the *doing* part of the equation:

> Whenever we ask about a sentence, 'What does it mean?' what we expect is instructions as to the circumstances in which the sentence is to be used; we want a description of the conditions under which the sentence will form a *true* proposition, and of those that will make it *false*.
>
> (Schlick 1936:340)

I am not speaking here of absolute truth or of absolute falsehood – such hypothetical states are hard to come by in the hardest of sciences, let alone in 'epistemologically challenged' disciplines such as our own – but rather of the ruling out, as far as possible, by logic and by methods of empirical observation, of obvious errors. We can never be *certain* of our propositions: 'despite what she says, this child has been sexually abused'; 'this young man knows what he is doing, really'; we can only be temporarily encouraged or discouraged according to the results of tests which rein in the tendency of the human mind to fill in the spaces between observations. This sort of thing:

> I found that those of my friends who were admirers of Marx, Freud and Adler were impressed by a number of points common to those theories, and especially by their apparent *explanatory power*. These theories appeared to be able to explain practically everything that happened within the fields to which they referred. To study any of them seemed to have the effect of an intellectual conversion or revelation, opening your eyes to a new truth hidden from those not yet initiated. Once your eyes were

thus opened, you saw confirming instances everywhere: the world was full of *verifications* of the theory.

(Popper 1963:5)

When reference to possible interior goings-on seems to help the investigation along – as perhaps with the concept of 'attitude', the level of inference should always be kept at the lowest possible level. This position on what counts as evidence in the assessment of human behaviour gives findings in this field their relatively greater robustness and replicability. But, however heuristically useful, are they a true account of human experience, or even of the necessary limits of scientific enquiry?

The problem with radical behaviourism is that it fails to distinguish between the person who sits, head in hands, on a railway platform for ten minutes because his train has been cancelled (again); and the person who sits in exactly the same position for exactly the same time who has recently lost a loved one and who may or may not jump under the next incoming service. The behaviour is the same, though the latent distinction may become clearer fifteen minutes later. The task of prediction for the Samaritans, railway police and social scientists is the same, for if asked what they were doing both subjects are likely to reply: 'waiting for a train'. Nevertheless, we know that the interior experience of these two people is different, and may be implicated in what happens next.

In the past we were forced to choose between the rampant subjectivity of mentalistic psychology – the idea that thoughts arise spontaneously from the conscious or unconscious mind and direct our behaviour (which is rather like saying that appetite causes eating); or the 'self-denying ordinance' of behaviourism, confining ourselves to exterior observations of eating time and speed, salivary flow, etc., ruling out all interior states from peckishness to ravenousness, including disguising one's hunger for reasons of social propriety.

Recent developments in psychology suggest that a science of cognition may not be the contradiction in terms it once seemed. Dennett (1991), a philosopher with a prodigious knowledge of biology and psychology, has laid out the following personal ground rules for such a project in a wonderfully provocative book:

(1) *No Wonder Tissue allowed.* I will try to explain every puzzling feature of human consciousness within the framework of contemporary physical science; at no point will I make an appeal to inexplicable or unknown forces, substances, or organic powers.

(2) *No feigning anesthesia.* It has been said of behaviorists that they feign anesthesia – they pretend they don't have the experiences we know darn well they share with us. If I wish to deny the existence of some controversial feature of consciousness, the burden falls on me to show that it is somehow illusory.

(3) *No nitpicking about empirical details.* I will try to get all the scientific

facts right, insofar as they are known today, but there is abundant controversy about just which exciting advances will stand the test of time. If I were to restrict myself to 'facts that have made it into the textbooks', I would be unable to avail myself of some of the most eye-opening recent discoveries (if that is what they are).

(Dennett 1991:40)

Studies of human perception (see Gregory 1970; Dixon 1976; Sheldon 1987a), and of the effects of localized brain damage (Sacks 1985), research on artificial intelligence (Boden 1981), and work on consciousness by neuro-scientists, are giving rise to imaginative theories regarding the nature of consciousness – but, and this is what is new, these theories are grounded in a developing body of *empirical* research. The model of consciousness that is emerging has the following features:

— The importance of evolutionary pressures is underlined, not only in respect of our basic physical reflexes, but for cognition too. Edelman's (1987) concept of 'neural Darwinism' (not so very far off from Homme's (1965) attempts to apply operant conditioning principles to thought) suggests that set patterns of information-processing are governed by early experience, while our brains are still developing. Particularly productive neural 'firing' patterns and combinations get laid down by the influence of the environment on brain microstructures. All this moves us even further away from the concept of the free-thinking 'I', in charge of all decisions – 'the Central Meaner', as Dennett describes this hypothetical entity. Rather, consciousness is a multi-layered activity, much of it automatic. There is no 'screen in the head' on which all options can be flashed, because if there were, there would be 'no one' to watch it:

> There is no single, definitive 'stream of consciousness', because there is no central Headquarters, no Cartesian Theater where 'it all comes together' for the perusal of a Central Meaner. Instead of such a single stream (however wide) there are multiple channels in which specialist circuits try, in parallel pandemoniums to do their various things, creating Multiple Drafts as they go. Most of these fragmentary drafts of 'narrative' play short-lived roles in the modulation of current activity but some get promoted to other, functional roles in swift succession, by the activity of a virtual machine in the brain.

(Dennett 1991:63)

— Consciousness, then, is 'future-producing', designed to answer the question, vital in evolution: 'what do I do next?'. Consciousness is no 'free-floating entity'; it is highly dependent on 'hard-wired' endowed circuits and on more adaptable 'preferred channel' ways of problem-solving, based on experience of the effects of our behaviour.

— Consciousness is less free of contemporary sensory input than many psychological models would suggest, and thinking is less free of 'yesterday's environments' with their attendant successes and failures of actions than some psychological models have led us to believe.
— Much of our behaviour is unconsciously formed in line with the above points. Range and complexity disguise the automaticity of set thinking patterns and set responses.

Does all this mean that we are machines after all? Let us examine this question, and consider the next obstacle to acceptance of cognitive-behavioural models: the charge that these procedures assume that people are really programmable 'machines' which, it is alleged, denies the essential humanity of those who come to us for help.

Figure 2.2 Sydney Harris 'I think you should be more explicit here in step two' (after Dennett)
Source: American Scientist

FREE WILL VERSUS ENVIRONMENTAL CONTROL

All new heresies which suggest that human beings (or in this case, the experience of an inner conscious 'I') may not necessarily be at the centre of the universe give rise to uncomfortable feelings. Furthermore they appear to defy common sense. I *know* that the world revolves around me, and that I spontaneously cause things to happen in it, just as I know that the sun revolves around the earth and that the earth is flat. I see these things every day. Similarly, I know that my will is free and that if I wanted to, *really* wanted to, I mean, I could leave this writing table now for a pleasant walk outside. The fact that I forego this opportunity and continue to write is because I *want* to. Clear enough? It shouldn't be. As an explanation of my present actions it is pure tautology. It says nothing about causes, and does little to advance the reader's knowledge of the factors leading to my present behaviour. A more complicated explanation is that in the past I have had pleasant experiences (experiences that I have learned to connect with comfort or excitement, feelings of satisfaction, control over my circumstances, and so on) as a result of doing things like this at the expense of other, perhaps more immediately pleasurable activities.

So again, because of my learning history, as I sit here I have emotions that arouse images of similar future events: hearing again the lovely sound of a manuscript hitting the bottom of a post-box; holding a bound copy one day; a favourable review, perhaps; the approval of colleagues; the image of an interested reader and so on. These are the reasons why my present behaviour continues. In addition, there is the anticipation of aversive consequences lying in wait for me, should I do anything else: walking across a field but as a *wastrel* (mental camera pans back to reveal lonely figure in bleak landscape – after David Lean). My behaviour is following a pattern, as does all behaviour, though it is not always an easy task to identify the controlling factors, especially not from the outside, where, in the present case, it might look as if I were just sitting at a table with a fixed expression.

Were one of these controlling factors to change, or a new one to emerge – the noise from outside my window of a low-flying aircraft, or the news that the deadline for this book had been extended, then my behaviour would change markedly, and fall under the control of a new set of variables. Does this mean that I am a robot? I certainly don't feel like a robot, nor do I experience the behaviour of other people as robotic, and it may be that this is the important thing about free will and determinism. We have the experience of free choice, though we do not choose our choices, nor do we choose the thought patterns which accompany their prospect and execution.

Skinner (1974) argues that the absolute prediction of human behaviour from its causes would be a task similar in complexity to that facing a physicist trying to predict the individual trajectories of all the droplets in a rainstorm (probably a gross underestimation of the problem). But the fact that it cannot be done does not mean that such trajectories do not exist or that they are not the result of known forces. Nor does it mean that we should not go in for the behavioural equivalent of 'weather forecasting'. Nor does it mean that we should not look at local conditions so long as we remember that our little maps of hypothetical cause and effect are part of larger ones. First there are small problems of helping a person with a learning disability to acquire skills in self-care (local weather), then there is the wider problem of discrimination in society (climate).

Rather than fretting over the issue of free will or questions of self-determination, the concern of those of us who wish to use psychological knowledge for good should be to widen the range of possible responses the individual can make to his or her environment – including responses which seek to change it.

In response to such a discussion Dr Johnson once said, striking a rock, 'we know our will is free and *there's* an end on't!' (Boswell 1740). With due deference, given what we have learned in the behavioural sciences in the last century, it would be more reasonable to argue that our 'will' is an inference from our behaviour – which is *not* free. However, given the enormous complexity of this interaction of stimulus and response, we *feel* that it is (and there's an end on't?). As before, a quantitative change from one single, simple reflex to a multiplicity of stimulus–response connections produces a qualitative change in appearance, and behaviour turns into a *process* in the same way that a series of film stills is turned into movement and drama by the rapid motion of the movie projector. The stills are there all the time and are the invisible components that give rise to the perception of behaviour on the screen. Action and interaction become a *flow* of behaviour, or a *stream* of events.

However, we need to remember that even streams have their component parts, right down to the individual molecules of hydrogen and oxygen that are their building blocks. At this microparticle level we are increasingly led to believe that 'building blocks' is quite the wrong sort of term, and that chaos rages (Gleick 1988). But this may have less to do with indeterminism than *indeterminability*, though as an empiricist I have to accept that the two are effectively the same, for now.[1] The view of interaction taken here is that discrete elements in this process of influence by the environment, and re-influence by the individual, are blurred by the speed and complexity of events. Such a view acknowledges multiple causation and recognizes that what is often regarded as the cause of something is merely the last of, or the most conspicuous part of, a great many preconditions necessary to its occurrence (Verworn 1916). In this way it can be said that operating the switch *caused* a light bulb to illuminate, but in fact many other complex factors were at work to bring this about.

Sir Karl Popper suggests that a proper challenge for determinists is to predict the exact moment at which his cat might jump on to his writing table, and to draw the exact outline of paw marks where it will land (Popper 1982). Can't be done. Yet how equally silly to see this as a completely indeterminate sequence. Cats are genetically equipped for jumping; their instincts make them feel safer when high up, they learn readily to associate places where their human food- and comfort-providers sit, mainly in the mornings perhaps, and so forth. In any case, I fancy that had B. F. Skinner been given a day or two with this cat we may have seen something worth watching.

It is often said, all these philosophical diversions aside, that social workers should be practical people, which is often simply politician-speak for 'shut up and do as we tell you'. It is true that we are mostly concerned with the nearby causes of unhappiness (local 'weather'). These influences are usually the most predictable and the most tractable, but they are not the only ones with which we are concerned. We also have a duty to persuade our clients to think more rationally, less self-punishingly about larger-scale political factors ('climate'). A case in point is unemployment. This causes depression, family and relationship difficulties, increases crime, adversely affects health, damages the welfare of children and produces widespread social dislocation. It is usually discussed by politicians (where they feel that they can do nothing about it) as a macro-economically determined phenomenon (a curious convergence of view, this, between conservatives and old-style Marxists). Yet most public measures taken against it are individual, psychological and motivational in character. For example, the recent re-labelling of the unemployed (in true Orwellian fashion) as 'job-seekers' – are the homeless soon to become 'house-seekers' one wonders? What little help is provided ('job-clubs') reinforces a view among victims that it is *their* fault, that they should try harder, present themselves better and so forth. A little positive cognitive-realignment and re-attribution in such cases, based on the facts, is the opposite of shaping individuals into social conformity and denial of choice.

Being Utopian at heart, social workers have a fickle relationship with theories (see p. 6). Any sniff of a constraining implication and they are set aside for something more supportive of the best in human ambition. Thus, behaviourism is a 'closed-system', is 'determinist', is 'controlling', is 'dangerous' in the wrong hands – where other therapeutic approaches, however ineffective, are not. This chapter, and Chapter 8 on ethics, are offered as a corrective to such views in the hope of persuading readers that these are matters to be wrestled with, not selected for comfort's sake. Here is a final note of dissonance for those of you who yet retain such views. It comes from the keyboard of Richard Dawkins (1976; see also 1982) – a brilliant biologist, a neo-Darwinist, and a materialist:

> The point I am making now is that, even if we look on the dark side and assume that individual man is fundamentally selfish, our conscious foresight – our capacity to simulate the future in imagination – could save us from the worst selfish excesses of the blind-replicators. We have at least the mental equipment to foster our long-term selfish interests rather than merely our short-term selfish interests. We have the power to defy the selfish genes of our birth and, if necessary, the sefish memes[2] of our

indoctrinations. We can even discuss ways of deliberately cultivating and nurturing pure, disinterested altruism – something that has no place in nature, something that has never existed before in the whole history of the world.

(Dawkins 1976:215)

3

LEARNING THEORY AND RESEARCH

This chapter will review the different theories of learning from which the techniques known collectively as cognitive-behavioural therapy, or cognitive-behaviour modification, are derived. Such an account is necessary for two reasons. First, so that the person applying the techniques will understand the reasons for what he or she is doing, rather than just dipping into a bag of therapeutic tricks and hoping to come up with the right approach. Second, so that a proper assessment of the client's problems can be made. In this field, there are no general purpose procedures, and decisions about which techniques to use are based upon certain well-established findings as to how behaviour (including problematic behaviour) and its cognitive and affective accompaniments are acquired in the first place.

Until recently, an exercise such as this would have been relatively straightforward, but as the reader will see, more recent research into the role of cognitive variables and their effects on overt behaviour (Bandura 1977; Hollon and Beck 1994; Eysenck and Keane 1990; Dennett 1991) has tugged behavioural psychology out of its previously neat and tidy shape. While all this is very exciting it makes the task of the newcomer more difficult. Let us apply a good behavioural principle and start off simply, moving on to more difficult and speculative issues later. Here is a list of basic theoretical assumptions:

(i) By far the greater portion of the behavioural repertoire with which individuals are equipped is the product of learning. This vast range of possible responses is acquired through lengthy interaction with an ambivalent physical and social environment.

(ii) Genetic and other physiological factors also influence behaviour in a more general sense, and there is an interaction between these and environment through inborn influences on intelligence, temperament and personality, and through predispositions to mental disorder (Eysenck 1965; Thomas *et al.* 1968; Heatherington and Parke 1986; Sheldon 1994a).

(iii) Two broad processes of associative learning account for the acquisition and maintenance of motor, verbal, cognitive and emotional responses. These are: *classical or respondent* conditioning, based on the work of the

44

great Russian physiologist I. P. Pavlov, and *operant or instrumental* conditioning, based on the work of the American psychologists E. L. Thorndike (1898) and B. F. Skinner (1953). To these influences must be added *vicarious learning*, or *modelling*, which process contains elements of both classical and operant associations (Bandura 1969).

(iv) Consciousness, and the ways in which we process information about past, present and predicted future environments – which bundles of stimuli, contingencies and imaginings include self-observation and appraisal of our own behaviour – , are a deeply mysterious, but not mystical set of phenomena. Thinking, too, follows patterns and is rarely far removed from the effects of external influences. In other words, above the level of simple reflexes, we do not simply *respond* to stimuli, we *interpret* them first, but not haphazardly (Bandura 1977; Dennett 1991).

(v) Behaviours that we judge to be 'maladaptive', 'abnormal' or 'self-defeating' are learned in exactly the same way as those that we are disposed to call 'adaptive' or 'normal'. Any apparent differences between the two are a property of the attributive and evaluative judgements we make about behaviour, rather than of the properties of the behaviour itself or its origins.

(vi) The behavioural and cognitive-behavioural therapies owe their existence to learning theory – really a vast body of experimental evidence on how humans adapt themselves to their environments by a process akin to 'behavioural natural selection' – by which strains of action, patterns of thoughts and feelings thrive, perish, or lie dormant according to the *effects* that they have. Each dimension of learning has given rise to therapeutic approaches logically consistent with the basic research.

(vii) Properly applied, these therapeutic derivatives have a direct and beneficial effect on a wide range of problems and are not threatened by a re-emergence of 'symptoms' in some different form (Rachman and Wilson 1980).

The next thing of which the reader needs to be made aware is that there is not one master learning theory from which all these principles are derived, but many different, overlapping theories, some of which have led to broad theoretical consensus, and others to continuing disputes. However, before we can proceed to examine these differences, we need a general definition of learning. There are many available, but they tend to range from the general but vaguely unsatisfactory, to the meticulous but, for practical purposes, barely usable. The common ground between them is that the concept of learning applies to the *associative processes* whereby new and relatively durable responses are added to the individual's repertoire. The following simple outline will meet our immediate requirements. (Those with an appetite for extended technical definitions should consult Hillner 1979 and/or Gray 1975.)

45

Learning may be defined as a relatively permanent change in behaviour that occurs as the result of prior experience.

(Hilgard, Atkinson and Atkinson 1979:18)

Three qualifications are immediately necessary even to this short, formal definition. First, and contrary to the everyday meaning of the term, there need be no intention on anyone's part to *impart* learning for it to take place. Nor need there be any *intention* on the part of the learner to acquire new information or behaviour. Second, we must exclude all effects due to fatigue, illness or the influence of drugs. Third, the effects of learning may not be immediately apparent. A newly acquired potential for behaviour can be stored in memory until circumstances are propitious for its performance.

The next question is, *how* do organisms learn? As I have indicated, arguments continue over the precise nature of the process, but five related influences are usually cited.

(i) Classical conditioning: whereby the temporal-spatial association of one stimulus with another – already capable of producing a certain response – leads eventually to responding to either stimulus alone.

(ii) Operant conditioning: where the acquisition of new responses occurs as a result of our experience of the rewarding, punishing, or relief-giving consequences of behaviour.

(iii) Vicarious learning: where new responses are acquired by observing the behaviour of others and the outcomes that their actions produce.

(iv) Cognitive influences governing the *interpretation* of stimuli.

(v) Genetic-environmental interactions, whereby learning some things is easier or harder than others.

Let us now examine the implications of what has been proposed so far in more detail, beginning with factors rooted in our biology.

GENETIC INFLUENCES

Mention the possibility of innate influences on behaviour in social work circles and you are likely to hear the background hissing once reserved for the characters with black hats and moustaches in silent movies. There are good Pavlovian reasons for such irrational reactions: (a) the mistaken identification of all genetics research with right wing political ideology in general, and the manipulations of Sir Cyril Burt in particular; (b) a perceived conflict with allegedly more 'democratic' notions of social engineering to secure the needs of individuals; (c) unflattering professional implications for social workers who, if such influences were valid, would be condemned to struggle vainly against fixed human potentialities. These views are plain wrong. Modern genetics research stresses biological and environmental *interaction* (Berger 1985; Thomas *et al.* 1968; Gottesman 1991). However, if there are predispositions within us that make some things easier to learn and adjust to, and some things harder, then arguably we had better know about them – for ethical as well as technical reasons, as the following illustration reveals.

Case example

I recently interviewed a client with an autistic son who (with limited assistance from the helping professions) had worked out a rough and ready behavioural management scheme for herself. It worked reasonably well when applied consistently, but left her feeling guilty. She was guilty about 'regimentation', guilty about having occasionally to resort to medication, and guilty that she and her husband might have failed to co-operate fully with a recent course of psychoanalytically-flavoured family therapy which they had found bizarre. Focusing on the irrationality of such feelings and their deleterious effects, congratulating her on her skills as an amateur behaviour therapist and putting her in touch with a regional support group, produced considerable relief. There was little else that could have improved upon her existing approach, nothing to do except to reinforce it and to try to remove from her any irrational guilt over the limits of her influence on a predominantly physical condition.

A bare knowledge of genetic influences is important, therefore, in telling us what *not* to do (or to imply) through our professional behaviour.

INNATE INFLUENCES ON CHILDHOOD DEVELOPMENT

The word 'sterile' often appears before the phrase 'nature/nurture debate' in textbooks, indicating, to me at least, that the authors have given up on the most important topic in psychology. This is understandable but regrettable, and is largely due to the immense methodological problems involved in unravelling the cable-knitted strands of these influences. Yet significant work has been done that avoids the simplistic approaches of early research, and the balance of probability has steadily shifted away both from the sporting environmentalism of the 1960s and 1970s and the a priori genetic explanations of an earlier era, towards the centre, the point at which two strong sets of influences interact to produce typicalities in behaviour and emotions The careful and persistent longitudinal work of Thomas *et al.* (1968) represents this shift rather well.

Here is the issue – a brave one to take up at the time:

> As physicians we began many years ago to encounter reasons to question the prevailing one-sided emphasis on environment. We found that some children with severe psychological problems had a family upbringing which did not differ essentially from the environment of other children who developed no severe problems. On the other hand, some children

were found to be free of personality disturbances although they had experienced severe family disorganisation from parental care.

(Thomas *et al.* 1968:1)

Thomas *et al.* observed (with acceptable levels of reliability) substantial qualitative and quantitative differences in the behaviour of a sample of babies (n=181) and rated them along the following dimensions:

(i) The level and extent of motor activity;
(ii) The 'rhythmicity', or degree of regularity of functions such as eating, elimination and the cycle of sleeping and wakefulness;
(iii) The response to a new object or person, in terms of whether the child accepts the new experience or withdraws from it;
(iv) The adaptability of behaviour to changes in the environment;
(v) The threshold of sensitivity to stimuli;
(vi) The intensity, or energy level of responses;
(vii) The child's general mood or 'disposition', whether cheerful or given to crying, pleasant or 'cranky', sociable or otherwise;
(viii) The degree of the child's distractability from what he or she is doing;
(ix) The span of the child's attention and degree of persistence in an activity.

They then classified the children (according to the profile created by their positions on these continua) as *'easy'*, *'slow-to-warm-up'* and *'difficult'*, and followed them up over the next twenty-odd years. They were concerned to see whether children who exhibited, for example, low levels of conditionability and high levels of fractiousness early in childhood posed greater problems for parents as they grew up, and whether patterns of over-representation in referral for psychological help would emerge. Here is a summary of their findings:

(i) Temperamental characteristics tended to remain stable over the years, 'slow-to-warm-up' babies growing into quiet schoolchildren, active outgoing babies into active, outgoing teenagers.
(ii) The categories employed had considerable predictive value. For example, 70 per cent of the children from the 'difficult' group (parents did not know of this classification) developed behavioural problems requiring professional intervention, whereas only 18 per cent of the 'easy' children did.
(iii) Temperamental–environmental clashes were readily understandable in terms of the child's early behavioural profile and were often reversible once a consistent, 'with the grain' environment or set of contingencies was engineered. For example, active, outgoing, hard-to-condition babies who moved on to controlled classroom conditions tended to kick over the traces. Children from the 'difficult' group generally exhibited many problems of frustration control and needed extra help to acquire a tolerable measure of this.
(iv) Attempts by parents to counter adverse temperamental tendencies were often effective. However, the further down the shoulders of the distribu-

tion curve the child was in early life, the greater the effort and persistence required to modify this as the children grew up.

This important research, part of a series, with findings well replicated elsewhere (see Heatherington and Parke 1986) does not carry the authority of a separated twin study. It does not, for example, control for experiences in the womb (though this does not substantially alter the argument). What it does is to reinforce something that parents have been saying to us for years, namely, that children are *different* right from the start, that they are not just pieces of organic blotting paper, soaking up environmental influences, rather they are active contributors to the process of interaction with their parents. A growing body of evidence counsels us to take more seriously the child's individual contribution to the learning equation:

> At a very early age, human babies show signs of a strong urge to master the environment. They are limited in what they can do by the slow development of their skill in controlling their own movements. Thus it is fair to call them 'helpless' in the sense that they cannot manage the environment well enough to survive unaided. This makes it all the more interesting to discover that the urge to manage the environment is already there at the time of this helplessness and that it does not appear to derive from anything else or to depend on any reward apart from the achieving of competence and control.
>
> (Donaldson 1978:110)

The upshot of all this is that we must realize that some expectations and some plans will be easier for some children to go along with than others. Here is what most parents think they are going to get when they have a baby:

> John was my touchy feely baby. From the first day in the hospital he cuddled and seemed so contented to be held that I could hardly bear to put him down . . . We took him everywhere because he seemed to enjoy new things. You could always sit him in a corner and he'd entertain himself. Sometimes I'd forget he was there until he'd start laughing or prattling.
>
> (Heatherington and Parke 1986:85)

And here is the kind of testimony about the realities of child rearing that we should, perhaps, be listening to more open-mindedly:

> Nothing was easy with Chris. Mealtimes, bedtimes, toilet training were all hell. It would take me an hour and a half to get part of a bottle into him and he'd be hungry two hours later. I can't remember once in the first two years when he didn't go to bed crying. I'd try to rock him to sleep but as soon as I'd tiptoe over to put him in his crib his head would lurch up and he'd start bellowing again. He didn't like any kind of

changes in his routine. New people and new places upset him so it was
hard to take him anywhere.

(Heatherington and Parke 1986:85)

The disappointment and guilt created by such experiences can lead to the
pathologization of temperamental differences, the blaming of the victims, and
a vicious circle creating a risk of child abuse – as the following case example
shows:

Case example

A breathless member of the public telephoned social services to say that her
neighbour, a young woman, was pacing the garden rocking her baby with
exaggerated movements and yelling at it to be quiet, and that she feared for its
safety. The subsequent interview revealed the following.

Since bringing the baby home three months ago he had slept irregularly and
unpredictably, crying most nights and throughout the day. The parents had
tried attempting to regulate feeding; had made use of 'demand' approaches;
and had tried to ignore fractiousness – but were always defeated by the child's
persistence. The child had been examined by a paediatrician, and the health
visitor had called regularly to advise on the removal of obvious provocations
for the behaviour. The parents were tired, angry, disappointed and beginning
to row. Mother especially felt that the problem was due to some failure of hers.
Medical staff unwittingly reinforced this view by telling her the obvious – none
of which advice worked. More worryingly, the mother admitted to growing
hostility towards the child and to a difficult-to-dispel feeling that he was crying
on purpose and choosing his moments for maximum disruptive effect. She
confessed to shaking the child and coming close to hitting him.

The main point of intervention in this case was the vicious circle that had
been set up by the child's behaviour, producing anxiety, guilt and strife
between the parents, making them in turn less reliable and consistent. A joint
approach was organized involving the paediatrician, health visitor, GP and the
social services, and formal records began to be kept – which identified (a) a
very challenging level of fractiousness, but (b) that the mere keeping of records
reduced these problems a little and made the parents feel more able. Probably
the most telling impact came from the paediatrician who again examined the
child, found nothing medically wrong and voiced the opinion that the problem
was 'constitutional' and little to do with the standard of care available. This
authoritative re-framing of the problem greatly increased the willingness of the
mother to help draw up and stick to a hyper-reliable set of routines rather than
cast around for different solutions. She also felt able to ask her mother for help,
which previously she had been too ashamed to do. The baby continued to be
difficult to pacify, but the parents coped with increasing confidence, sharing
the care more equitably within a pre-planned framework. Most importantly,

they had the knowledge that some babies are just like this, and have to be survived.

BIOLOGICAL INFLUENCES ON PERSONALITY

The most powerful influences affecting the kind of people we become are experiential. Yet in a strange way we each become more, or less, than the main drift of our experience would predict. We develop a discernible 'personality' quite early in childhood (Dunn 1980; Goldsmith 1983). Although we speak (often in a circular way) of someone's personality as if it were another kind of organ inside them – 'David's gregarious behaviour is a product of his outgoing personality', etc. – all that can be said for the term is that there *are* roughly reliable, seemingly unique patterns to our behaviour which others use as a basis for attributions and predictions about how we might behave in particular circumstances and what we are likely to do next. We also make judgements about the thinking patterns of others, which we infer from their behaviour.

The main clue to personality factors at work – whether due to biological difference, a particular pattern of learning, or both – is when behaviour and emotional expression appear to transcend contingencies, the pressures and temptations of the here and now. This in turn depends upon the strength of these contingencies. Thus, although extroverts may be much less noticeable than usual in the examination hall, they will probably suck in louder breaths, ask for more windows to be open/closed than others. Similarly, although introverts are usually less visible all round, the right combination of deinhibiting social conditions can produce untypically outgoing behaviour.

This concept of extroversion–introversion (Eysenck 1965; Gray 1975) has proved remarkably robust in experimental tests (Goldsmith and Gottesman 1981). Its mixed reputation is based upon a misunderstanding that it is a theory of *types*, that is that the human race contains two different kinds of people, the inward-looking and the outward-going. Rather, we should think of a bell-shaped distribution of traits, with most of us in the middle demonstrating a well-adapted and flexible mixture of behaviour, and smaller and smaller numbers on the steepening shoulders of the curves showing less and less current-contingency-inspired flexibility in our actions.

On the one side of the curve we have what might be thought of as 'stimulus-hungry' individuals, prone to sensation-seeking behaviour on the basis of nervous system differences which automatically reduce external stimulation. Contra-intuitively, these are the extroverts, the signals from the environment are 'filtered' and therefore they seek to pre-amplify them by their outgoing behaviour. Thus we can think of strongly extroverted individuals as people with, as it were, 'Citroen 2CV nervous systems' – slow to rev up, requiring considerable amounts of external stamping on the gas pedal to get things moving. On the other hand, some people are 'stimulus amplifiers', that is, prone to sensation shyness, possessing, as it were, 'Ferrari nervous systems' which require only gentle external stimulation before they fire up to uncomfortable levels. To repeat the point: most of us are VW Polos, comfortable with pottering along and capable of occasional bursts of speed depending on the circumstances.

We appear to inherit and to develop these optimal arousal ranges (Scarr and McCartney 1983) and much of our behaviour and our planning is dedicated to keeping ourselves within them. Therefore some learning tasks are more difficult for some people to address – anything requiring persistent self-control and delayed gratification on the extroversion dimension; anything requiring overcoming of inhibitions and acting on first impulse, on the introversion dimension. There are, therefore, *gradients* of learning for all of us. Sometimes acquiring new behaviour is a downhill affair, sometimes a long, hard climb.

Note that no particular combination of personality and environmental configuration is more favourable. Introverts find reflection and considered action easier, and the demands of sociability harder. Extroverts find impulse control more difficult but spontaneity easier. Either predisposition can get one into trouble or frustrate the process of getting out of it. Both wings of the continuum require that we adjust the demands of our therapeutic programmes. Consider the difference of approach required for the impulsive, somewhat paranoid young man in the case described on pp. 154–5, and the shy, almost phobic young woman whose case is outlined on p. 121, and the point about 'gradients of learning' should become clear – read ahead.

Next, in line with the list on p. 46, we turn to the processes by which, against this biological background, learning occurs.

CLASSICAL CONDITIONING

Classical conditioning is a term first applied to the work of Pavlov by Hilgard (1948) to distinguish his principles from those of the developing *operant* model. An alternative term for this process of stimulus association *is respondent* conditioning. Interestingly, few readers on encountering the name 'Pavlov' will not have conjured up an image of a bearded man in a lab coat accompanied by a bored-looking dog – which is quite a good example of classical conditioning in action. Pavlov's work dates from the turn of this century and his real achievement stems from his painstaking methodology and his careful analysis of results; from the detail and the accuracy of his findings, rather than from their novelty. People throughout history have felt their mouths water at the thought of food – though none is present. Animal owners throughout the centuries have banged food pails and watched their animals come running. But then, apples fell from trees for thousands of years before Newton.

Pavlov's experiments were designed to settle an argument over the nature of certain 'psychical' secretions from the salivary glands of animals. 'Psychical' here refers to secretions of saliva present *before* the presentation of any food

– a reaction presumed to originate spontaneously from the mind of the animal (Pavlov 1897). Crossing into the psychological domain, Pavlov soon found himself lacking a satisfactory means of investigating this phenomenon and so turned back to the methods of natural science:

> In our 'psychical' experiments on the salivary glands, at first we honestly endeavored to explain our results by fancying the subjective condition of the animal. But nothing came of it except unsuccessful controversies and individual, personal, uncoordinated opinion. We had no alternative but to place the investigation on a purely objective basis.
>
> (Pavlov 1897:183)

Pavlov's procedure was as follows: a dog underwent a small operation to facilitate the collection of saliva directly from the cheek gland. The dog was then trained to stand quietly in a harness. The laboratory was soundproofed and the experimenters observed the proceedings through a glass screen. Thus, there was no possibility of extraneous sounds or movements distracting the animal. The sequence of the experiment is as follows. A bell is rung – the animal reacts only slightly to the new noise. No salivary flow is recorded. Next, a quantity of meat powder is delivered to a food tray in front of the dog. He salivates and eats it. After a few pairings of the bell (or light, or range of other originally neutral stimuli) with the food, the dog begins to salivate to the sound of the bell alone. He continues to do this over many trials, even though no food is forthcoming. The dog has learned a new response.

Let us look at this process of associative learning schematically, to see what is involved (Figure 3.1).

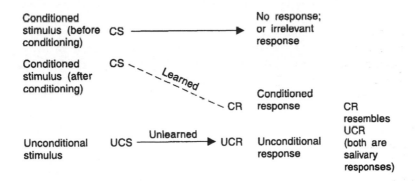

Figure 3.1 A diagram of classical conditioning
Source: Adapted from *Introduction to Psychology*, fourth edition by Ernest R. Hilgard and Richard C. Atkinson, Copyright 1967 by Harcourt Brace Jovanovich, Inc. Reprinted by permission of the publisher.

The association between the unconditional stimulus and the unconditional response exists at the start of the experiment and does not have to be learned. The association between the conditioned stimulus and the conditioned response is a learned one. It arises through the pairing of the conditioned and unconditioned stimuli followed by an unconditional response (salivation to food). The conditioned response (salivation to the bell) resembles the unconditional one (though they need not be identical).

There is considerable misunderstanding about the role of animal studies and their relevance in advancing our knowledge of human behaviour. Much of the basic experimentation in the behavioural field has involved the use of animals. The function of these experiments is to investigate the truth of relatively simple propositions under better controlled conditions than would normally be possible with human subjects. Once this first stage in the research has been satisfactorily completed, then adaptations of the same procedures, now better understood, can be applied to human subjects to check on the transferability of results.

An example of this progression is to be found in the celebrated study of fear acquisition through classical conditioning, carried out by Watson and Rayner (1920). The subject of this experiment was a toddler known to history as 'Little Albert' (in parody of Freud's celebrated analysis – by post! – of a boy with a phobia of horses, called 'Little Hans'). Freud's theories of phobia acquisition held sway at the time. These identified repressed castration threats as the likely cause, the horse acting as a symbol of powerful masculinity – notwithstanding less florid explanations based on the fact that Little Hans had once stood next to a dray horse which had dramatically collapsed and died. Watson and Rayner wished to challenge the received wisdom by seeing whether a phobia could be created in the laboratory. The procedure was as follows: a tame white rat (CS) was introduced into a play pen containing little Albert, and the latter began to play with it without fear. (Fear of small animals is not innate in man, though see (i) below). However, during subsequent trials, whenever the rat was introduced, a fire gong suspended over the pen was struck vigorously to produce a loud noise (UCS). A fear reaction to sudden loud noises *is* innate in humans, and so this produced an unconditional fear response (UCR). Soon little Albert became distressed just at the sight of the small animal, even when its presentation was not accompanied by a loud noise (CR). A new, conditioned response (fear and avoidance of small furry animals) had been acquired. Classical conditioning is particularly important in the acquisition of new emotional responses (see Chapter 4, and the case example on p.57).

Whilst in the field of conditioning there is plenty of evidence that new fear responses can be generated by simple contiguous association, it is erroneous to assume that all fear responses develop in this way. Later work (see Davey 1981) suggests that conditioning is a more complex phenomenon than envisaged by Pavlov. In this research there are three important trends to note:

(i) If Pavlovian concepts were universally true, then it should be possible to condition a fear reaction to anything. The fact that certain kinds of objects (CSs) can set up conditioned reactions much more easily than others, and that some pose formidable difficulties, raises questions about the simple paired-association model. It appears that perhaps as a result of natural selection, there are certain stimuli, e.g. animals and insects or other mobile, intelligent, scurrying organisms with an adaptive, potentially-predatory capacity, of which we are especially prone to learn to be afraid. Further, that there are other objects and events where associations just will not stick. The idea of a continuum of 'preparedness' and counter-preparedness is increasingly important in research on this topic (Garcia and Koelling 1966; Seligman 1971; Hillner 1979).

(ii) Some investigators have raised doubts as to the distinctness of classical learning procedures and have put forward single process theories (favouring an exclusively operant analysis of learning; see Williams and Williams 1969). Later in this chapter the reader will see that the two models do overlap at certain points (see p. 65). In this book the view that there are two distinct learning processes is retained, partly as a heuristic device and partly because, as yet, the research that threatens this position is insufficient to justify a radical reappraisal.

(iii) Since it is possible for human subjects to have powerful fears of circumstances and animals which they have never encountered and are unlikely to come across, it is clear that cognitive variables are involved in fear conditioning. Thus, in the absence of any real snakes (they kill more people than any other kind of animal abroad, but are scarce in the UK, though there are plenty of reptile phobics) we acquire a fear of an image, presented to the accompaniment of distaste or anxiety. Here perceived parental distress may be the original UCS, the child's anxiety in the face of this the UCR, the snake image the CS, and the eventual fear reaction to the *idea of* snakes, the CR.

Case example

I had little fear of thunder and lightning as a child until I went to stay with my grandmother and observed her storm preparations. At the first sign of threatening weather (which she was an expert at predicting) she would open the front and back doors to allow for easy entry and exit of thunderbolts, turn off the electricity ('because it attracts lightning'), turn all the mirrors in the house to the wall for similar reasons, and retire to a cubby hole under the stairs, just as she had done during air raids in World War Two. My thoughts were: if this strong, competent, 17-stone lady on whom my well-being usually depends is running for cover, then I had better join her fast. Diagrams in the *Boys' Book of Science* and a little natural exposure put paid to this nonsense later.

Stimulus generalization

Let us return to Watson and Rayner's work, since the next stage in the experiment illustrates a clinically important phenomenon called *stimulus generalization*. Once the conditioned response was established, similar responses could be obtained to a variety of like stimuli, for example, other small animals, parcels of furry material, or a fur coat. This effect was noted also by Pavlov who found that having conditioned dogs to salivate to the sound of a bell, the same kind of response could then be induced by other noises of a broadly similar kind.

This phenomenon of generalization gives us a clue to the biological purpose of stimulus association. It has great survival value for the organism, and anything that confers a biological advantage is likely to have been selected in the evolutionary process. Clearly, the conditioned reflex is a winner in this respect for nature cannot 'foresee' all eventualities and therefore it can work only to a very limited extent through specific genetic endowment. Faced with the problem of changing, and highly variable environments, nature instead confers *conditionability*, and, if you like, *programmability* – or the ability to learn about the functional relations between objects and events in the environment by association. Thus, well before the food enters the dog's mouth, its upper digestive tract is prepared for it and is ready to break it down chemically for its nutritional value. The earlier this process begins, the shorter what would once have been a highly vulnerable feeding episode, and so the better from the point of view of survival. If an animal can learn to respond to stimuli which reliably precede the opportunity to feed and have the digestive process under way, so much the better. Try it yourself. It is a crisp autumn morning, and standing in the garden, you smell Sunday lunch cooking – roast lamb and mint sauce (vegetarians can substitute mushroom flan or, if all else fails, imagine licking half a lemon). If the conditions are right, the response that will have taken place (saliva filling the mouth) is another example of classical conditioning. This particular response is established through the past pairing of actual food with images of food, and words that eventually come to represent and signal the likely presence of food.

Because stimuli naturally impinge in groups, it is biologically advantageous for those reliably associated with each other to have the same general effect. Imagine a member of a primitive species of *Homo erectus* not endowed with this facility thinking to himself: 'now I've seen those large stripy cats before and I know they can be quite nasty, but I wonder what the smaller spotted ones do?', and the long-term value of stimulus generalization should become clear. Once an association has been formed, it can itself form the basis of new learning. Thus the process of classical conditioning 'strings together' stimulus connections and an absence of birdsong in a clump of trees can eventually come to evoke a fear reaction consistent with the above example. If all this seems fanciful, in terms of today's sophisticated living conditions, imagine coming back from holiday and encountering a near-silent room full of previously sociable colleagues – 'too damned quiet' still applies.

We have seen that conditioned reflexes provide different forms of reliable early warning for the organism. They allow the body to gear itself up to cope with potentially advantageous or potentially threatening situations. The 'four Fs', as Dennett (1991) calls these imperative drives: fight, flight, food and procreation. Our state of constant readiness in this respect is governed by the autonomic nervous system, which acts through the glands and the smooth muscles, to help us to gain an *edge* over our potentially hostile environment. Thus we do not have to wait until the burglar we suspect we have heard downstairs actually hits us over the head before we begin to react to the out-of-normal-context sounds he is making. An unusual noise at night will set our pulses racing, our muscles will stiffen ready for action, our pores will open, sweating will begin so that we can cool our body efficiently if strenuous activity follows, our pupils will dilate so that we can make best use of what light there is, the blood-clotting mechanism goes to 'amber alert' in case we are injured and so forth. Similarly, we do not have to wait to be told that because we have failed adequately to prepare for an unexpectedly important meeting, we have entered a sequence of events where we stand at risk of losing the esteem of our colleagues and our employers, possibly of losing our livelihood, of being discredited socially and so on. The chairperson need only look from the surprisingly well-stocked files of others, to the vacant table in front of us, and this is stimulus enough to trigger an emotional reaction based on a long chain of associations, stretching back from self-regard to more basic concerns about survival. As far as our bodies are concerned, we might be getting ready to take on a medium-sized bear. The fact that under modern social conditions, to run away from a threat, or to punch it in the eye, is seldom an adaptive response (though some meetings do give rise to satisfying thoughts in this direction) is neither here nor there. Evolution has not yet caught up with this fact, and so conditionability has its side effects. The following case example demonstrates this point.

Case example showing the origins and development of a phobia

Mrs Wood, aged 40, was referred to the social services department for 'support' by her somewhat exasperated family doctor. In his view Mrs Wood suffered from agoraphobia, a 'dependent personality' and a number of unspecified 'psychiatric difficulties'. Knowing how to motivate social workers, the doctor also said that he had some worries about Mrs Wood's young son, because not only had Mrs Wood barely left the house in the previous three years, but very little had been seen of the child – a stimulus which is reliably associated with being grilled before a child abuse enquiry (UCS).

57

Background

During the first interview Mrs Wood was wary of discussing her problems, and still reacting to her doctor 'washing his hands' of her case and passing her on to social services and the out-patient department of the local psychiatric hospital – which, of course, she could not possibly reach. During the second home visit Mrs Wood was more forthcoming, and the following patterns in her problems emerged.

She described herself as 'always having been a nervous person'. She recounted stories about dismounting from her bicycle as a child whenever a car came up behind her, going some distance out of her way to avoid a dog, feeling very shy and conspicuous as a teenager, and so forth – a range of normal-enough fears, but noteworthy in their combination and extent. She reported a strong and persistent fear of hospitals and of all medical encounters, probably stemming from her mother's bloodcurdling accounts of the birth of her younger sister. Her mother had nearly died in childbirth, and had filled the early years of her children's lives with graphic stories of medical mismanagement. Mrs Wood became pregnant 'by accident', comparatively late in life. In order to persuade her to have the baby in hospital, the doctor had played up the dangers of a home confinement, raising her already high level of anxiety about the birth.

One hot summer's day, when she was seven months pregnant, Mrs Wood had fainted while crossing a footbridge spanning a small river near her home. 'I was sure I was going to fall in, and when I came round, people said an ambulance was on the way and I panicked. People were trying to hold me down, covering me with clothing.' She fought to get free: 'I knew I had to get away, I got very upset, and eventually I persuaded someone to take me home. When I got in I was shaking all over. I shut and bolted the doors, back and front . . . I was sure that the ambulance was going to call at the house . . . I hid out of sight of the windows . . . and eventually (it took about an hour) I calmed down, and sat waiting for my husband to come home from work.' 'Catastrophic' or even 'paranoid' thoughts of this type are an important feature of panic reactions.

Mrs Wood had her baby at home, against medical advice, painfully, but without serious complication. She tried to go out several times after that but never got further than the front garden, or, if at night, as far as the front gate. She reported the following feelings at each attempt: 'Shivering; awful feelings in the pit of my stomach; pounding heart; light-headedness.' In the daytime everywhere seemed 'very bright and stark'. She felt conspicuous out in the open, 'almost as if I might be struck down'. Her breathing felt loud in her ears and her biggest fear was that she would collapse again.

Mrs Wood eventually gave up these attempts and remained indoors for the next four years. For the first two of these she reported that she didn't really miss going out: 'the family were very good, they took the baby out, got the shopping, they are marvellous; so are the neighbours'. Later, however, Mrs Wood began to experience feelings of dissatisfaction and frustration with her confined existence and felt shame when she could not attend her mother's funeral. When Mrs Wood felt she *had* to go out, for example to peg out washing, she reported making a quick dash, hoping no one would see her or try to talk to her, and 'great relief' when she got back inside. 'I think there must be something seriously wrong with me . . . in my mind . . .' was initially her best idea as to the causes of all this.

If we examine this case in the light of classical conditioning theory, the following pattern emerges.

— Mrs Wood may have possessed a predisposing personality for strong fear reactions (see Claridge 1985); certainly her accounts of her previous life showed her to be eminently conditionable to a range of not objectively threatening circumstances.

— Against a background of heightened anxiety about pregnancy, dreading the thought of the possibility of having to go into hospital, Mrs Wood experienced a traumatic incident (UCS) which aroused in her a powerful fear reaction (UCR).

— This incident, when paired with the previously neutral stimulus of the footbridge and other stimuli associated with being out of doors (CSs), produced a conditioned response to these stimuli. Even after the incident itself had passed, the pregnancy was over, she was perfectly well and the crowd no longer in sight, she still experienced fears associated with this context.

— Mrs Wood reported that her panic state was made worse by the attempts of would-be helpers to restrain her until the ambulance came. Natural escape behaviour was prevented, thus intensifying her fear.

— This conditioned fear response quickly generalized to virtually all outdoor circumstances, even though objectively they barely resembled the circumstances of her collapse. Furthermore, every time Mrs Wood tried to go out of doors she was punished for the attempt by her powerful emotions (setting up a 'fear of fear' reaction) – even though she saw such feelings as annoying and irrational.

— Every time Mrs Wood managed to escape from the outdoor circumstances that elicited the conditioned fear response, her strongly aversive feelings were reduced or terminated. This strengthened avoidance behaviour and made future experiments less likely.

— Mrs Wood's family and friends rewarded her long-term maladaption to her phobia by relieving her of many of her responsibilities regarding her child, and by reassuring her that they did not mind her staying behind. The impression grew, strengthened by early non-cooperation with the treatment scheme, that Mr Wood rather liked having his wife at home and dependent upon him.

It will not have escaped the reader's attention that as we move from laboratory to examples of conditioning in the natural environment, it has become more difficult to specify the key stimuli combinations with the same precision. Was it the already-learned fear of hospitals which became connected with particular outdoor circumstances? Or was it, perhaps, loss of consciousness, embarrassment at this, or fear of loss of control? Or was it, perhaps, a fear of falling helplessly into the water? All of these were mentioned during interviews. To what extent did fears for the unborn baby play a part? To what extent did the unsympathetic words of the family doctor predispose Mrs Wood to what happened? It is likely that all these factors were influential in producing the unconditional fear and panic response. In the natural environment, stimuli tend to come in untidy bundles, as do responses, and it is often difficult to tease out their different effects. Mrs Wood remembers particularly the idea of being 'a prisoner of the crowd', the fear of hospitals, and the narrowness of the footbridge. She also had a vivid recollection of the brightness of the day, of being helpless out in the open. Her memories cover the key stimuli but we have only a limited idea of their relative importance. The analysis is not as neat as the one provided by Pavlov in his carefully controlled experiments, but it is one made within the framework he constructed, and is dependent upon exactly the same general principles (the therapeutic programme used in this case is described on p. 228).

Now we turn to some other dimensions of the classical conditioning process.

Classical extinction

In Pavlov's experiments, if the bell was rung repeatedly without any food ever appearing, the conditioned salivary response eventually disappeared. This too is biologically advantageous since there is no survival value in responding forever to only temporarily reliable associations. The process is called *extinction*, and it is an important feature of operant conditioning too (see p. 62). However, well-conditioned responses such as the phobia discussed above are very resistant to extinction; they take a considerable time to 'unlearn'. This may be because of a repeated pairing of key stimuli; because, as in the present case, of one very dramatic conjugation; because, as in the Wood case above, the new behaviour can acquire 'positive' secondary consequences not readily apparent to outside observers, or because the fear association is kept alive by mental rehearsal.

Experimental neurosis and learned helplessness

Following his work on classical conditioning, Pavlov and his co-workers conducted a series of experiments to investigate how animals cope with being conditioned to respond to contradictory or ambiguous stimuli. Such situations are prevalent in the complex social environments of human beings, and so the findings have relevance outside the field of animal behaviour.

The experimenters conditioned animals to anticipate food on the presentation of a particular visual stimulus. For example, the animal was taught to salivate to a circle of light but not to an ellipse (Shenger-Kristovnikova 1921). It was then made increasingly difficult for the animal to distinguish between these stimuli, by arranging for the circle to become narrowed at the sides, and for the ellipse to flatten out. Another variation in such (rather cruel) experiments involved the random substitution of consequences – so that the animal was unable to predict whether food or pain would follow a given stimulus (see Masserman 1943). The effects of these studies were that the animals' behaviour became agitated and very uncharacteristic – hence the term 'experimental neurosis'. Later, and this is the important point, when the original stimulus conditions were reinstated, animals lost their ability to make even crude discriminations, and the experimenters began to use words such as 'depression' and 'catatonia' to describe their immobile state. In other experiments animals just accepted shocks rather than take an easy escape route because they had been unpredictably shocked in the past for so doing.

This work has given rise to research aimed on the parallels between the artificial environments of these animals, and those found in human society. Some of the most fruitful recent work is that of Seligman (1975) whose learned helplessness theory is of great interest to cognitive-behavioural therapists. Seligman's view, based on analogue studies with humans, is that when an individual learns through experience that there is little or no reliable connection between stimuli, and that his or her behaviour has little effect in modifying the environment of consequences (reducing painful effects and boosting pleasant ones), their behaviour first becomes erratic as they try to re-establish some control, but if this fails then, just as in animal experiments, they gradually withdraw, since the environment does not support attempts positively to adapt to it. Neither conditioned emotional reactions, nor the anticipation of pleasure, nor the arousal states useful in combating threats, serve any useful, predictive or strategic purpose and so they die away, leaving the individual in a state of apathy.

Such formulations will have a ring of truth to anyone familiar with the case histories of some psychiatric patients under treatment for reactive depression, or to anyone familiar with the backgrounds of clients labelled as 'inadequate personalities', or of those said to belong to 'problem families' and so forth. Behavioural approaches help to combat such states by attempting to re-establish some order and predictability in the circumstances of clients by helping them to understand their experiences, and, in a sympathetic, step-by-step way, by teaching the skills necessary for the reassertion of some control over their unpredictable environments (see p. 95).

OPERANT CONDITIONING

The term operant conditioning (together with its synonym, instrumental conditioning) refers to the way in which organisms operate on their environment, which in turn selectively strengthens, or *reinforces* certain patterns of behaviour at the expense of others. This can happen either accidentally, or because the environment has been specifically programmed to support certain behaviours and discourage others, as in the workings of families, organisations, or through the rules of the classroom.

The root principle of operant conditioning is that *behaviour is a function of its consequences*. Parents who respond favourably, first to the random gurglings of their infant, then to specific noises, then to approximations of words, are making use of this principle and helping along the acquisition of spoken language – for which the biological facilities already exist. Similarly, the schoolchild who notices that an unplanned act of disruption produces a level of peer approval previously unknown will be more likely to repeat the behaviour in future. The lecturer who tries to set his audience at ease by starting with a joke, but gets puzzled frowns rather than the good-humoured laughter he anticipated, will be unlikely to repeat the exercise for a while.

An operant, then, is a sequence of behaviour, often exploratory in nature, not under the direct control of an experimenter, that produces an environmental consequence. A useful analogy here is that of sonar or radar. Individuals manoeuvre themselves through their physical and social environments according to the 'return signals' they receive from it in the form of consequences and symbols of impending consequences. The more (or less) pleasurable the environmental feedback, the more (or less) likely are they to engage in the behaviour again in similar circumstances.

The groundwork for this deceptively simple theory of stimulus–response learning was carried out by E. L. Thorndike (1898). However, the extension and detailed investigation of the theory was the life work of B. F. Skinner (1953, 1974). Skinner's contribution was to investigate with great precision the large number of variables that influence the course of learning through experience of consequences; to formulate this into a comprehensive theory; and to apply the theory very successfully to human behaviour. A description of Skinner's basic animal experiments will be useful in clarifying first principles.

A hungry pigeon or rat (not both) is placed in a glass-sided box (now called a 'Skinner Box') which is equipped with a food dispenser which, once discovered, is capable of being operated from inside by means of a disc or a lever, or from outside by the experimenter. The advantage of this device, from the point of view of the experimenter, is that the ratio of the delivery of food to the animal's rate of correct responding (called the *schedule*, (see p. 72) is readily controllable. Therefore, the experimenter has power over the main environmental contingencies that affect the behaviour of the animal. These can be systematically varied and any resultant shifts in the pattern of responding accurately recorded. The results of these experiments are recounted below.

TYPES OF REINFORCEMENT

There are two main types of reinforcement: positive and negative. Both processes *increase* the frequency, and/or magnitude, and/or speed of a response. Another way of putting it is to say that positive and negative reinforcers increase the probability of a response, or that they 'accelerate' certain sequences of behaviour.

Positive reinforcement

In Skinner's famous experiments a rat or a pigeon was placed in a special box and left to its own devices. Eventually, through random exploratory activity (operant behaviour) the food release lever is nudged and a food pellet drops into the tray. The release-operating behaviour then occurs more frequently, and is said to be positively reinforced by the food consequence. The term 'reinforced' simply means strengthened, and refers to the fact that, as a result of a certain consequence, the particular sequence of behaviour leading up to it is demonstrably more likely to occur under similar circumstances in future. Therefore a positive reinforcer is a stimulus which increases the frequency of the response that it follows.

Reinforcers are therefore defined exclusively in terms of their effects. Corn is unlikely to strengthen the disc-pecking behaviour of a bloated pigeon, and so it is not a positive reinforcer in that instance. The everyday term 'reward' is too vague to describe this process since it is derived mainly from the intentions of the would-be rewarder, or is used because the stimulus being delivered belongs to some general class of things or happenings *usually* experienced as pleasant by *most* people, or usually responded to predictably by an animal. In fact, there is hardly such a thing as a universal reward. This has long been recognized in the old adage: 'one man's meat is another's poison'. Appetites also change dramatically over time and from setting to setting. The praise given by the elderly schoolteacher for a certain style of dress, although intended to reward the behaviour which produces this effect, will usually have the opposite effect. The policeman who ticks off an unruly football supporter in front of his pals is intending to punish, and thereby inhibit rowdy behaviour, but he may well positively reinforce it by conferring hero status on his subject.

Negative reinforcement

Negative reinforcement is a clumsy term and in my experience causes students of learning theory more trouble than anything else. So let us start with a simple everyday example. Sometimes when I am writing my dog paces back and forth beside me, emitting panting and occasional coughing noises. He has been shaped into this strange pattern of behaviour by previous experience. Having tried all kinds of stimuli to get me to give him access to the great outdoors, he eventually hit upon coughing. Perhaps on some previous occasion of genuine throat-clearing, fearing for my carpets, I had jumped up and opened the door for him. But aetiology aside, the lesson has been well learned, and the deal is that he paces, pants and coughs until I let him out for a sniff around the garden. In his case such behaviour has been *positively* reinforced by me. He gets his way a lot of the time and so the behaviour is well established in his repertoire. In my case, the behaviour of leaving my writing table, just in case he isn't fooling this time, and to get rid of the distracting noise is *negatively* reinforced. Contingent on certain behaviour from me, an unpleasant set of stimuli (noise and anxiety) are terminated. So dogs condition people too!

Here is another example of the negative reinforcement of behaviour. A man with a drinking problem wakes up feeling awful. He feels anxious, low and he has a craving for more alcohol. His family eye him suspiciously and take him to task over the condition in which he came home the night before. He goes into the garage, pours himself a tumbler of vodka from his secret store and soon begins to feel better. The craving subsides, the world is a brighter place and quickly takes on a pleasantly out-of-focus aspect which distances him from his troubles and anaesthetises him to the pain of everyday living. He takes another swig to intensify this effect. This man's initial drinking behaviour was negatively reinforced. In the short-term alcohol had the effect of reducing aversive stimulation (withdrawal symptoms, sensitivity to disapproval), in the long-term its effects on others will probably lead to an intensification of aversive experiences, and so the vicious circle continues.

A useful way of clarifying the difference between positive and negative reinforcement is to imagine the usual Skinner box equipped with a loudspeaker or an electrified floor. To turn off an unpleasant level of sound or electric shock for a while, the animal operates a lever. On this occasion the behaviour is negatively reinforced since it *removes* a negative stimulus rather than providing a positive one. Any sequence of behaviour that reduces the effects of aversive stimuli will be readily repeated when the organism is faced with similar circumstances in future. So, analogously, we can think of the drinking response of the alcoholic 'switching off' or at least 'turning down' the level of unpleasant physiological stimulation from within (anxiety, craving) and as distancing him from unpleasant social stimulation from without. Actions performed in the face of pain, anxiety and deprivation states are sometimes negatively reinforced in the same way. The learning that results is acquired through a kind of 'relief conditioning' process.

To sum up: a negative reinforcer is a stimulus which, if *removed* contingent upon a certain response, results in an *increase* in the probability of that response in similar circumstances in future. This is the case with obsessional behaviour where lining up the furniture, or repeatedly scrubbing one's hands, reduces high levels of anxiety, usually within the context of a 'superstitious' cognitive rationale (see Rachman and Hodgson 1980). At a less threatening level, the influence of negative reinforcement patterns is visible in much of the *avoidance behaviour* that people exhibit when confronted by a challenging task. When working at home I am prone to make large pots of very complicated soups which need lots of stirring – 'avoidance soup', as it is known to members of my family.

Conditioned reinforcers   *extinction also works here.*

Conditioned reinforcers provide an important point of connection between the classical and operant models reviewed above. This term describes the process by which anything which is regularly associated with the reinforcement of an operant will eventually acquire an independent reinforcement value of its own. If then we were to switch on a flashing light every time we positively reinforced the disc-pecking behaviour of a pigeon with food, we would expect, from our knowledge of classical conditioning, that the pigeon would eventually respond to the light alone. The light becomes a conditioned reinforcer, since eventually it itself reinforces the disc-pecking behaviour of the pigeon. The extent to which the pigeon's behaviour can be maintained in this way depends upon a number of factors. The first is contiguity: the proximity of the light and the interval of time that elapses between delivery of the goods and the light. The second concerns the number of times the light and the food are paired – the more often this happens (up to a point) the more reinforcing the light becomes. However, this power of 'reinforcement by proxy' is lost relatively quickly when all food is withheld (extinction).

One further animal example to get this clear. Animal trainers have a problem in trying to reinforce items of behaviour at a distance. They cannot constantly be popping eatables into the mouths of their charges after every piece of clever behaviour and there is a limit to the extent to which behaviours can be chained together, so that reinforcement need only occur at the end of the sequence. This is where conditioned reinforcers come in. In the training of dolphins for public performance (the really interesting question here being why performing animals reinforce the zoo-attending behaviour of humans) the trainer needs something to stand 'in lieu' of fish when the dolphin is doing tricks in the middle of a large pool. He (silly ass) uses the sound of a whistle which has been repeatedly paired with feeding. This sound eventually becomes a reinforcer in its own right. In turn, certain attending, emotional and motor responses in the crowd are reinforced by the relative absence of controls. Skinner (1971) has proposed that the less conspicuous the controlling features of complex behaviour, the more interesting and credit-worthy it becomes; hence the attraction of apparently non-directive dolphin training. It represents a high degree of control over a usually-hard-to-manipulate part of the environment (a basic human drive) and we find this vicariously pleasurable: 'look no hands; look no fish!'. Might this be why walking around a supermarket with a phobic client seems somehow less skilled than reviewing the alleged dark, visceral origins of such conditions in a consulting room?

These examples give us a clue to the function of conditioned reinforcers in everyday life. Stimuli, in the form of attention, praise, grades and so forth, maintain responding when larger-scale positive consequences are long delayed, as when someone is studying for a diploma or working with a difficult case, where outcomes lie well in the future. These symbols or tokens are secondary events associated through learning with a 'primary' pay off, such as greater prestige or more money. However, the reader might like to consider just how 'primary' these reinforcers are. There is nothing *intrinsically* satisfying about any of the above examples. They are each a link in a chain leading back to genuinely primary, biologically-based reinforcers: warmth, shelter, food, sex and so on (see Figure 3.2). But then men and women sometimes forego these things to obtain dignity, justice, prestige, or even diplomas. Such motives become functionally autonomous; and so, in our case, which reinforcers are really primary?

Generalized reinforcers

There is, however, another aspect to this process. A situation where particular conditioned reinforcers were linked only to particular primary deprivation states, or primary needs, would limit responsiveness drastically, and produce stereotyped and ultimately not-very-adaptive behaviour. But in the natural environment, in most cases, conditioned reinforcers *generalize.* That is, they become associated with more than one primary reinforcer. A wide range of responsiveness is maintained thereby because of the increased likelihood that one or other of the primary deprivation states, or something very close to it, is likely to be present at any given time. Money is a good example of a generalized reinforcer. We associate it with, and can procure with it, a wide range of goods and benefits, and therefore whatever deprivation state we happen to be in, or whatever sources of stimulation happen to be near us at the time, there is a good chance that money will enhance the possibilities of satisfaction. For this reason tokens are used in certain behaviour modification programmes, for example those aimed at shaping the pro-social behaviour of institutionalized psychiatric patients. These tokens can then be exchanged for a wide range of goods and services (see p. 174). If you think all this rather artificial and mechanistic, feel in your pocket and consider the purpose of the tokens you will find there.

Skinner also cites sensory feedback, and the successful manipulation of the environment as examples of generalized reinforcers:

A baby appears to be reinforced by stimulation from the environment which has not been followed by primary reinforcement. The baby's rattle

Figure 3.2 Gary Larson, 'Jurassic Calendars'
Source: Gary Larson, *Jurassic Calendars*. Far Side © Farworks, Inc. Dist. by universal
Press Syndicate. Reprinted with permission. All rights reserved.

is an example. The capacity to be reinforced in this way could have arisen
in the evolutionary process, and it may have a parallel in the reinforcement we receive from simply 'making the world behave'. Any organism
which is reinforced by its success in manipulating nature, regardless of

the momentary consequences, will be in a favoured position when important consequences follow.

(Skinner 1953:78)

This example has implications for the question of how artistic behaviour and creative endeavours are to be explained in behavioural terms (Skinner 1974). Further examples of generalized reinforcement are provided by approval, attention, affection, esteem, control and so forth.

In cases of disruptive children referred to me, inappropriate attention is undoubtedly the commonest source of unwitting generalized reinforcement of bad behaviour. Attention usually precedes, and is concurrent with, primary reinforcement in a social setting, and because of this it acquires its own behaviour-strengthening effects. It becomes worth having even when mixed in with irregular amounts of other stimuli intended to deter. Because these contingencies operate in a vaguely reliable way, the behavioural connection of attention with pleasure is eventually quite difficult to remove.

To sum up: a generalized reinforcer is a conditioned reinforcer which strengthens several types of behaviour in several situations.

Some further general points about reinforcement

(i) The reinforcement status of a stimulus is established by observing the *effect* that this has on behaviour through experiments: whether through the controlled experiments of researchers, or through the less well-controlled assessment procedures employed by therapists. The principles at least, are the same.

(ii) We are not surrounded by stimuli which it is possible to classify on an a priori basis as reinforcers. These potential properties are not of the stimuli so much as of the organism on which they impinge and its previous learning experience. Such questions are decided by observation of *effects*.

(iii) Behaviour is reinforced, not people. To say that Ms A is trying to reinforce Freda is sloppy and misleading, except as a form of deliberate shorthand where all concerned know that it is Freda's assertive behaviour that is the target of positive reinforcement.

(iv) Reinforced responses can be thought of as 'semi-automatic', in the sense that sometimes we behave in a very stereotyped way in response to contingencies, and think about it afterwards. Sometimes we think about the reasons for our behaviour *as* we behave. At other times stimuli give rise to memories, thoughts and feelings about potential actions which we perform later, and which are affected by these. In any case the consequences produced play an important role in determining how often, and in what circumstances, these responses are used in future.

(v) 'Unconscious' learning can occur; that is, we may not always be able to specify the precise nature of the reinforcement contingencies that elicit certain responses from us – as when we find ourselves repeating patterns of behaviour which are against our interests without understanding why.

(vi) Patterns of positive and negative reinforcement are often inextricably intertwined. The taste of the vodka in the example on p. 64 would be positively reinforcing, and the (probable) build-up of 'frustration' (state of physiological arousal) in my dog which my opening the door for him would put an end to, would ensure that his behaviour as well as mine also receives negative reinforcement. Incidentally, I have had two dogs now that do this and I am beginning to think seriously that it may have nothing to do with reinforcement *per se*, but be due rather to pressures in the animal-companion–carer system.

THE SHAPING OF BEHAVIOUR

By selectively reinforcing features of a behavioural performance, or by reinforcing only those responses that occur at a certain level, we can gradually alter the nature of a response. Skinner worked with pigeons in this way to produce unusual neck-stretching movements and eventually a repertoire that included playing ping-pong with their beaks! Using the same basic principles Isaacs *et al.* (1966) shaped the behaviour of a chronically withdrawn schizophrenic patient whose typical behaviour consisted of sitting silently and staring into space. During a ward meeting the therapist pulled out a piece of gum, and noticed that the patient's eyes moved in his direction slightly. The patient was given the gum and once the response was established, performance levels were gradually increased. The stages in this were: head turning; eye contact; holding out a hand; then responding with more complex speech. At each stage only slightly exceptional behaviour was reinforced, and this is the key feature of operant shaping. Referring to the shaping power of the natural environment, Skinner had this to say:

> Operant conditioning shapes behaviour as a sculptor shapes a lump of clay. Although at some point the sculptor seems to have produced an exclusively novel object, we can always follow the process back to the original undifferentiated lump, and we can make the successive stages by which we return to this condition as small as we wish. At no point does anything emerge which is very different from what preceded it. The final product seems to have a special unity and integrity of design but we cannot find the point at which this suddenly appears. In the same sense an operant is not something which appears full grown in the behaviour of the organism. It is the result of a continuous shaping process.
>
> (Skinner 1953:91)

Shaping, when systematically applied, is a therapeutic technique of considerable importance (see Chapter 6), as when a social worker selectively congratulates a parent for responding more matter-of-factly and calmly to an over-demanding child. Over time, reinforcement becomes conditional on longer and/or more complex sequences of behaviour.

Sometimes the shaping of verbal behaviour is important for therapeutic purposes. For example, in the case of an excessively shy and unassertive individual, speech containing personal references, expressions of opinion, or statements of intention, might be selectively strengthened by increased attention and signs of approval.

FADING

Fading is the process whereby control of a sequence of behaviour is gradually shifted from one set of reinforcers to another. This process is central to socialization, where, for example, parents gradually fade out the regular positive reinforcement of sitting at the table for meals until the behaviour is maintained by purely non-verbal signs and approval and by conversation, plus the signalled threat of disapproval for breaking social rules. Similarly, a reinforcement programme that begins by encouraging adaptive behaviour in a child with the use of sweets or toys can hardly continue in that vein forever. Apart from the possible side-effects of obesity and dental caries, satiation effects will quickly reduce the effectiveness of such programmes. In any case, the aim of behavioural programmes is to bring adaptive behaviour under the control of 'naturally occurring' social influences. Fading in this type of programme can, if necessary, be accomplished by the use, alongside material reinforcers, of praise, affection and so on, so that the former can be given less often or in smaller quantities as the behaviour comes to be maintained by conditioned reinforcers.

Although fading is a common enough feature of daily life and of childhood experience, my impression is that far too little attention is given to it in therapeutic settings. Perhaps it is the fault of the still-dominant medical model which tempts us to think in terms of 'cure' rather than adaptation. Or perhaps it is the setting up of behaviour modification programmes that reinforces our own therapeutic behaviour because it is the most exciting part? The relatively mundane business of ensuring that any effects produced can be maintained in natural settings smacks a little of 'after-care' and is (mistakenly) seen as a less important activity. Getting clinical psychologists out of their Portakabins to help with this is notoriously difficult – perhaps we are using the wrong reinforcers? Nevertheless, research into the long-term effects of some quite impressively conceived behavioural schemes shows just how dangerous it is to assume that behaviour changed in one setting will stay changed in another when artificial reinforcers are no longer available (see Lovaas 1967). This point is particularly important in residential and hospital social work, where in the past, 'train and hope' programmes, as they are called in the business, have resulted in wastefully high levels of relapse, which could easily have been avoided.

DISCRIMINATIVE STIMULI

Figure 3.3 A failure of discrimination – H. M. Bateman cartoon
Source: 'The man who asked for a double scotch in the Grand Pump Room at Bath', in H. M.
Bateman (1975) *The Man Who . . . and Other Stories*, ed. J. Jensen. Reproduced by permission
of Eyre Methuen Ltd and London Management Ltd. © H. M. Bateman 1975. The original of
this cartoon is on display at the City Art Gallery.

Discriminative stimuli (usually abbreviated to Sds) are stimuli which (as a
result of learning) signal to us that reinforcement may be available for particular
forms of behaviour. They are especially important in complex social settings
and much of the process of human socialization is taken up with establishing
finely tuned responses in relation to such cues. Where they have not yet been
learned, behaviour can seem 'out of place' – as when enquiring children
innocently ask: 'Why *are* you a bore, Uncle Ian?' Social gaffes of various kinds
can often be put down to a failure to attend to available discriminative stimuli
(see Figure 3.3).

    These stimuli are important in our work with clients, in that, if we learn
what signals tend to precede particular behaviours, we may be able to intervene
at this early point in the sequence. In addition, clients can sometimes be taught
to attend to these signals in a critical way, and to institute pre-rehearsed
self-control procedures (see p. 205). If feelings of boredom reliably trigger
excessive eating, or a particular sort of conversation within a peer group

reliably predicts aggression, then action can sometimes be taken to divert behaviour into another channel. Attention to these antecedent factors can allow us to interrupt a sequence of problematic behaviour *before* it becomes fully developed. Thus, in the case of a child, withdrawal of attention or a small pre-signalled sanction might be used, whereas later much stricter or more elaborate measures would be necessary, bringing with them unwanted side-effects (see p. 75).

Stimuli can also acquire a negative signalling value. These have the sub-title *delta stimuli* (SΔs) and come to indicate by regular association that no pleasurable consequences are likely to occur, or that an aversive outcome is in prospect.

In cases where a client's behaviour is 'over-generalized', where, for example, he fails to discriminate between those people who are out to punish him for previous misdeeds and those who wish to help him, an extra emphasis on identifying the differences in settings, behaviour, probable intentions, demeanour, function and so on, may aid future discrimination. Probation officers have particular problems in this regard because of their association with punishment and the courts.

Let us now consider the effects that different patterns or *schedules* of reinforcement have on behaviour.

SCHEDULES OF REINFORCEMENT

So far we have been discussing the way in which different stimuli, and connections between stimuli affect the elicitation and maintenance of behaviour. The next set of considerations stems from the fact that stimuli impinge, or can be artificially presented, in different *sequences*. This can have a marked effect: (i) on the rate and level of acquisition of responses; (ii) on the way responding is maintained; and (iii) on the resistance the behaviour shows to extinction (Ferster and Skinner 1957). Therefore, such factors are of considerable clinical importance.

The following factors are the most potent in their effects on behaviour: (a) the number and ratio of responses receiving reinforcement in a sequence; (b) whether this pattern is regular or irregular; and (c) the interval between responses. Each of these will now be discussed in turn.

Fixed ratio schedules

Descriptions of this type of schedule are usually abbreviated to FR, with an index number following, giving the number of responses which has to occur before reinforcement takes place. Thus FR6 equals six responses of a particular kind before reinforcement occurs. Natural environment contingencies rarely provide so regular a pattern. A piece worker who receives payment according to the number of items of work produced is on an FR schedule, as is the schoolchild who gets a star for every three marks of B+ and above.

FR schedules have the effect of speeding up responses: the more items of appropriate behaviour performed, the greater the number of reinforcements supplied. Thus their chief characteristics are high and stable levels of responding, and (as with continuous reinforcement schedules – see below) the fact that their effects are relatively easily extinguished. Secondary features are that the accuracy of the responses monitored on this schedule need be no more than adequate to obtain reinforcement (think of car factories); that the number of outputs rather than the quality of outputs is what is being reinforced (think of the Universities' obsession with publication rates). Indeed, if the ratio of response to reinforcement is high then a certain amount of 'trimming' occurs, that is, embellishments (which might provide opportunities for shaping) are dropped in the interests of speed, and following reinforcement for a long sequence the frequency of responding may well drop temporarily as another long series looms up. Obviously, if the ratio is too large then the behaviour extinguishes altogether in the normal way.

Fixed ratio schedules are used in practice when a high, fast and regular rate of discrete and easily definable responses is required. The rate can be varied so that it is favourable to start with and then increased later by gradual steps.

Continuous reinforcement

This is said to be occurring when every occurrence of a target behaviour is reinforced and is the way in which most behavioural treatment programmes start off. The aim is to establish and strengthen a particular sequence as quickly and effectively as possible, and it is therefore worth knowing that experimental evidence shows clearly that reinforcement on a continuous schedule works fastest and best in this regard. If a client only rarely engages in eye contact, then every single appearance of this behaviour should be positively reinforced with whatever works – perhaps increased attention, perhaps a smile, perhaps a favourable comment. Once the new behaviour is established, a different approach is required to maintain it.

Behaviour monitored on a continuous reinforcement (CR) schedule is easily extinguished. That is, if reinforcement stops, apart from the possibility of a brief 'spurt', to test out the contingencies operating, the response rate drops like a stone. This fact has obvious implications for practice, and in particular for the question of how to maintain desirable behaviours without artificial reinforcement after the social worker has left the scene. Anyone concerned with advising on behavioural programmes will be familiar with this 'straight up and straight down' phenomenon present in case data, where adequate behaviour is maintained on a continuous schedule until the client has 'improved', then the case is closed. Three months later it is re-referred with the client in virtually the same state, and behaviour modification is said 'not to have worked' or to have produced only short-term, 'symptomatic' benefits. The real point is that no thought has been given to 'immunizing' the new behaviour against extinction by exposing it to little irregular periods of non-reinforcement. To resist the onslaught of natural environment contingencies behaviour is best *developed* on a continuous schedule and *maintained* on a variable schedule (see below).

Differential reinforcement of other behaviour (DRO Schedules)

Another way to speed up acquisition is through providing a set of contingencies which 'contrast' one particular behaviour with others in the repertoire. To do this we continuously reinforce the desired sequence while placing nearby, competing, less desirable behaviours on extinction (as in the case discussed on p. 79).

Intermittent and variable schedules

There are two categories of intermittent schedule: (i) ratio schedules; and (ii) interval schedules. In the case of a ratio schedule, reinforcement occurs after a certain number of responses; that is, it might be given for every three conversations held with one particular nurse. In the case of an interval schedule, reinforcement occurs after a given amount of time has elapsed; that is, it might he given for every 20 minutes spent in the rehabilitation unit. The next important influence is whether the ratios and the elapsed intervals of time determining reinforcement in the two cases above are fixed or *variable*.

These schedules have very powerful behaviour-maintenance effects and provide built-in resistance to extinction. With variable ratio (VR) schedules, reinforcement occurs for an average number of responses. But the important thing is that the precise ratio of reinforcement to responses is variable over a given period. Thus, reinforcement may be experienced for every sixth, tenth, fourteenth and tenth response – in sequence. This schedule would be called VR10 since the mean is ten. A good example of a VR schedule in everyday life is the fruit machine, where excitement and persistence derive from the unpredictability of reinforcement.

With complex versions of this schedule the individual cannot easily predict when the next 'score' will occur, and so, not only is the response maintained at a high and stable rate, but the quality of response is good since there is often experimentation to 'perfect' it and so bring on the reward; the response can thus be shaped. Where reinforcement or punishment of a particular kind occur on a *very* variable schedule this can lead to what Skinner has termed 'superstitious behaviour' (Skinner 1953). The organism guesses at the contingencies associated with certain consequences, and tries out variations in behaviour to see whether this makes a difference or changes its luck. Throwing salt over the left shoulder after a spillage to avoid bad luck is an everyday example of this.

I wave at single magpies to forestall widowhood, and the practice has never let me down. The little rituals displayed by examination candidates (four pens, three pencils, two sharpeners, the lucky rubber, etc.) provide another example.

If VR reinforcement is terminated completely the rate of responding tends to stay level for a considerable period just in case the next sequence produces the long awaited pay-off. However, while resistance to extinction is a considerable advantage when the issue is how to maintain new behaviour acquired in therapy, it is an equally considerable disadvantage when trying to remove maladaptive behaviour from the repertoire. Most behaviours acquired in the natural environment are reinforced on variable interval schedules. Jamie's mother does not respond with cuddles every time he has a tantrum; she did so at first (continuous reinforcement), then she decided against this mollycoddling and ignored the next two upsets. The third was a really bad one and she felt that she couldn't ignore it, and that something must be the matter. The next tantrum was ignored completely. During the one after that Jamie was smacked. In the one after that Mrs B tried pleasant diversionary tactics. When the social worker called six months later she advised Jamie's mother to ignore tantrums from now on 'so that they would extinguish'. Nineteen disasters later mother gave up the scheme and told the social worker that behaviour therapy sounded like a load of old nonsense. The social worker replied that it was 'certainly not a panacea' and was given to wondering intermittently if she still had her old copy of Melanie Klein at home (see Figure 3.4).

In natural settings even more complex schedules operate, with the different types reviewed here combining and alternating to produce different effects on behaviour. Knowledge of these different patterns can help the social worker correctly to identify them during assessment and to develop combinations of techniques, either to counter them, or to exploit them for therapeutic purposes.

PUNISHMENT

Punishment requires detailed discussion, not because it has a special place in the repertoire of behavioural techniques, but because of its controversial nature. First, it is important to distinguish punishment from negative reinforcement. It is commonly believed that negative reinforcement is just a fancy term for punishment, but this is not the case. Punishment is the effect of applying an aversive stimulus contingent upon a certain response, thus *decreasing* the probability that the response will be emitted in similar circumstances in future. Imagine a Skinner box where the pressing of a lever always resulted in a shock or a loud noise. This punishment would result in a *reduction* in the performance of this response, or more likely, its complete suppression.

The aversive stimuli may also take the form of contingent removal of positive reinforcement – as in the deprivation punishments of childhood. Two terms which the reader may encounter in the literature are: 'positive punishment', for the presentation of an aversive stimulus; and 'negative punishment'

Figure 3.4 'Bitter Sweets'

Source: Posy Simmonds, *The Guardian*. Reprinted by permission of A. D. Peters and Co. Ltd.

for the withdrawal of a positive stimulus. The important points here are: (a) that in both cases the effect of the stimulus is to weaken the response that it follows; (b) negative punishment (deprivation) is less likely to produce unwanted escape or avoidance behaviour.

Thus the use of the word punishment in the behavioural psychology literature is somewhat different from our everyday understanding of the idea. First, it does not necessarily imply that anyone is deliberately setting out to inhibit certain behaviour. Second, there is no implication that the subject was necessarily doing anything 'wrong', or that the aversive event was retributive in character. Through trial and error, or accident, certain environmental or internal physiological consequences occur that inhibit the behaviour with which they are associated. In other words, punishment is a naturally occurring phenomenon as well as something people do to each other deliberately.

Many of our clients live in extremely punishing environments, which is why so many of them withdraw from the constructive problem-solving attempts that often look, to those not directly involved (e. g. tabloid journalists), like *obvious* solutions to their difficulties. An example of this kind of suppression of adaptive responses is the familiar situation of the 'multi-problem family' who, on balance, experience fewer aversive consequences by 'muddling through' than by attempting to get to grips with their difficulties (a syndrome also not unknown to social workers with unmanageably large caseloads). When choice-making behaviour, or self-assertion in any direction leads to punishment, then apathy results. Another familiar example of this phenomenon is that of the psychiatric patient whose attempts at communication with the outside world produce adverse reactions, resulting in the gradual closing off of this source of reinforcement, and the potentiation of alternative, day-dreaming and fantasy responses.

Social workers need therefore to know about the effects of punishment since, unfortunately, it is a prevalent feature of the environment of those with serious personal and social problems. Indeed, it is the most common method used for the control of all kinds of social deviance. It is favoured for the following reasons.

(i) It is easy to formulate punishment contingencies – much easier than trying to discover precise deficits in social skills which result in inadequate performance, and easier still than trying to find reinforceable behaviour incompatible or competitive with maladaptive behaviour. Interestingly, and perhaps for this reason, when students in my psychology classes are presented with case material describing deviant behaviour they usually spring immediately into discussions about ways of suppressing such behaviour through punishment, though in other contexts they would be firmly against such approaches.

(ii) Rewarding low-level adaptive behaviour in the context of a serious maladaptive performance calls for clear discriminations – not only on the client's part, but on the part of outside observers. Often the community and its representatives are unable, or unwilling, to make such fine distinctions; to do so would look too much like condoning the bad behaviour that happens to occur nearby. It is safer and more comfortable to attribute behaviour entirely to durable, internal predispositions which might be susceptible to 'short sharp shock' approaches. Therefore, however effective the results, nothing nice can be allowed to happen to juvenile delinquents, they must be reformed through suffering – or not, as the case may be.

(iii) The short-term suppression of unwanted behaviour that punishment can bring often reinforces the behaviour of the punisher (positively and negatively). Furthermore, he or she is seen to have done something definite and clear-cut about the problem.

(iv) Another reason for the popularity of punishment is that it is believed to act as a source of vicarious suppression for similar behaviours in others, as in 'making an example' of offenders *pour encourager les autres.*

But there are many problems associated with the use of punishment.

(i) Naturally enough, it induces escape behaviours in those on whom it is used. These can be at least as maladaptive as the original problem-behaviour, and the negative reinforcement of successful responses in this class can give rise to a new generation of difficulties. For example, a child may learn that he can escape punishment by lying really convincingly.

(ii) Punishment gives rise to revenge motives. A good way of avoiding its unpleasant effects is to remove, or act against, the source of these. If this is the social worker, however benign his or her intentions, they may be left either with no one to work with, or with a client who will regard every suggestion as a signal to do the opposite.

(iii) Punishment alone, whether arranged or accidental, gives no guidance as to what alternative behaviours might be more effective than the response that is being discouraged.

(iv) Punishment acts as a *general* suppressant. It tends to have a 'blanket effect', removing wanted as well as unwanted responses from the repertoire, sometimes leaving nothing much for the therapist to work with.

(v) Unless powerful, punishment has only short-term effects, and influence based on visible coercion is influence easily disregarded once the heat is off (Festinger 1957).

(vi) Punishment can easily generalize to its users. Someone who makes regular use of it will find it hard to use positive reinforcement effectively with the same client in the future.

These problems need to be kept in view when the social worker is putting together programmes that have a necessary control element, particularly when they involve children. These points do not add up to a case for the complete abandonment of punishment as a technique, rather they are intended to serve as a reminder that most of our clients already inhabit environments rich in aversive stimuli, and only rarely will it help to add to these artificially.

There are occasions when punishment can be used quickly to suppress behaviours that interfere seriously with attempts to reinforce other performances. Lovaas (1967) used contingent electric shock to suppress self-injurious behaviour in autistic children. Left to extinguish by itself this behaviour continued until hundreds of self-administered blows were recorded. In some cases, two shocks reduced this rate to zero – where it stayed for good, allowing physical restraints to be removed and a language–teaching programme to begin.

The important point in this example is that punishment was used briefly, and in the context of a wider programme reliant upon positive reinforcement principles. Analogously, it is debatable (distinguish from desirable) whether the occasional slap in the context of a normally loving and affectionate family does any harm. It might help the child to discriminate between behaviours constituting mild naughtiness and more seriously offensive behaviour. However, there is always the negative modelling-effect to be considered (see p. 8).

Social workers cannot have their heads in the clouds about punishment. It is not a very large feature of the repertoire of behavioural procedures appropriate to our field, but as an *effect* it is all around us. Some clients may even see the very presence of a social worker in their homes as a punishment, however benign and liberal our own interpretation of our role.

Case example showing the effects of operant consequences on behaviour

Mark, aged 10, was referred to social services via the education social work service (the department held a supervision order on an elder brother following three instances of theft). Junior school staff were greatly concerned about Mark's disruptive behaviour in class and were beginning to use psychiatric terminology to describe this. Expulsion was likely unless something could be done and there was official concern regarding the amount of physical punishment used at home following these incidents.

In common with that of his brother, Mark's childhood had been somewhat troubled. A history of marital difficulties between parents, and two lengthy periods of separation from them while in the care of relatives had been the most distinctive features. Family life seemed to have settled down of late and the social worker handling the case had filed increasingly optimistic reports about this. However, it was known that parents had often disagreed to the point of violence about disciplinary practices in the home – mother favouring the strict enforcement of rules, but father, when present, following a 'boys will be boys' philosophy – this, perhaps, to excuse some of his own wayward behaviour. In addition, Mark was not a bright child and had reading difficulties requiring remedial teaching – with which he rarely co-operated.

With the somewhat hesitant co-operation of the school authorities an investigation of Mark's disruptive behaviour began in its natural setting. Student social workers took it in turns to observe lessons. They were introduced just as 'students' and spent periods sitting unobtrusively at the rear of the classroom to observe and record his behaviour. Data recorded by these observers revealed the following. (a) 'Disruptive behaviour' usually meant 'Mark leaving his desk or group activity'; but after that he would occasionally make loud noises, slamming down objects, teasing, hitting and pinching other pupils, and generally interfering with their work. (b) Some teachers had more difficulty with Mark than others. (c) The most common methods of dealing with Mark were: reasoning with him, or speaking sharply to him, both of which seemed to have only a marginal and temporary effect; trying to distract him, which only worked in the short term; placing him outside the door – to which he did not seem to object at all and which, again, had no effect on his subsequent behaviour. By and large teachers tried to ignore him, most operating what the head teacher referred to as a 'sleeping dogs' policy where they could.

The working hypothesis developed in this case was that Mark's classroom behaviour was largely a product of the following contingencies. (a) When Mark was at all well behaved (which records showed was a fair proportion of the time) he was ignored. Most teachers were wary of him and left him alone. (b) Conversely, whenever Mark caused or threatened a disturbance he received immediate attention from his teacher on virtually every occasion. (c) Attempts to punish Mark were ineffective, not only because they were admirably half-hearted, but because of his immunizing exposure to much more serious forms of it at home. (d) Mark's reading difficulties sometimes made it hard for him to join in lessons – he was bored and a little embarrassed by this and escaped from these conditions by amusing himself with other more interesting if dubious pursuits.

The reinforcement patterns thought to be operating in this case are as follows.

— Mark was *positively reinforced* with attention for bad behaviour (a commodity in short supply at home, for *any* behaviour). A further contrast between consequences of good and bad behaviour was provided by the fact that teachers would stay away from him when he was not being difficult, and in any case saw all too little to reward in what they called 'his attitude to schoolwork in general'. Thus teachers were only persuaded to reward extended runs of positively good behaviour, and these occurred rarely.

— Mark's tendency to get out of his seat, and his disruptive behaviour, were also *negatively reinforced*. The work was difficult for him to succeed at because he did not possess the skills required, and so became bored. If called upon to contribute to class work, he usually tried, but made a mess of things. Thus leaving his seat and disruptive behaviour had the effect of terminating or reducing boredom, embarrassment and worries about failing. On one occasion, Mark automatically placed himself by the door after a confrontation with a teacher.

Results from the attempt to reverse these reinforcement contingencies – to provide positive reinforcement for remaining seated and concentrating on school work, and none for disruptive or aggressive behaviour – are shown on p. 135 and the methods used discussed on p. 166. This approach is called *differential reinforcement* and its principles are central to behavioural practice.

MODELLING AND VICARIOUS LEARNING

So far, we have examined (a) the means by which new responses are generated through stimulus association, often in chain-like fashion (classical conditioning); (b) the way in which responses are established in the repertoire or lost from it as a result of the consequences they produce (operant conditioning). We turn now to a third process, derived in part from the other two, and called, variously, *observational learning, vicarious learning, modelling*, or *imitation*. Different authors give somewhat different meanings to these terms, but since there is considerable overlap, I suggest that for practical purposes they be treated as virtually synonymous. This works so long as we remember that 'modelling' generally implies social imitation.

These processes are the means by which new responses are acquired, reinforced, or extinguished, *at a distance* (vicariously), through observation of the behaviour of others. A large proportion of the behavioural repertoire of each of us is developed in this way, not through direct personal experience, but through watching what others do in particular circumstances and how they fare as a consequence. Its basis in simple imitation is visible in the biologically endowed, facial expression-copying of small babies (see p. 100).

Modelling is the process through which we learn the speech patterns of our parents and peers; learn to act like our favourite film star; pick up the rudiments of a new dance style; learn how to behave in strange surroundings; how to approach strangers for amorous purposes; how to intimidate others; come to approach decision-making in as neurotic a way as our parents; learn how being aggressive gets people their way, or not.

Modelling is a powerful influence in human socialization and its importance has been enhanced considerably by the arrival of the mass media. Through modelling we select, observe and learn to imitate in approximate form elements of the behavioural performances of others most days of our lives. When we are in interesting or demanding circumstances, under threat, or in strange surroundings, we become avid modellers, searching in the behaviour of others for clues as to how to behave. Similarly, at certain stages in socialization, during adolescence in particular, models are actively sought and copied as the young person experiments with different styles of behaviour. Paradoxically, this copying is done as a way of establishing a *distinct* identity – this is only achieved later when judicious editing, fluency and the combining of different perform- ances produces a genuinely unique style of behaviour.

As in the case of the other forms of learning reviewed above, we can acquire both useful or destructive, good or bad, self-enhancing or self-defeating, confident or fearful responses through observational learning. The process is exactly the same. Albert Bandura (the foremost researcher in this field) makes the point that were operant conditioning the only means by which human beings could acquire a behavioural repertoire, then the planet would be littered with the mangled corpses of those whose responses had been ineffective in controlling their particular bit of the environment:

> In laboratory investigations of learning processes experimenters usually arrange comparatively benign environments in which errors will not produce fatal consequences for the organism. In contrast, natural settings are loaded with potentially lethal consequences that unmercifully befall anyone who makes hazardous errors. For this reason, it would be exceedingly injudicious to rely primarily upon trial and error learning and successive-approximation methods in teaching children to swim, adolescents to drive automobiles, or adults to master complex occupa- tional and social tasks. If rodents, pigeons or primates toiling in contrived situations could likewise get electrocuted, dismembered, or bruised for errors that inevitably occur during early phases of learning, few of these venturesome subjects would ever survive the shaping process.
>
> (Bandura 1969:143)

Skinner's analysis of what happens when we observe the behaviour of someone else and then perform it ourselves takes the standard operant view outlined as follows:

$$Sd \text{——————} R \text{——————} Sr$$

Here Sd represents the discriminative stimuli present in the modelled perfor- mance, R denotes an overt matching response, and Sr the reinforcing stimulus which follows this performance.

It will be immediately apparent that although this explanation may ap- proach sufficiency in very controlled conditions of deliberate response-matching where considerable prior learning has taken place (for example, a dancing class), but for many everyday modelling situations it is inadequate. First there is the problem of acquisition, that is, how the observer comes to acquire the new set of responses in the first place. Second there is the problem of the retention of a modelled behaviour pattern for days and weeks before it is performed overtly. We may go to the cinema and observe a particularly cool, collected performance by an actor and not try to re-enact aspects of this until we are next confronted with the office panic-monger.

An experiment to demonstrate the role of reinforcement in modelling was performed by Bandura (1965). Children watched a film of an actor displaying aggression. The reinforcement conditions under which this behaviour was performed were systematically varied. In one sequence the actor was punished; in another, rewarded with praise and sweets, and in another, no particular consequences were seen to result from his behaviour. Immediate post-exposure observations of children from the audience showed notably higher levels of aggression. The highest and most varied levels of aggressive behaviour came from the groups who had seen the model's aggression reinforced or attract no negative consequences. For them the violence was seen to pay off, so they imitated it at the next opportunity.

Post-performance reinforcement undoubtedly plays a part in the modelling process as this experiment demonstrates, but as a complete explanation it too is somewhat inadequate. Paying attention to what other people do in interesting or stressful situations is likely to be reinforcing in itself. (Bandura's argument that modelling can occur in the absence of reinforcement seems a bit thin.) He means, one supposes, deliberately presented reinforcement. However there is likely to be plenty of naturally-occurring generalized reinforcement for response-matching surrounding any behavioural performance which is distinct enough to catch our attention. Also there is a key role here for the *anticipated* reinforcement (Sd) of any imitation which will add new response-options to the stock. Individuals with a wide range of possible responses to whatever circumstances they happen to find themselves in, are more likely to be able to obtain satisfaction, and more likely to be avoid aversive stimuli. In this sense, the knowledge that novel response-options are being stored in memory as behavioural 'capital' for later use might itself reinforce attentional and response-matching behaviour.

The rest of the modelling process occurs in symbolic, that is, cognitive form. We think ourselves into the role of the performer, imagine and, to some extent, experience the emotional accompaniments that he might be experiencing (easy in the cinema and on television because of the cues provided by the accompanying music). Next we anticipate how successful we would be in performing this behaviour and what the probable outcome would be for us in given circumstances. A child who watches others breaking down a fence with consummate skill need not perform similar behaviour on the next fence he comes across. A variety of different conditions (Sds), some of them social in origin, will determine when the behaviour 're-emerges'. In the meantime, aspects of the performance are represented in memory waiting to be called up for future circumstances.

Another form of modelling where covert factors (feelings this time) play a large part in the acquisition process has been called *empathetic learning*. The fact that we tend to 'feel along' with the performances of a model (as a result of a lengthy process of classical conditioning) tends to make us want to re-perform the behaviour to obtain internal, emotional reinforcement from the various states of arousal previously known to accompany it. In the example of the child breaking down the fence, according to Bandura and Rosenthal (1966) the behaviour would be re-performed by an observer with the aim of re-producing, perhaps in amplified form, the emotional 'kicks' that once accompanied watching someone else do it.

Case example

In 1964 I went to see *Grand Prix*, a banal motor racing film with action scenes shot from car-mounted cameras. Walking out of the cinema I was met with a wall of sound. The night air was thick with blue smoke as hundreds of teenagers revved up their ageing Ford Anglias and Austin 1100s and raced each other down the Bristol Road, seats all the way back, arms straight, windows down. When my girlfriend asked why I was driving like a maniac I replied that I had *always* driven fast, hadn't she noticed? and that anyway it was skill that mattered. This behaviour lasted for about ten miles (when I remembered that I was supposed to be practising being cool and impervious to influence).

The current status of this theory as an explanation of modelling is viewed by Bandura as similar to that of the operant conditioning model. Such factors may well be at work, and may play a relatively large part in modelling under certain conditions, but they are background rather than central features in most cases:

> Sensory-feedback theories of imitation may therefore be primarily rele-vant to instances in which the modeled responses incur relatively potent reinforcement consequences capable of endowing response-correlated stimuli with motivational properties. Affective conditioning should therefore be regarded as a facilitative rather than as a necessary condition for modeling.

> (Bandura 1969:132)

In other words, the cognitive, problem-solving content of modelled perfor-mances can be sufficient to secure imitation.

Research in this field has had considerable impact on practice in the form of programmes to teach child-management skills to parents with children at risk (Deschner 1984), to equip psychiatric patients with the social and other skills necessary for survival in the community (Trower *et al.* 1977), and to provide violent offenders with alternative cognitive and interpersonal skills so that hostile impulses can be brought under control (Kazdin *et al.* 1989).

COGNITIVE-MEDIATIONAL THEORIES

Theories of observational learning which emphasize the importance of the mental representation of the sequence to be re-performed are called *cognitive-mediational theories* (Bandura 1969, 1977; Eysenck and Keane 1990). They concentrate on the hidden stages that occur between observation and performance. Two systems are said to be at work here to represent a performance in our heads for later retrieval: a process of imagination and a verbal process. Performances are encoded into particular image-sequences and word symbols and stored in memory.

Let us look now at an experiment that demonstrates the role of such symbolic representation in modelling (Bandura 1969). In this study children were asked to pay attention to filmed sequences of complex behaviour. One group of children were just instructed to watch carefully; one group was asked, as well as paying attention, to speak along with the models on the screen and describe and label the model's behaviour out loud; another group were instructed to watch attentively, but to count rapidly at the same time (this to prevent the encoding of information). When asked to re-create the sequences they had seen, the children in the 'verbal-labelling' group were much more effective in their performances than the next group (the watch-silently group) and produced yet more accurate responses than the group that had had to engage in a competing activity.

Most of us will have had the experience of talking ourselves through a difficult or unfamiliar task – either out loud, as in childhood, or subliminally ('under our breath'): 'Right now, that's the gasket back on, and now I put the *large* locating screws on the *left* so as not to mix them up with these *smaller* ones over *here*. . .'. The point here is that it is the encoding and organizing of complex modelling stimuli by the brain that ensures accurate reproduction. Similarly, the more complex and unfamiliar the task the more likely we are to open an extra channel of sensory input to guide our actions, to lay out components in order, or to talk out loud and then listen to what we are saying. Cartesian models of mental functions (see Chapter 2) have seeped into Western culture and therefore it is easy for us to underestimate the extent to which consciousness is dependent upon sensory input. Try Dennett's little experiment (1991). Ask a group of people to imagine a three-by-three crossword grid. Next tell them that the words down are *gas*, *oil* and *dry*, and ask them, what are the words across? The usual results are: (a) people have more difficulty with the task than either they thought, or 'screen in the head' notions of consciousness would suggest they should have; (b) the fingers of the subjects positively twitch for something to write on, or, since this is forbidden, any set of external feedback mechanisms (drawing on one's hand, talking to someone else, using window panes to represent the grid, etc.).

The more complex the information, the greater the degree of organization and splitting into sections required, as in those instances when we have to depend on the promptings of manuals and schedules of various kinds. By the same token, we can reinforce ourselves for both approximate performances and during the mental rehearsal of a complex performance. This occurs through the tagging on of images of ourselves coping with, and mastering the problem against which we plan to use the modelled performance – pictures of approving smiles from our peers as they see us deal deftly with a sticky situation. Also, through self-talk. 'Good, you're doing fine'; 'That went down well'; and so on. The therapeutic derivatives of this phenomenon (discussed in Chapter 7) largely concern attempts to render clients more aware of the stages in their cognitive responses to challenging situations and what they 'say' or do not 'say' to themselves about their attempts to address them.

So far we have seen that offshoots of both classical and operant conditioning procedures play a part in getting us to attend to, and reproduce for ourselves, the behaviour of others. But neither of these processes fully accounts for this form of learning, which is made possible only through cognition, which allows us to re-enact, in symbolic form, the little dramatic performances we have selected from the behaviour of others and that we anticipate (sometimes wrongly) will be useful to us. The following diagram from Bandura (1977) (Figure 3.5) provides an economical summary of the various stages of the modelling process. The reader will see that the first list of factors is associated with the characteristics of the modelled stimulus, and what it is about it that we selectively perceive and attend to ('attentional process'). The second list relates to the coding, organization and storage of a 'mental script' of the performance. The third set concerns the rehearsal of modelled performances, and the fourth the factors that decide the place of the performance in the repertoire, how often it is likely to be performed, whether it will be developed further, or lost and so on.

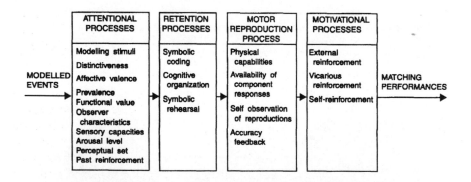

Figure 3.5 Component factors governing observational learning in the social learning process
Source: Bandura (1977). © Albert Bandura 1977. Reprinted by permission of Prentice-Hall, Inc., Englewood Cliffs, NJ.

THE USES OF MODELLING

Modelling procedures are useful in a wide range of circumstances, particularly the following.

(i) To remedy behavioural deficits. Clients often just do not have the behaviours or the thinking strategies necessary to solve their problems in repertoire. They may simply never have learned them, or they may have lost them because of intervening experiences. In this case there may be little or nothing for therapists to shape. Some of the most heartrending problems ever to confront us are the result of a failure to learn basic human characteristics because no examples were available nearby:

> That girls are raped, that two boys knife a third,
> Were axioms to him, who'd never heard
> Of any world where promises were kept,
> Or one could weep, because another wept.
> (W. H. Auden, 'The Shield of Achilles')

(ii) To reduce interfering anxiety. When individuals are forced to cope despite considerable social and behavioural deficits, their actions usually become stereotyped and awkward. Knowing this they tend to avoid any circumstances ($S\Delta$) where they are unlikely to perform well, or will be punished, and experience anxiety. Anxiety can enhance a performance up to a certain level, but beyond this optimum level interferes progressively with performance (Hebb 1972 – also see p. 107), resulting in increasingly inadequate and poorly discriminated behaviour. This, in turn, sets up a vicious circle leading to greater anxiety and more generalized avoidance. Modelling techniques can be used to demonstrate and teach better coping behaviours more likely to lead to reinforcement. The rehearsal of these new behaviours, to a point of reasonable competency, usually carries with it a 'desensitization' component. Fears are lessened both by vicarious extinction and by operant extinction – that is, by watching someone else perform the target behaviours without apparent anxiety, feeling sympathetically relaxed thereby, then practising under relatively benign conditions and with increasing competency.

(iii) Modelling can also be used to re-establish behaviours which were in the repertoire of the individual but which have been lost or suppressed because of lack of available reinforcement or through punishment. If these are present at a very low level, then shaping is likely to be a lengthy and labour-intensive process. Sometimes short-cuts can be attempted by modelling the required behaviour and showing it obtaining reinforcement – as in programmes to re-establish social skills lost through long-term institutionalization.

In my view, we have now passed the point where exclusively behaviouristic conceptions of learning can account (without undue contortion) for the phenomena under review.

COGNITIVE LEARNING

Several writers have argued that there is a type of learning – leading to the acquisition of new and visible responses – which is substantially independent of (distinguish from uninfluenced by) the different associative mechanisms on which classical and operant conditioning depend, and on which modelling effects have been seen partly to depend. There are various labels for this: *cognitive learning*, *insight learning*, *latent learning* and so forth. Each of these terms refers to an overlapping set of concepts that lay stress on the importance (particularly in complex learning tasks) of selective perception, understanding, prior knowledge, attribution, imagination, memory factors, concept formation and creative intelligence – allegedly the results of various forms of 'cognitive structures'.

Let us take the notion of 'cognitive structure' first. Skinner's view is simply that private events lie outside the boundaries of a true science, except to the extent that their influence can be reliably plotted in 'black box' fashion by referring to overt behavioural correlates. However, to the extent that this can be done, he argues, we do not need to bother with hard-to-get-at internal processes of mediation, since we already have a more parsimonious, and therefore superior theory (Skinner 1974). Skinner's analyses, though economical and often persuasive, often leave one with the feeling that they are too 'pat'. Even though both are concerned with rewards and punishments, the mental leap from the Skinner box to the roof of the Sistine Chapel is hard to make in one go. Creative problem-solving and artistry are surely something entirely different? Indeed, investigators of the origins of complex learning argue that crude and uncoordinated stimuli affecting an individual ought to result in crude and uncoordinated responses – unless, that is, something extra is added inside the 'black box'. The extra 'something' must be the effect of complex cognitive structures, that is, symbolic, mental 'maps' stored in memory, from which, and to which, items are added and subtracted, and between which interchanges can take place to create new orderings of information, and hence new response options.

Take virtually any two words and conjoin them and an entirely new image with entirely new meaning and implications arises. Try 'golden' and 'mountain'. Few, if any of us has seen such a thing (at dawn, in the desert, something close perhaps), yet we have no difficulty conjuring up the image, or even a newly-created folk tale to match. Indeed, we have to work very hard to produce grammatical word sequences with no apparent meaning: 'Colourless green ideas sleep furiously' is the standard example from philosophy, but note (a) the *quest* for meaning that this triggers, and (b) that to anyone brought up on Bob Dylan songs, or interested in conservation politics, even this comes close to sense.

In case I am giving you cause for concern, consider that much of our daily mental activity when we are not 'on task' is taken up with divergent speculation at least as unusual as this. In the longer term it pays off; it generates novel, humorous and creative insights and solutions once in a while. We are probably all intuitively aware of something like this going on when we come across a new idea that functions, at both a conceptual and an emotional level, as a key piece in an incomplete jigsaw puzzle enabling us to see a new 'picture'. We also have inside our heads the facilities to put items of information derived from incoming stimuli on 'hold'; dredge up concordant information from memory, run a series of simulations vaguely akin to computer models, select the best one (that is, the best match and the one most likely to lead to reinforcement) and then behave according to this programme, changing course in the light of feedback on the environmental effects produced.

The main idea here is that of *anticipated reinforcement*, gauged through the setting up in systematic form of 'thought experiments': 'Now what would happen if I did x rather than y?' The answer is likely to be based on prior experience of similar situations. One such famous thought experiment was that of Galileo, who in fact had no prior need to drop weights from bell towers to prove that (counter-intuitively) heavy and light objects fall at the same rate. He simply imagined what would happen if a wire were to be attached between the objects making them into one; would the assembly fall according to its combined weight, or the heavier pull at the lighter? No. QED. Cognitive postulates of this type have given rise to the notion of *coverant conditioning* (Homme 1965), where 'operant thoughts' derived from prior experience are reinforced or extinguished according to whether they add constructively to a problem-solving formula likely to pay off for the individual when it is translated into behaviour. Thus, when we think of solving our financial problems by robbing a bank, the thoughts are usually extinguished quite quickly by other associations about the possible consequences, except where, 'just for the fun of it' (that is, for the emotional feedback), we deliberately control the mental drama to make sure we get away undetected.

Analyses of this type of problem-solving behaviour in traditional stimulus–response terms are also available (Skinner 1974), but they are exceedingly complex and cumbersome and quite often the game is just not worth the candle.

The view that environmental influences do not simply enter the brain as stimuli and leave as responses, in ping-pong fashion, is hard to resist. Just what kind of cognitive 'pinball machine' they do go through before they re-emerge over time as effects, and often pretty divergent and unusual effects at that, is a major growth area in psychological research.

One can trace this interest back to the Greek philosophers; the introspection of Wilhelm Wundt (1907); the 'metabehaviourism' of Tolman (1932); the observations of Vygotsky (1962) that thinking in language follows from the social pressure to communicate with others about things and actions, not the other way around; the work of Jean Piaget (1958) on stages in intellectual development; to modern precoccupations with the principles of artificial intelligence and attempts to apply them to the study of human behaviour (Boden 1981). The complex models that are emerging have one thing in common: they all serve to refute Cartesian notions of a separate, internal, calculating system directed *sometimes* by the 'will' towards problem-solving activity in the exterior world. They all stress the 'incorporatedness' of the dynamics of the external world, past and present, in consciousness. It has taken us a long time to catch up with the assumptions of Australian Aboriginal culture in this regard.

For practical purposes the important question is, can we successfully inter-vene through the medium of language to alter cognitive patterns, beliefs, 'mental maps', attributions, ways of seeing and so on, so that more adaptive *behaviours* are generated? Let us address the problem through an analogy. If we think of cognitive structures as forming a proposed plan for a building project (future behaviour), could we alter the shape of the eventual building by changing the plan – or does it all still depend largely on how the builder has done things in the past (learning history); whether he has the skill to do anything different (repertoire); whether he could be bothered to work on a building of a different shape (short-term reinforcement); whether such a building would 'work' or whether it would collapse in the face of environmen-tal stresses (long-term reinforcement)? These questions need to be approached with caution. As we saw in Chapter 1 the automatic assumption that changing thinking changes behaviour has often led to ineffective methods being used in the past (Sheldon 1986). In fact, we know rather more about the power of induced behavioural change to alter thinking.

What, then, is the form of a 'cognitive structure' and what effects can these be seen to have on behaviour? It could be argued that once again we are in danger of reifying an activity and making it into a 'thing'. Certainly we have combinations of neurons programmed to fire in certain combinations rather than others, but this is hard for most of us to imagine. The contents of the skull are dense. It is dark in there. But it is often imagined to be hollow, and filled with the light and sound of experience. So we heuristically infer that we have cognitive structures because the private processing of information about envi-ronmental contingencies tends to follow certain patterns. We quickly learn that stimuli are not always what they seem, that not all brightly coloured tablets are sweets and that not all 'sincere offers of help' are sincere offers of help, and, a point worth repeating, that sometimes the *absence* of stimuli predicts much:

'Is there any other point to which you would wish to draw my attention?'
'To the curious incident of the dog in the night time.'
'The dog did nothing in the night time.'
'That was the curious incident,' remarked Sherlock Holmes.

(Conan Doyle, 'Silver Blaze':326-7)

Given the niche-filling pressures of natural selection (e.g. camouflage), responding to the surface features of stimuli would always have been dangerous
for our primitive ancestors – as in different ways it still is – and so the behaviour
of *interpreting* readily attracts reinforcement. As an activity, it contains the
following elements.

(i) An examination of sensory data in great detail.

(ii) The action of looking at the *context* of stimuli (a pie cooling in the kitchen
evokes quite a different set of responses from a pie cooling in a field).

(iii) Responding to the images which stimuli evoke in our heads through
classical conditioning. For example, if I write *red car* it is virtually
impossible for you not to 'see' a red car. This image may be followed by
an association with Redcar (the place), then with horse racing, or with
any other number of items linked with the image by prior knowledge or
experience.

(iv) Attempts to establish causality and intent (a hand placed unexpectedly
on the shoulder can mean friendly support or the sack).

(v) The action of looking at relations between stimuli: two sets of stimuli are
not just one set plus one set. Their conjunction can produce quite
different implications. The client who assures her social worker that
things are getting better to the accompaniment of non-verbal signals of
anxiety might be said to be 'adopting a strategy' (for any one of several
different purposes). Only further interpretation of these conjoined
events, perhaps followed by some careful encouragement and probing,
will discover the true meaning or intent contained in the behaviour, that
is, the effect it is designed to have, or the internal state it is designed to
conceal.

(vi) Stimuli produce a range of conditioned associations previously stored in
memory. These are the raw material on which future computations about
how best to behave are made. In addition they help to trigger and sustain
emotional reactions which then enter the equation themselves as inhibi-
tors or enhancers of particular behavioural options. Thus if we recall that
last time we were in a particular kind of fix we 'brazened it out' and this
image is accompanied by very pleasant feelings enhancing recalled actions, then unless there are powerful contra-indications present in the
current situations, we are unlikely to hesitate for long before repeating
this sequence.

(vii) We use the facility of language (inner speech) to talk to ourselves about
contingencies: 'Now wait a minute (warily), someone must simply have

dropped this pie, there's *bound* to be a logical explanation, bit surreal though, shades of Magritte. . . Wait 'til I tell the family'; (image of astonished and attentive family).

(viii) The use of previously reinforced and shaped problem-solving strategies. We manipulate data in pre-set ways. There are many possible variables here. For example, we may have learned that speed in decision-making is the crucial thing, and so select a course of action on the basis of little detailed evidence that this plan will pay off. Or we may tend to 'weigh' such issues (scan and re-scan the data) because we have learned that precipitate action leads to regrets later (see p. 108). Similarly, we may approach a problem (a complex set of contingencies) on the assumption that it provides yet further evidence that others are out to get us. Or, in the absence of any well-practised methods of computing likely outcome, that it provides yet further evidence that we are getting 'past it' and can't cope any more. These *thinking styles* give rise to 'self-concepts', that is to views of our likely efficacy in influencing the environment, our abilities in discriminating among complex stimuli and so on.

(ix) 'Insight learning' may occur. The process here is one of scanning outer (environmental) stimuli, and inner (physical/emotional stimuli) and by manipulating, or even deliberately suspending, the rules by which such events are assessed, coming up with highly original responses. In man, these creative responses often attract generalized reinforcement (see p. 66). They produce a satisfactory feeling of cleverness. Together these factors give the experience of 'insight', or creative-problem solving, its unique 'Eureka!' feel. In addition, most kinds of problem-solving, however refined, take place against a background of negative reinforcement possibilities provided by worry and anxiety. We often experience profound relief when we reach a tenable solution to a problem which has been bothering us, or use our 'wits' to escape a seemingly unavoidable obligation.

(x) The development of rules. Human beings can produce what seem like entirely novel and spontaneous responses because they learn the abstract rules that govern the relation and succession of stimuli, and the likely effects of particular actions. Rule-following behaviour is sparked off by hosts of discriminative stimuli present in the environment, and the application of existing rules to new combinations of stimuli can lead to new combinations of responses. This kind of computation gives to human behaviour its special 'knight's move' characteristics.

It could be objected that not all thought processes are so heavily strategic as in the list given above. Cognitive patterns of these types give us important clues as to how clients develop problems, and why they are resistant to extinction (therefore they will be discussed in more detail in the context of a review of assessment procedures in Chapter 5). For example, in the case of 'daydreaming' or contemplation, the thoughts we experience are not driven by an urgent need to come up with a quick behavioural policy. The philosopher Gilbert Ryle had this to say about thinking of this kind:

> Not all pondering or musing is problem tackling. While some walking is exploring and some walking is trying to get to a destination, still some walking is merely strolling around. Similarly while some meditating or ruminating is exploratory, and some, like multiplying, is travelling on business, still some is just re-visiting familiar country and some is just cogitative strolling for cogitative strolling's sake.
>
> (Ryle 1949:28)

This is an important distinction, but not one which seriously threatens the analysis already developed. We know from studies in physiological psychology that the brain cannot easily do nothing, not even in sleep. It is just not 'wired up' that way (see Blakemore 1977). The system is at an optimal level of arousal when it is working away. Much below this level, as in sensory deprivation experiments, strange things begin to happen. These are symptoms of 'stimulus hunger' and can include hallucinations and depersonalization (see Heron 1957). We can all experience something a little like them on long motorway drives.

Ruminative thoughts, although not about urgent behavioural decisions, are nevertheless likely to be connected to more distant general contingencies. Thus, outside depressive illness, we ruminate about our long-term future without too much anxiety, and without feelings that a solution must necessarily be found quickly. External stimulation of even a slightly unusual kind disrupts this 'coasting along' and replaces it with thought patterns geared more directly to short-term problem solving. There is undoubtedly a role for reinforcement here too, and it is likely that relatively non-specific thinking would be maintained by conditioned reinforcers (see p. 65).

If these assumptions are roughly correct, then there is no reason to view private, cognitive events as in some way disconnected, non-physical phenomena which have little to do with behaviour, nor to assume that they obey principles markedly different from those contained in the various theories of learning reviewed above. This said, we are all aware that some sequences of complex thought exist in the form of object, event, or picture *symbols* rather than in fully formed 'photographic' images or fully formed words and sentences. These bio-electrical flashes 'stand for' things and concepts allowing us to compute from sensory experience or memory with astonishing rapidity. Musical memory, for example, conjures up images (the Bach Cantata no. 140, horses, banks and overdrafts – curse them) but does not depend upon these. Abstract thought is a challenge to cognitive psychology's attempts to say what thoughts are a bit like – speech, pictures, sounds, smells. In the end, we may have to accommodate the view of the philosopher who, on being asked what he thought in, answered, 'I think in thoughts'.

If the phenomenon of interpreting and thinking about stimuli and their response connections complicates matters rather, then the fact that, in man, 'the environment' virtually always includes 'the social environment', multiplies these complications many times over. 'A response to a response to a response' is a common-enough occurrence in everyday life. Sane people do not try to draw such complex interrelationships schematically, but this is not to say that they completely defeat a rigorous analysis.

The American psychologist Albert Bandura has developed such an analysis stage by stage over the last thirty-odd years and this enduringly useful model is known as social learning theory (Bandura 1977).

SOCIAL LEARNING THEORY

This is a formulation that rests heavily on theories of vicarious learning (see p. 81). The formulation shares many of the assumptions of the cognitive theorists, and yet in Bandura's view it is compatible with many of the basic tenets of traditional behaviourism. As a theory, then, it is well placed to integrate a number of current trends in the discipline.

Here are two quotations that should give you the flavour of social learning theory:

> Stimuli influence the likelihood of particular behaviors through their predictive function, not because they are automatically linked to responses by occurring together. In the social learning view, contingent experiences create expectations rather than stimulus–response connections. Environmental events can predict either other environmental occurrences, or serve as predictors of the relation between actions and outcomes.
>
> (Bandura 1977:59)

And as to the question of determinism, and whether behaviour and the learning function is powered from inside or outside the individual:

> Environments have causes, as do behaviors. It is true that behavior is regulated by its contingencies but the contingencies are partly of a person's own making. By their actions, people play an active role in producing the reinforcing contingencies that impinge upon them. As was previously shown, behavior partly creates the environment, and the environment influences the behavior in a reciprocal fashion. To the oft repeated dictum, 'change contingencies and you change behavior', should be added the reciprocal side, 'change behavior and you change contingencies'. In the regress of prior causes, for every chicken discovered by a unidirectional environmentalist, a social learning theorist can identify a prior egg.
>
> (Bandura 1977:203)

You will have gathered that questions of ultimate causality do not worry Bandura much. The fact that man is above all things a social animal means that he both creates, and is created by, these special environments. It is Bandura's view that behaviour within this huge closed circuit is dominated by two sets of influences:

Outcome expectations: the estimate of a person that given behaviour will lead to certain outcomes.

Efficacy expectations: representing the conviction that one can successfully execute the behaviour required to produce a specific outcome.

These two influences are differentiated because a person can believe that a particular course of action will produce certain outcomes, but may have serious doubts as to whether he or she is capable of performing the behaviour necessary to bring these about. Or, he or she may feel that a given objective is within his or her grasp, but does not value it.

These are the constituent parts of Bandura's concept of *perceived self-efficacy.* According to him all psychological change procedures, whatever their type, are mediated through this system of beliefs about the end result of an action and the level of skill required to perform it adequately (see Figure 3.6).

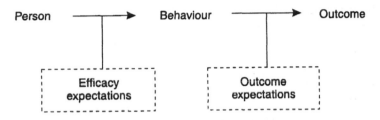

Figure 3.6 Efficacy and outcome expectations
Source: Adapted from Bandura (1977). By permission of Prentice-Hall, Inc., Englewood Cliffs, NJ.

Of these two elements, efficacy expectations are the most important. Attempts to modify outcome expectations by verbal persuasion alone have relatively weak and temporary effects, particularly in the face of contradictory experiences. Similarly, so-called placebo effects, though they may have an enhancing effect on therapy, are unlikely to provide a sufficient basis for lasting change, and will rarely serve in place of a logically constructed programme of help (Bergin and Garfield 1986). The main effect on outcome expectations is through the strengthening of efficacy expectations. Bandura (1978) lists the following sources of efficacy expectations.

(i) Performance accomplishments: gained through participation, and desensitization to threats inhibiting an approach to the feared circumstances. (Bandura sees reinforcement simply as an *incentive-giving or regulating* influence, cognitively mediated and reflected upon.)

(ii) Vicarious experience: gained through watching others perform (modelling).

(iii) Verbal persuasion: by suggestion, explanation, guided self-instruction, interpretations and so on.

(iv) Reducing fears associated with particular performances by *imagining* oneself coping in a step-by-step manner. Other approaches include: relaxation techniques; biofeedback; exposure (imagining worse fears for lengthy periods as a way of extinguishing them – see p. 217).

Bandura suggests that the main effort of the would-be helper should go into directly modifying thoughts and feelings which affect perceived self-efficacy. This is in line with many of the treatment procedures and styles already made use of by social workers. But (referring to research into pathological fears), Bandura adds a word of caution – and this is the point where his theory is connected to main stream of cognitive-behavioural practice:

> Developments in the field of behavioral change reveal two major divergent trends. This difference is especially evident in the modification of dysfunctional inhibitions and defensive behavior. On the one hand, explanations of change processes are becoming more cognitive. On the other hand, it is performance-based treatments that are proving most powerful in effecting psychological changes. Regardless of the method involved, treatments implemented through actual performance achieve results consistently superior to those in which fears are eliminated to cognitive representations of threats. Symbolic procedures have much to contribute as components of a multiform performance-oriented approach, but they are usually insufficient by themselves.
>
> (Bandura 1977:78)

All this is in line with the review of outcome studies contained in Chapter 1. However, there are objections to Bandura's theory which fall into three groups. First, those which object to it on the grounds that it is less *parsimonious* (economical) than existing formulations, and that the predictions made by the theory can be adequately explained by existing knowledge. (See, for example, Eysenck's cogent analysis; Eysenck 1978.) The argument here is that there is no need for Bandura's theory, since classical conditioning theory does the job of explaining in a more simple, and more easily verifiable way. Second, there are objections that Bandura's theory contains ambiguities (Teasdale 1978), particularly in the precise differences between outcome and efficacy expectations. Third, there is the view that there is as yet too little experimental evidence to support Bandura's contention that behavioural change only occurs through a strengthening of perceived self-efficacy.

At this stage, then, cognitive-mediational theories of this type still need to be approached with caution. They offer the possibility of a meeting ground for therapists of different cognitive and behavioural persuasions. In addition, they are attractive in that they deal in an ungrudging fashion with the private 'world within the skin' which, however awkward in scientific terms, we all have experience of. Further, they are likely to be welcomed by those working outside controlled clinical settings, who have to rely to a considerable extent on programmes that aim to develop self-control (see p. 210).

Against these attractive features must be weighed the fact that the classical and operant theories of behavioural change have served us very well and continue to do so. They are sophisticated theories, well grounded in scientific research, and they have given rise to exceptionally reliable and well-documented therapeutic approaches. I have already given some indication of the places where existing foundations of behavioural change are relatively inadequate, and will not repeat these points here. The question of whether cognitive-mediational theories and their therapeutic offshoots can plug these gaps remains to be seen. My own position is that existing theories provide a barely adequate explanation of the various problems that fall within their scope. A strong skeleton structure, if you will. This provides a secure framework on which to base experiments in areas where the therapeutic implications of existing theories are difficult or indeed impossible to implement. (For example, the hard-to-motivate families struggling with a range of problems at once, which make up a solid proportion of any social worker's caseload.) As long as the established standard of evidence, and the established ways of evaluating therapeutic outcome are kept in sight, what is there to lose (except possibly some time spent in chasing red herrings)? Certainly there is much to gain, providing that we proceed according to the results of the kind of research reviewed in Chapter 1, and not in pursuit of a new fashion for novelty's sake.

We have seen so far that the special nature of human behaviour is conferred on us through what Pavlov called 'the second signalling system' – language, and through it the facility for inner speech and symbolic imagery, which enables us to act upon the environment in an extraordinarily strategic way by conducting mental experiments to see what might happen if we did A or B, *before* we actually do it. On the face of it, then, there is a prima facie case for supposing that in some cases we may be able to intervene effectively in the causal chain at this point: (a) by suggesting an alternative evaluation of the data on which the client is basing decisions; (b) by challenging actions based on negative self-concepts which do not seem to us justified by the evidence or by any comprehensive view of the individual's future potential; (c) by trying to substitute different imagery from that evoked by existing stimuli; (d) by trying to get the individual to consider new evidence on their existing view of personal efficacy; (e) by presenting a different interpretation of the likelihood of certain positive or negative consequences occurring; (f) by trying to reinforce a different pattern of self-commentary to run alongside particular actions. To this list I would add the rider: that effectiveness is likely to be strongly

97

influenced by the extent to which the therapist can ensure that the trial *behaviours* that occur as a result of such approaches are reinforced.

4

EMOTIONAL REACTIONS

Behavioural science has often been accused of neglecting the emotional dimension of human existence. While this view continues to surprise those of us familiar with the extensive literature on this topic within this discipline, it is perhaps an inevitable reaction. Any field that has in the past so discouraged inference to internal goings-on, and has ruled out introspection and subjective assessment as in valid approaches to scientific or clinical phenomena, must tread this ground very warily (see Skinner 1974). The argument that behavioural psychologists have probably done more than those of any other school to try to put the investigation of the nature and influence of emotion on a secure scientific footing fails to convince. The general public, and more than a few social workers too, balk at the necessarily unemotional treatment of emotion when it becomes a subject of study. They prefer to hear more subjective descriptions of its admittedly marvellous range and subtlety. This reflects a belief that it is better simply to experience emotion, rather than to analyse it. Anyone who has had to take *As You Like It* apart, line by line, or to dissect a Mozart piano concerto note by note will tell you there is something to be said for this point of view. But if we wish to understand something as completely as possible – even something as intensely personal as emotion, then we have to analyse it thoroughly. This is certainly the case if we wish to use our knowledge to help someone with 'an emotional problem' – that undifferentiated catch-all of social work assessment. We need to know what emotions are, what instigates them, whether they cause behaviour or are a concomitant upon it, what is their relationship to cognition and whether, or how, they can be changed. Sometimes this can even leave us with a greater respect for that which has been analysed.

Certain basic forms of emotional responding are inborn, for example, fear, crying, smiling and so on. This does not mean that they are unaffected by environment, which shapes these reactions from the moment of birth and teaches us how to cry so as to attract our parents' attention, and later when to suppress crying, and what to fear and what not to fear.

The three-week-old infant in Figure 4.1 is actively copying the facial movements of the adult – it is too soon for this to have been learned. This later

99

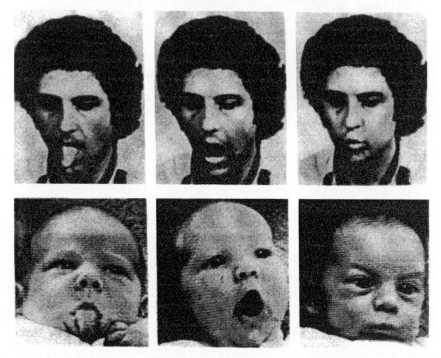

Figure 4.1 Imitation of facial gestures by two- to three-week-old infants
Source: Harris, P. (1972) in K. Connolly ed. (1979) *Psychology Survey No. 2*, London: George
Allen & Unwin. Reprinted by permission of the publisher.

becomes a reciprocal shaping process with adults copying and amplifying the
facial expressions of babies. Very young babies show greater signs of pleasure
and interest at the sight of the human face (or even a drawing of it) than to all
but the most dramatic stimuli of another kind. The human face is our main
source of information as to what an individual feels and intends, with non-
verbal behaviour in general and, later, speech in second and third place.

The experience of basic emotions is closely allied to physiological changes
that occur in the body predominantly as a result of external stimulation (but
not entirely; remember colic). The relevant systems lie within the sympathetic
nervous system – mentioned already as giving rise to fight and flight reactions
– and within the parasympathetic nervous system which acts in juxtaposition
to this. The relationship between the two is analogous to the dual-control of
limb movements by extensor and retractor muscles.

When some aspect of the environment acts upon us and triggers either a
primary physiological reflex, or a powerful conditioned reflex of the 'Oh Lord,
here comes the boss' kind, a number of biologically functional (but not
necessarily socially functional) things occur rapidly together inside our bodies.

— Heart rate increases, vasocontraction puts up the blood pressure, and hormonal release (adrenalin) maintains this.
— We start to breathe more rapidly.
— Skin pores dilate to aid cooling of the body.
— The blood sugar level rises to meet the potential increase in energy demands from the muscles.
— The pupils of the eyes dilate to let in all available light.
— The salivary flow dries up and keeps our throats clear for rapid mouth breathing.
— Blood flow is directed to the vital centres (that is, the brain and large muscles).
— Movements in the gastro-intestinal system are greatly reduced and in extreme cases the bladder and rectum contract.
— The capacity of the blood to clot is strengthened by chemical and enzymic action.
— Muscle tone increases.

As previously discussed, these mechanisms, derived from evolution, help to prepare the body for action (fight/flight) in the face of danger. Other stimuli evoke different combinations of effects – as in the case of sexual arousal where some of the above mechanisms are involved, but are accompanied by powerful sensations of pleasure and the release of different hormones – which reactions, as we all know, can be conditioned to other previously neutral stimuli such as smells, sounds, objects, touch.

Neuro-physiologists have located specialized centres deep within the brains of animals which seem to be responsible for producing pleasure and pain. Olds (1956) began the experimental study of this by inserting fine electrodes into the brains of laboratory rats. The rats in these experiments operated a lever controlling a mild electric current, continually foregoing food, water and the opportunity to mate so to stimulate themselves. They did this to the point of complete exhaustion. A small repositioning of the electrode produced equally strong pain and avoidance reactions. It is likely that similar centres in the brains of humans provide the physiological basis for reinforcement.

There are several theories of emotion that build upon these basic physiological components. These are now discussed in historical sequence.

According to the James–Lange theory of emotion (see James 1890) it is our perception of combinations of physiological changes of this type that we call 'emotion'. Hence James's famous dictum that 'We do not run away because we are afraid – we feel fear *because* we run away'. Fear is both the product and the precursor of the most obvious and effective types of action for bipeds to take. The *cause* of our behaviour here is the escape-behaviour-provoking stimulus, whether genetically programmed (as in the case of large, looming objects, loud noises, sudden movements) or learned by association. The bodily

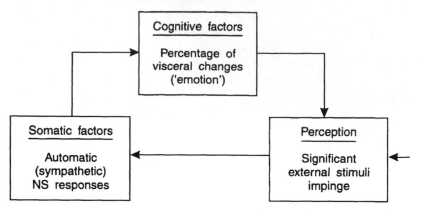

Figure 4.2 Emotional arousal (James–Lange theory)

changes experienced are, in the first place, concomitant not causal (see Figure 4.2).

However, this theory has long had its opponents. It fails, for example, to explain convincingly how we come to be able to appreciate the subtle differences between varieties of emotional experience. The bodily changes described above, though they may occur in slightly different combinations or at different levels of intensity, are relatively crude. One critic (Cannon 1927) pointed out that the nerve supply to some of these internal organs is insufficient to account for the tremendous speed and intensity of emotional reactions. Having tried (and failed) to induce replica emotions in individuals by chemical and other means (for example, the injection of adrenalin) he turned his attention to the role of the thalamus in the brain's central core. In association with the Danish physiologist, Bard, he developed the view that this centre acted as a kind of 'telephone exchange' for incoming stimuli, redirecting 'messages' to both the cerebral cortex and (via the sympathetic 'trunk lines') to the other organs of the body concerned with emergency action. The key difference here is that (counter-intuitively, since we feel that emotions originate elsewhere in the body) the *brain* is the seat of emotion (see Figure 4.3).

More recent research has identified centres for the processing of emotion-arousing stimuli in the hypothalamus and the limbic system. One ingenious method of studying the relative parts played by concomitant visceral responses and by higher centres is to study people with spinal cord lesions placed in emotion-arousing circumstances, or volunteer subjects given temporarily-paralysing drugs. In this way the dimension of visceral stimulation is controlled out. There is no doubt that people affected in this way, either by accident or by experimental design, experience something similar to ordinary emotion, which they are disposed to act upon. But it seems from descriptions

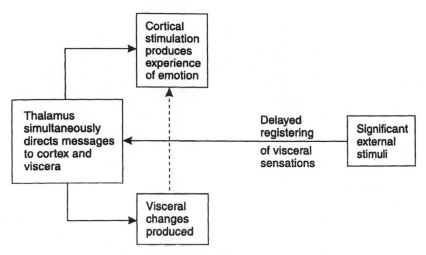

Figure 4.3 Emotional arousal (Cannon–Bard theory)
Source: Adapted from Hilgard, Atkinson and Atkinson (1979). © 1979 by Harcourt Brace
Jovanovich. Reprinted by permission of the publisher.

to be qualitatively different from what most of us feel. Here are the comments
made by a clinical subject in one such study:

> It's a sort of cold anger. Sometimes I get angry when I see some injustice.
> I yell and cuss and raise hell . . . but it doesn't seem to have the heat. It's
> a mental kind of anger.

(Hilgard et al. 1979:336)

COGNITION AND EMOTION

The dominant theme in present day research is that of the role of cognition,
appraisal and memory in emotion. It may be (in line with the James–Lange
theory) that the visceral changes we experience as emotion are relatively
undifferentiated (in line also with the Cannon–Bard conclusion) but that an
'overlay' of cognitive factors gives them their special and subtle 'flavours'.
Most of us are familiar with pictures in social psychology texts which show
contorted faces or specific gestures and ask us to guess the emotion being
expressed. Without the help of the usual contextual clues it can be very difficult
to do (see Figure 4.4 overleaf).

There is common sense in the view that waiting for an important exam to
begin, and going out on a first date produce, objectively, if not subjectively,
rather similar sets of feelings: a tightening of the abdominal muscles, palpitations, an inability to think straight and so on. An increasingly accepted view

Figure 4.4 Young women in a state of ecstasy at a rock concert,
not showing pain or grief

is that fine gradations of emotion are the result of the cognitive labelling and
the attribution of visceral experience according to the nature of the evoking
stimulus and our memories of similar experiences. This view opens the way to
an amalgamation of the various themes discussed so far (see Figure 4.5).

Thus in some cases of mild arousal, cognitive variables will be predominant:
in other cases of strong arousal, physiological variables will largely control
behaviour, and thinking will merely reflect upon this or attempt to 'steer' us
on our careering course.

Where clients have learned that a particular collection of stimuli is hazard-
ous and respond with a high level of physiological involvement (experienced
as fear or, if arousal is less strong, future-oriented and continuous, as anxiety),
this is certain to inhibit cognitive information-processing about how best to
respond. Whether the threat, say of being in a group of strangers, has special
properties in itself for the individual based on myth, knowledge, or hearsay,
or because of a prior learning experience, or because the situation is associated
with other feared happenings, makes little difference. The vicious circle of high
emotional involvement, attempted escape behaviour, and/or faulty and in-

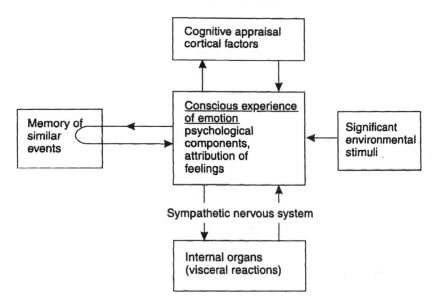

Figure 4.5 Theories of emotional arousal

hibited adaptive performance, increases the likelihood of an adverse reaction and of confirmation of the original association. Phrases such as 'cognitive restructuring', or 'cognitive appraisal' – used to indicate how crude physiological reactions are turned into more subtle and specific emotional experience – are somewhat metaphorical.

What mechanisms are at work? In a series of ingenious experiments, Schacter and his co-workers (Schacter 1964, 1965; Schacter and Singer 1962) sought to implicate *causal attribution* (see p. 112). Here is a good summary of the key factors, some of which were suggested to Schacter *et al.* by earlier research:

In usual, everyday circumstances Schacter believes that cognitions and arousal are highly interrelated, one leading to the other and vice versa. Sometimes, however, they are interdependent. This is exemplified by Maranon (1924). He injected 210 patients with epinephrine, which is sympathetic-like in its effects, and recorded their introspections. 71 per cent reported only physical effects and 29 per cent reported in terms of emotion, but the labels which they applied to their feelings were of the 'as if' kind. They said they felt 'as if' they were afraid. Maranon could only produce 'genuine' emotional reactions by providing them with appropriate cognitions. Schacter suggests that the 71 per cent who did not show this effect in Maranon's study had a perfectly appropriate cognition to explain their altered state – the injection. This point led Schacter on to the question which guided much of his subsequent research: what would be the result of a state induced by a *covert* (non-explicable) injection of epinephrine?

(Strongman 1987:88)

Schacter's volunteer subjects, who knew they were to be given a drug under medical supervision, were led to believe that this was 'suproxin' – allegedly a vitamin-based compound. In fact they were injected with either epinephrine (itself harmless) or a saline placebo. This experiment exposed subjects to three different conditions: (a) 'epinephrine-informed', where subjects were told of possible 'side-effects' such as arousal, palpitations, flushing, faster respiration, etc.; (b) 'epinephrine-ignorant', where nothing was said to prepare subjects for the effects; and (c) 'epinephrine-misinformed', where subjects were misled into expecting very unlikely 'side-effects', such as itches and headaches.

It was then contrived that subjects would wait in a room to allow the 'suproxin' to become absorbed, and then they would be asked to complete certain 'vision-tests'. In fact, the rooms contained experimental confederates who exhibited two types of behaviour: (a) anger, supposedly in response to the increasingly demanding and personal nature of a questionnaire which subjects were also asked to fill out; (b) euphoria, where the confederate behaved in an outgoing, excited way and flew paper aeroplanes, or played basketball with paper balls. The responses of subjects were observed through a two-way mirror.

The outcome measures in this experiment were (a) a self-report questionnaire, embedded in which were two scaled questions about mood states: 'how irritated, angry or annoyed do you feel now?'; (b) covert observations as to the extent to which the behaviour of naive subjects came to match that of confederates (admittedly somewhat 'soft' measures). The results showed that when subjects had no explanation for their induced emotional states they made sense of them in line with the environmental conditions – modelled anger and euphoria – in which they were placed. Subjects who had an explanation (the injection and a true expectation of its effects) did not – though they felt exactly the same bodily reactions.

These fascinating, if ethically unsettling experiments lend support to the proposition that cognition – more precisely, interpretation and attribution – play a major part in giving to our relatively crude physiological 'surges' their unique sense of implication.

Current research suggests a continuum, from strong feelings with little cognitive justification – 'I do not like thee Dr Fell, the reason why I cannot tell' – to the more typical interplay of cognition and emotion typical of everyday life (Lazarus 1982), through to background moods such as mild anxiety or uneasiness where ruminative cognitions play the dominant role. This model suggests that therapeutic opportunities exist in the extinction of arousal which has been conditioned to certain objects, social situations or places (as in the case discussed on p. 57), and in reviewing with clients any unlikely or self-damaging patterns of thinking – 'no one would be able to understand or forgive me if I gagged over my food and spoiled everyone's evening' (as in the case on p. 000). Given the continuum discussed above, it makes most sense to construct programmes which contain both elements, and which to some degree educate clients about the origins and the biological functions of emotions.

ANXIETY

Anxiety is anticipated punishment. It is a strong motivational force in our lives, acting through the negative reinforcement opportunities it provides to propel us into early, pro-active, precautionary modes of behaviour. It is easy to see how it was selected by the evolutionary process on 'better safe than sorry' principles. Indeed, a measure of background arousal, a tingle of anticipation or a frisson of danger, helps us to engage effectively with problems, both at a cognitive and a behavioural level – that 'firing on all four cylinders', 'mid-season form' feeling which we learn to associate with competence and mastery.

The problems associated with arousal are demonstrated in Figure 4.6.

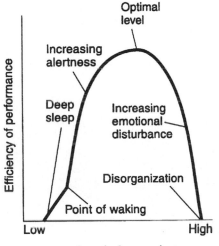

Figure 4.6 Emotional arousal and performance
Source: Hilgard, Atkinson and Atkinson (1979) (After Hebb 1972). Reproduced by permission of the publishers.

The relationships on this graph are: performance accomplishment – as measured in many different studies of task-efficiency in the psychological laboratory; and measured level of arousal. The most important dimension is the rapid fall-off of performance-efficiency which follows optimal arousal.

Only modest additional increments are required before emotions begin seriously to interfere with, and thus to disrupt efficiency. (Members of the new 'goading' schools of management and 'total quality assurance', please note.)

'Anxiety', whether as one more source of unhappiness; as something that leads to maladaptive associations (e. g. social phobias); as a basis for self-defeating avoidance, or in the form of generalized anxiety states (see DSM III[R] 1987), is a constant feature of our work with clients. Cognitive-behavioural techniques for dealing with excesses of this everyday phenomenon are based on the following aims:

(i) Greater understanding of the nature and origins of anxiety – why it is useful in some situations and maladaptive in others.

(ii) Accurate attribution of sources of anxiety, which tend quickly to generalize.

(iii) Clear identification of the origins of threat, from most to least provocative, and from most to least rational, so that priorities can be assigned to dealing with the sources of this.

(iv) Counselling to encourage the client in a rational, step-by-step approach to problem-solving, and coping mechanisms for keeping 'catastrophic' thoughts at bay.

(v) Relaxation, exposure and desensitization approaches.

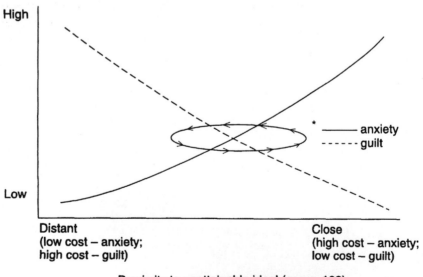

Proximity to unattainable ideal (see p. 109)

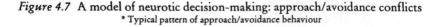

Figure 4.7 A model of neurotic decision-making: approach/avoidance conflicts
* Typical pattern of approach/avoidance behaviour

(vi) Reinforcement (self, or extraneous) for attempts to gain more control of the environment of provocative stimuli, particularly in the face of unreasonable demands.

Some clients are trapped between competing emotional states. In certain neurotic conditions, for example, clients, as a result of vulnerable personalities (see Claridge 1985; Eysenck 1965) and adverse life experiences, set off in pursuit of unattainable, self-defeating life goals (e.g. to be as good a person as my mother's sacrifices require) and so hover between anxiety-avoidance on the approach trajectory, and guilt-driven behaviour on the withdrawal trajectory (see Figure 4.7).

But remember that not all emotions are inappropriate for the circumstances in which they arise. In cases of bereavement and profound loss, one may have more concern for clients who are not (one hopes temporarily) swamped by strong feelings of loss, anger and doubt regarding the impracticality of any future, independent existence. Such emotions need to be acknowledged, absorbed, and confirmed as normal – 'the price we pay for loving' and, in most cases, worth it.

In other cases, e.g. in probation, child guidance and child abuse work, we may occasionally feel that clients are not anxious *enough* in the face of the consequences which lie in wait, and carefully monitored doses of motivating anxiety may have to be introduced.

Thus far in this book we have been considering the contextual and theoretical factors which we need to understand, change or draw upon to be effective practitioners of this approach. The focus of the book now shifts to consideration of skills and techniques, beginning with assessment.

5

ASSESSMENT, MONITORING AND EVALUATION

Issues arising from assessment and evaluation will be handled together in this chapter to emphasize the need for would-be helpers to consider a method of evaluating programmes from the outset. Unless data are gathered early on during assessment, to represent the current type and frequency of problems, this begs the questions: evaluation in respect of what? Against what prior standard or level? Unless we have an accurate measure of the pre-intervention profile of a problem, then, however rigorous the follow-up procedure, we can decide very little about our effect upon it. Or, as American computer programmers more graphically put it: 'garbage in, garbage out' will be the most likely result.

In social work, our main experience is with qualitative evaluation (attempts to assess what *kind* of change has occurred), rather than with quantitative methods (deciding how *much* change has occurred). Conversely, the behaviour therapies have, until quite recently, been dominated by the latter consideration. However, outside very controlled conditions, evaluation exclusively in either form is nonsensical. There is little point in knowing whether a client now spends more hours per week in conversation with other people than previously unless we also have some idea of the difference this has made to his or her life and what is felt about these new activities. There is always the argument that the clients would not persist in new behaviour if they did not find it congenial, but this underestimates the demand effects present in therapeutic programmes, and it also assumes that everyone conducts long-term follow-up assessments, which is naive.

Case example

Let me confess something about a case I handled in the short, 'pharisaic' phase of my career as a behaviour therapist. The client was a cripplingly shy young woman who had been variously diagnosed as depressed, schizo-affective, and as suffering from a 'personality disorder' (not bad going in a short life). The quantitative measure selected for evaluating a comprehensive programme comprising assertion training, positive self-statements and general social support was 'time spent per day outside the hostel' (where she tended to stay in

110

her room, avoiding all social contact). The early results were excellent: a rapidly rising line on the graph, followed by a reassuring period of stability. Then a first year student (knowing no better) asked the question: 'what kind of places do you visit?' The client revealed that she had been given a list of possibilities but had lost it, and that she usually went to a park three hundred yards away, equipped with a book, which she hardly ever read, and counted off the minutes until she could return. She did this, it emerged, to please me.

There is no good reason why qualitative data about changed thoughts and feelings cannot be gathered in a rigorous way and used to supplement estimates of amounts of behavioural change as the main criterion of relative success and failure, and this is the approach adopted in this book.

DISTINGUISHING FEATURES OF COGNITIVE-BEHAVIOURAL ASSESSMENTS

The following discussion provides an outline of cognitive-behavioural assessment and distinguishes it from other approaches with which the reader may be more familiar.

(i) This form of assessment is concerned with who does what, where, when, how often and with whom; it is also concerned to identify the absence or withholding of behaviours which it would normally be useful and reasonable to perform. It deals also with the consequences which actions have for all the parties involved in them – those who are said to *have* the problem and those for whom someone else's behaviour is said to *be* a problem. The emphasis here is on both visible, problematic behaviour, and the absence or the inadequacy of adaptive behaviour – where this could be used to reduce negative consequences for the client. Thus, early on in assessment, decisions need to be taken about (a) what behaviours are in excess: that is, what do the client and the people influencing him or her do too much of? For example, aggressive behaviour well above what could be regarded as an unguarded response to everyday frustrations; (b) what behaviours are in deficit: what does the client do too little of? For example: 'Mary has not spoken a word to any other resident of the hostel since she came here four weeks ago'; (c) what behaviours occur in the wrong place or at the wrong time? For example: 'Fred approaches people in the street and tells them about his personal problems, which reinforces their idea that he is an odd person.' To some extent, this is an artificial distinction, since in the third example it could be said that the client *lacked* self-control or adequate means for dealing with frustration. However, it is useful in practice, and serves to remind the assessor to look out for what behaviour is and is not there.

(ii) Behavioural assessment is concerned also with private sensations, such as doubts, worries, fears, frustrations and depression. It was noted in Chapter

111

2 that evolution has released humans from purely reflexive reactions to contemporary stimuli. Classical conditioning ensures that yesterday's learning environments exert a contemporary influence from inside us, through fears, anxieties and selective perceptions – sometimes profitably, sometimes self-defeatingly. We are driven to look for *meaning* in stimuli and we plan ahead, behaving a little like amateur scientists. By these cognitive processes we sometimes achieve breakthroughs in understanding and in preparing for the uncertain future, but we are equally capable of misreading evidence, taking undue note of limited data, and seeing what we expect or want to see (Sutherland 1992; Sheldon 1987b). The key concept here is *attribution*, which means the assignment of causes and motives to the behaviour of others and ourselves (Heider 1958; Bem 1967). Clients talking about their problems often reveal patterns of either unconvincingly *internal* attributions or of unconvincingly *external* attributions. For example: a depressed person who feels that he has let his family down badly but can give only a few minor examples as to how, based largely on hindsight. Or, conversely, a child with a history of aggression and delinquency whose explanations reveal an unlikely pattern of irresistible provocation from peers, and criminal carelessness by shopkeepers. Cognitive-behavioural assessment seeks to investigate such sequences of thoughts and interpretations: 'I am unlovable'; 'I am bound to fail'; 'I am too smart to be caught'; 'I am the victim of a conspiracy'; they strongly influence how people respond to stimuli from the environment.

However, it should be noted that all of the internal conditions referred to give rise to behavioural excesses or deficits: self-preoccupation, ineffective or ritual activity in the case of worrying; motionlessness, fixed expression, lack of social response, lack of attention to dress and hygiene in the case of depression. People either *do* or *do not do* things as a result of emotional states and adverse patterns of thinking, and before-and-after comparisons of these observable things provide the acid test of whether what clients *say* they feel as a result of therapy is quite reliable. Having both kinds of information helps to reduce the influence of the 'demand effects' mentioned above – clients trying to please or to deceive by living up to expectations. However uncomfortable the idea may be, such distortions are a fact of therapeutic life.

(iii) Considerable emphasis is placed on contemporary behaviour and the thoughts and feelings which accompany it. The search for the long-lost causes of problems is, in the absence of major trauma, regarded with suspicion. This for the following reasons: (a) there is no guarantee that they will ever be found; (b) because the exercise is costly in time and resources; (c) when views as to the original causes of problems *can* be elicited they are not always agreed upon by the protagonists, nor are they necessarily valid; (d) dwelling on the history of problems can sometimes serve to intensify bad feeling and can distract from the necessity of doing something positive in the here and now. This said, the social worker must balance the above with the need for clients to understand the nature and development of their problems and the ways in which the various parties involved might have come to view things differently. One solution is to limit history-taking to brief accounts of the *aetiology* of the problem (the history of specific causes) and to emphasize to clients that problems are often reactivated every day by what people do or fail to do, and by self-fulfilling expectations. A crucial question here is: what maintains problematic behaviour in force, long after the original factors eliciting it have passed into history? Frequently Mr Smith scowls at Mrs Smith and decides to drink the rent money because of what happened yesterday and what he expects to happen today, not because of what allegedly happened on Boxing Day, 1987. However, if problems seem to be tied up closely with 'personality factors', that is, with typical, well-established and apparently predictable ways of responding which vary little across circumstances, then it may be useful to investigate the *learning history* of the client. This includes identifying behavioural excesses, deficits and failures of discrimination as in (i) above; trying to find out how particular reactions have come about; looking at patterns of reinforcement and secondary gain; and, concomitantly, why obviously ineffective responses have proved resistant to reinterpretation, extinction or change. This can help us to formulate a more accurate treatment plan, but it still leaves us in the position of having to work with the contemporary manifestations of problems.

(iv) At some stage clear decisions have to be made with clients about what sequences of behaviour need to be increased in frequency and/or strength and direction, and what sequences decreased in these ways. Further questions include: what new skills (e.g. arguing or negotiating without threats) would be required in order for the client to perform other, more adaptive sequences?

(v) This concern over contemporary events is part of a wider attempt to establish the *controlling conditions* that surround a given problem. This part of the assessment can be thought of as 'topographical' in that it is concerned with the surface layout of the problem, and the aim is, metaphorically, to produce a 'map' of specified daily activities. Thus, we are concerned here with such things as *where* things tend to happen and not to happen; what happens around the client or to him or her just *before* a sequence of the unwanted behaviour occurs; what happens around the client or to him or her *during* the performance of the behaviour; and what happens *after* the performance of the behaviour. This emphasis reflects our knowledge about the way in which opportunities for certain sequences of behaviour are 'signalled' by prior events ('Sd's) and how these are maintained by certain patterns of thoughts and expectations, and by prior knowledge of reinforcing consequences (Bandura 1977). Any natural correlation or variance in these factors provides useful extra information. A simple example would be when John wets the bed every night *except* when he sleeps with his brother or *except* when he stays at his grand-mother's. Or, when it can be seen that Mr Turner's bouts of excessive drinking and exhibitionism always result in his daughter coming to care for him until he feels better.

(vi) Cognitive-behavioural assessments are somewhat independent of the definitions and labels that others place on troublesome behaviour. We are concerned to find out what people who are said to have 'inadequate personalities' do and think; what 'hysterics' and other allegedly attention-seeking people do, don't do, and think; what it is that Mark says to make his parents describe him as 'insolent'; how someone with 'anti-social tendencies' actually behaves, and so on. There are good ethical reasons for building such a label-examining stage into our assessments, but it is also necessary if we are to keep the element of subjective attribution present in most assessments of problematic behaviour to a minimum. *Naming is not explaining*, however much we intuitively feel that it is. In arguing that Mr Williams's 'aggressive' behaviour is due to his 'person-ality disorder' (which we suspect he has because of his aggressive behaviour), we are guilty of the same tautological and worst-case-con-firming thinking that we often seek to change in our clients.

(vii) The need for flexibility is always stressed in texts on assessment. While it is a matter of common sense that assessment procedures that are rigid and forced will probably be self-defeating, there is an equal need to make assessments as clear and specific as possible. Our main concerns should be as follows. (a) To produce clear *formulations* of problems (see p. 123); that is, to put together a concise account of how problems have developed and what might be maintaining them. These do not have to contain 'established truth' – just a coherent, 'best available' view that is testable in practice. (b) A good formulation leads to *clear hypotheses* about what might affect the problems under review. That is, it should be the sort of statement that can be easily checked-up on. The statement: 'Mr Brown's low level of self-esteem is due to poor ego-development' is a bad hypo-thesis since there is little or nothing that could ever happen to disprove it. 'Mary's avoidance of people is likely to reduce if she learns how to start conversations' is better. If Mary receives advice on how to start conversations, begins to mix with others, and yet does not talk to them for long and does not stay in their company, then the hypothesis as it stands is probably wrong and the social worker knows something more about the problem. (c) Hypotheses lead to both long-term and short-term goals. These too have ideal characteristics and are similar to those just listed. The clear goal is one which provides definite feedback on progress towards some specific, and at least partially pre-defined, end-state. Thus we need to tell from the goals we set with our clients whether our assessment policy is on the right track or not. The objective: 'to improve communication in the family' has little real meaning of its own. What will family members do more of, less of, do differently, do in different combinations, or in different places, as a result of family communication being improved? Obviously, 'circumstances alter cases'; the point is that some pre-described states – representing whatever behavioural, cognitive and emotional factors are held to be involved – should be the targets of intervention (see p. 127).

Now that we have gained an overview of this approach we can start to examine the stages of assessment in more detail (see Figure 5.1 overleaf).

OBTAINING A GENERAL DESCRIPTION OF PROBLEMS

The ideal shape for any assessment procedure is, metaphorically, that of the funnel or tun-dish: wide open to start with and tapering off thereafter. The first stages of cognitive-behavioural assessment are little different from those recognizable to most social workers already; thereafter there are some important differences of emphasis:

(i) Obtain a general description of the main problems from as many different points of view as time permits.

(ii) Find out whom problems affect and in what ways, and invite examples.

(iii) Trace their origins, course and development: when did they begin, through what changes have they passed and what has ever affected their course?

(iv) Get some idea of the different parts of problems and how separate or interactive they are.

(v) Assess existing motivation for change. For example, have the client and his or her family made any efforts to overcome these difficulties before, and if not, what prevented them? The question of how motivatable the clients and other significant parties are, however, is largely answered by experience.

(vi) What patterns of thoughts (pictures in the head, and/or internal 'conversations' with oneself or with others) or feelings precede, accompany and follow incidents representative of problems?

(vii) Obtain an impression of the assets available within and around the clients. The assessment of what is right rather than wrong with people easily gets overlooked.

There are two opposing categories of mistake that can be made at this stage. The first is that in the attempt to be task-centred and behaviourally virtuous, the interviewer can prematurely 'squeeze' out of the clients' stories all those things likely to complicate the business of reaching a clear decision in the case.

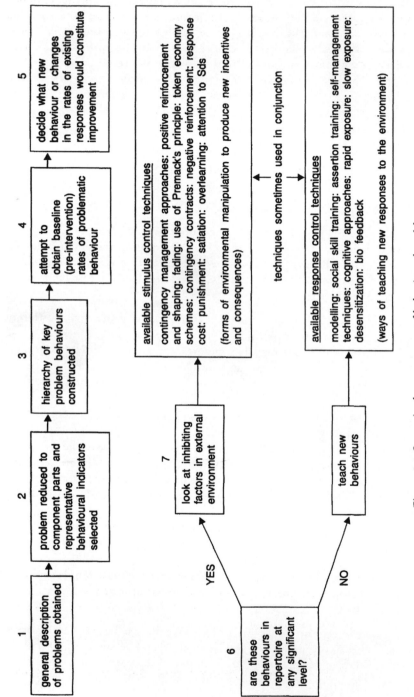

Figure 5.1 Stages in the assessment of behavioural problems

These effects are well known in both research and practice, as is the tendency for interviewers to 'shape' assessment data until it fits a favourite theoretical mould. Consider this chilling dialogue from the Orkney 'Satanic abuse' tapes between a child believed (on no good evidence, as it turned out) to have been sexually abused and her 'therapist':

> The questions come in coo-ing whispers to the child whom we will call Gwennie.

ADULT:	Where are the dickies and the fannies?
GWENNIE:	Don't know.
ADULT:	Can you write the word?
GWENNIE:	No.
ADULT:	. . . a word for when a dickie goes into a fanny?
GWENNIE:	Don't know.
ADULT:	Would you like to whisper?
GWENNIE:	No.
ADULT:	Is it yuckie inside and outside . . . is there any other word?
GWENNIE:	(anxious to please) Gooey?
ADULT:	(amid childish laughter) Oh, that's a good word . . . what does gooey feel like?
GWENNIE:	Here, this . . . (puts finger in mouth and pops).
ADULT:	What happened to gooey?
GWENNIE:	Don't know.
ADULT:	Has it got a colour?
GWENNIE:	(begins to count slowly up to four)
ADULT:	I wonder what this gooey is. Can you tell me?
GWENNIE:	No.
ADULT:	When you put the dickie into the fanny . . .
GWENNIE:	No. (angry) Now can I play? I am going to get my red car. This is boring. (Gwennie gets the car and begins to play.) Go and get me some toys.
ADULT:	When you put the dickie into the fanny it's yuckie and gooey and disgusting. Who hurt you most?
GWENNIE:	No one did it to me . . .
ADULT:	We won't write it down.
GWENNIE:	No one has been doing it to me. (Gwennie breaks into a scream) NOBODY HAS BEEN DOING IT TO ME.
ADULT:	You can play with the red car. We won't write it down if you want to whisper it . . .
GWENNIE:	(shouting even louder) I AM NOT . . . AND I AM NOT GOING TO WRITE IT DOWN.
ADULT:	If it's a name you can see written down you can point

> to it. (She shows the child a list of names of people on
> South Ronaldsay.) Is it a name you see written down?
>
> (Dalrymple 1994)

One has to try hard to imagine here what *contrary* evidence would (could ever) have looked like to this interrogator.

The danger at the other (safer) polarity is that sometimes, unless prompted, clients fail to give an adequate account of the whole of their problems because they have forgotten things, because they make narrowly based decisions about what is relevant and acceptable, or because they are responding to the theoretical interpretations of other professionals with whom they have been in contact. Social workers are particularly at risk here since, being but one stop up from the Salvation Army, they tend to see many people who have been worked with and abandoned by other sources of potential help.

All preliminary conclusions about the range, scope and development of the problem at which we arrive ought properly to be reviewed with the client. This 'reading back' helps to cut down the risks of misunderstanding, which are quite considerable in our field. Mayer and Timms identified this problem in the first British consumer research study and it has been present in most conducted since.

> There is almost a Kafkaesque quality about these worker–client interactions. To exaggerate only slightly, each of the parties assumed that the other shared certain of his underlying conceptions about behaviour and the ways in which it might be altered. Then, unaware of the inappropriateness of his extrapolations, each found special reasons to account for the other's conduct.
>
> (Mayer and Timms 1970:77)

An outsider sitting in on the first stage of a cognitive-behavioural assessment interview might, then, be struck only by the number of times the client was asked to give examples; by the concern of the interviewer to know what was *done* as well as what was thought and felt; and by the emphasis on what sort of events tend to precede, accompany and follow the peaks and troughs of problems. Figure 5.1 on p. 116 provides a guide to the stages of cognitive-behavioural assessment. This is an 'ideal type' compilation supplied for the purposes of clarification. In practice, some stages may have to be skipped or left until later, or the stages taken out of sequence. The important thing is to know that circumstances have required this, and to remedy matters as opportunities present themselves later.

Risk

This issue is placed near the head of the list of stages in assesssment to underline its importance. Sometimes, however, risks emerge later as the full picture becomes clear and it is a matter for continuous monitoring in certain cases. Child abuse inquiries have shown us how therapeutic involvement can lead staff into over-optimistic assessment of tractability and change (Sheldon 1987a). However, the principles of assessment and monitoring put forward here should make manifest risk more detectable. This said, it is beyond the scope of this volume to provide a full account of risk factors with the various client and problem categories which feature on social workers' caseloads (see Sheldon 1987a; Macdonald 1990). In any case they can, in their current state of development, serve only as a guide, prompting at least some conscious thought, appraisal and, if necessary, closer observation. We know, for example, that previous incidents of child abuse are the best predictor of future harm; that conditions of poverty, having children early, attributing motives to children beyond their developmental capacities, social isolation, a series of transient and unsatisfactory relationships – are all over-represented in our catalogue of tragedies. However, many young, inexperienced, poor, isolated parents looking for new partners do *not* abuse their children – in fact they perform daily miracles of coping. Further, we should be alert to the fact that while many depressed people are at their most vulnerable when emerging from medical treatment and entering into other therapeutic programmes or support schemes, for most these efforts accelerate and sustain their recovery rather than provide enough motivation for suicide. Sadly, hindsight is still the most reliable lawyer's guide.

Ways must be found of keeping qualified staff abreast of current research – which might mean expecting them to read books or use computer-based systems, and giving them the time to do it (for an example of a pilot scheme see Sheldon 1987b).

All the above assumes that someone has actually *made* a judgement about risk that *could* turn out to be wrong, so focusing our watchfulness and ensuring that we can learn from any 'near misses', since we can recognize them as such. However, many disastrous outcomes in cases are due to fudged assessments and *no* judgements rather than unexpectedly mistaken ones. Consider the most recent addition to our catalogue of child care disasters. This involved a 15-month-old child who eventually died of neglect in his filthy urine-soaked bed, notwithstanding the fact that the family had been a source of concern to the local authorities for some considerable time. Here are the observations of the policy manager, asked to compile a report on this tragedy:

> At no point between 1980 and 1993 did the department learn any more about the family's history, despite these early significant leads. Indeed throughout all our dealings with the family one can find nothing that could be recognized as a full or systematic assessment.
>
> (*Evening Standard*, 11 March 1994)

Staff using cognitive-behavioural approaches need regularly to remind themselves that selective and distorted perception is a part of the human

119

condition, not just a problem that their clients have. The good assessment 'shows it's working out'. If it is wrong it is wrong clearly and early. Risk assessment is not a function which can safely be left to service commissioners. Risks change and develop over time and require regular monitoring by those closest to them.

The next question is, 'who shall assess the assessors?' It is important that staff have access to supervision or consultation which does more than support them personally in their difficult decisions, but offers challenges, professional in character, to any apparently fixed view of risk or fixed ideas about the appropriateness of therapeutic decisions (Greenland 1985). These factors out of the way, it remains only to make the point that there is no such thing as a risk-free case or community care scheme, and sooner or later managers, politicians and the public at large will have to accept the fact. Providing the above criteria are satisfied and the work done has been good enough by professional standards (which a future general council will need to codify and enforce), then anything else that happens is an *accident*.

REDUCING PROBLEMS TO COMPONENT PARTS

Various suggestions are available as to how best to start this process. I advocate the 'visitor from outer space' approach (not recommended in cases of paranoia). This involves asking clients to say what an outside observer who knew nothing of the problem would see were he, she or it in a position to observe everything that went on. Clients often describe events in terms of their own part in them, or according to the effect that other people's behaviour has on them – leaving out important information about what other people do on the periphery. Another tendency is for parties to problems to diagnose 'intentions'. Remember that the statement: 'She snubs me every evening, just to put me down', can be read from the partner's point of view as: 'He's waiting for me every evening just looking for trouble, so I keep quiet.'

There is a third category of behaviour apart from deficits and excesses such as these; namely, 'failures of discrimination'. The reader will remember from Chapter 3 that behavioural sequences are often prompted by stimuli that signal either the likelihood of reinforcement (Sds) or of punishment (SΔs). Failures of discrimination are an important consideration in cognitive-behavioural work and the social worker should be on the look-out for them. People who consistently fail to match their social behaviour to that prevailing nearby, or the person who is boldly assertive to all and sundry regardless of whether anyone is set to deprive them of their rights or not, both fall into this category. They fail to identify, or at least do not consider it worthwhile to respond to, orientational signals from their surroundings.

A useful device for gaining some preliminary ideas about what might be sparking off problematic behaviour, and then maintaining it, is the 'ABC Chart'. A stands for Antecedents, B for Behaviour (the performance), and C for Consequences. These records can deal with thoughts, expectations, feelings, behaviour and interpretations of behaviour. It is an easy matter to instruct clients in their use and they provide valuable and detailed information (see Figure 5.2 overleaf).

Most of the cases dealt with by social workers feature compendium problems; they have lots of different parts to them and the bits often interact with each other. The best way to begin the process of specification is to find out from clients what things go together and what things they regard as separate entities. We begin then by pencilling in connections between events and bracketing off other events until we get some idea of how the whole system works. The next stage in the process of specification is to reduce each point of the total problem to discrete behaviours – as in the following example of a client described as 'socially withdrawn' by hostel staff.

Case example: Mary, a client displaying profound lack of social confidence

— Eye contact level is about a second every 3 to 4 minutes.
— Sentences are faltering and often left incomplete.
— Voice level is low with only occasional variations in pitch.
— There are sharp intakes of breath at unexpected moments in the middle of conversations.
— Replies to direct questions are always brief – sometimes merely labels.
— When someone comes in Mary walks immediately to her bedroom.
— Mary spends only a few minutes per week out of doors.
— Mary rejects all opportunities to meet other people unless forced to by relatives, when she remains largely mute.

Some problems are easier to reduce to their component parts than others. Generally speaking, the more interconnected and the wider the scope of a problem, the more difficult it is to decide where one piece of behaviour ends and another begins. In other cases problems may be mainly emotional in character and not reliably connected to a particular sequence of behaviour from anyone else. When people are very unhappy, or clinically depressed, then it is likely that this will show up in what they do not do. For example, they may pay no attention to dress, diet and hygiene and may spend long periods, head in hands, sitting in a corner. They may also express feelings of unworthiness. In less severe cases, emotions and behaviour are not so clearly connected. For example, the long-term unemployed client who feels a failure and whose marriage is going through a bad patch may behave in an exaggeratedly cheerful and solicitous manner, often making things worse thereby. Social strategies and over-compensations are unlikely to escape detection completely, but they can cloud the picture.

Next there is the possibility that the person in a family exhibiting the most

	A What happened just before?	B What happened?	C What happened afterwards?
12.30	I sat at the table and asked Billy to come for his dinner. Felt anxious because I know what he is like.	Billy wouldn't come and when I tried to make him he threw a tantrum. I felt angry. shook him and took him upstairs.	I took his meal. talked him round and gave him a cuddle. Felt relieved.
2.00	I was in the kitchen washing up. Felt weary and kept talking to Billy over my shoulder.	Billy kept calling me. more and more loudly. and cried when I wouldn't come. I felt angry.	Went into him after 5 minutes and coaxed him into a game. Felt hopeless.
3.30	I started to get Wendy's tea	Billy kept yelling for me. threw his toys about and tugged at an electric plug. Felt angry.	I smacked him. Felt guilty afterwards.
4.30	I was watching TV. Feeling tired.	Billy sat in front of the screen making noises. I ignored him for a bit. then I lost my temper and put him in the bath.	Went out to him to stop him kicking the door and offered him a chocolate biscuit if he would be quiet. He calmed down and I felt guilty about bribing him.
7.30	Told Billy it was time for bed. Felt anxious but tried to hide it.	Billy started to wail. I felt angry and took him upstairs but he kept coming down again.	Gave in and sat him by me until he went to sleep. 'Anything for a quiet life!'

Figure 5.2 An example of an ABC chart

disturbed behaviour may not be the person who really 'has' the problem. Children often react violently to family and marital difficulties either as a strategy for preoccupying or uniting parents, to punish them, or to guarantee attention that would not otherwise be forthcoming. Sometimes these reactions can be dramatic, as in a recent case of my acquaintance involving a boy of 9 who inflicted weals and bruises consistent with child abuse upon himself in the hope of forcing his father to return, and punishing his mother whom he (wrongly) saw as the cause of the separation. However, it makes little sense to proceed automatically to such conclusions, as happens in certain family therapy centres, seeing all problems of childhood as symptoms of a breakdown in the 'family system'. It is less reasonable still to assume that changing aspects of the way in which families function will automatically result in a disappearance of the child's behaviour which, whatever its original causes, may now be maintained by other factors. In a series of interviews with a large sample of ex-clients from a child guidance clinic making extensive use of family therapy procedures (Sheldon 1989), it became obvious that most respondents were 'natural behaviourists' in the sense that although most were prepared to accept that family dynamics had played a part in producing their children's difficulties, they still saw behavioural change in the referred child as the ultimate test of therapeutic effectiveness.

PROBLEM FORMULATIONS

Many textbooks warn of the dangers of 'one-off' assessments, and remind us that 'assessment is an ongoing process' – a truism calculated to produce nods of approval from most audiences. But there is an equal and opposite danger, namely, allowing new information to build up haphazardly on the case file. Many fat files in social services departments are defective in this respect, and unless there is a requirement for regular summarization, as happily there increasingly is, it is very difficult to get a clear idea of the social worker's thinking about the case. One answer to this problem is to regard assessment as a definite stage in case management which takes place as early as any 'first aid' considerations allow, comes to some preliminary conclusions which are written down as clearly as possible, but which will probably need revision in the light of experience. This is where case formulations come in. These summarizing statements represent the best-informed judgements available on the nature and causes of the problems with which the client and/or we are concerned.

Certain qualities attach to problem formulations. In some of my own research on recording and evaluating practice (Sheldon 1985), I have often encountered statements on files which, though they purported to sum up problems and guide future actions, were really no more than lists of alleged factors loosely thrown together with little information on where they came from, or how they interact. The good formulation should have some of the features of clarity and, in Sir Karl Popper's terms, the 'riskiness' that scientific hypotheses have (Popper 1963). That is, they should be phrased in such a way as to stand at risk of refutation by subsequent events. The entry: 'This case contains many interactive problems to do with finances, inconsistent parenting and pressures within the family system' takes us no further and it is difficult to imagine it ever being overturned by events. Here is an example of a good case formulation:

> Because of his lack of experience of children and his anxieties about discipline, Mr A tended, on joining the family, to crack down very severely on very minor infringements of rules – what he calls 'starting as you mean to go on'. However, the children's relationship with him is not sufficiently well developed that they are willing to accept this as his legitimate role. They see it instead as a rejection of them; as a desire to dominate them and to replace their natural father. Discussion of this problem with the family and the drafting out of an agreement setting out the obligations and expectations of both adults and children may be a useful temporary measure to reduce the present high level of conflict (rows and slaps) between Mr A and the children. A separate series of meetings with Mr A and Mrs L aimed at teaching Mr A how to express his positive feeling towards the children in a way that they can accept (including how to deal with rebuffs), should enable him to cope better with joint activities with the children. It will be a good sign if these increase beyond their present low level.

(Sheldon 1990)

Now of course none of the above need be true. Nor need the scheme outlined produce any worthwhile gains. It may be that the social worker's encouragement that Mr A should try to understand the children's apparent rejection of him and try to react differently to them does *not* result in his spending more time with them; or that it does, but they continue to hate it. It may be that the relationship with the natural father calls all the tunes. It may be that the rows between adults and children continue at their present level, or that there are fewer of them but when they occur they are nastier, involving more coercive statements and threats of physical force. In which case, this formulation has proved inadequate and the social worker needs to think again. Better to know; but this quality of feedback on the accuracy of our assessments depends absolutely on the extraordinary precautions outlined above. It almost never 'emerges' within 'wait and see' approaches to assessment. Clear and tangible objectives are the hallmark of all variants of behaviour therapy and probably account for a substantial proportion of their general level of success. However, a common defensive reaction of other kinds of therapist is to argue that this process is easier in the behaviour therapies than with other approaches. This is simply untrue. As we have seen these techniques are used against a wide range of complex and challenging problems. Such observations more accurately reflect the dangerous idea, common to the more traditional mentalistic approaches, that outcomes will look after themselves if the *process* is right. Research shows that nothing could be further from the truth.

PROBLEM HIERARCHIES – DECIDING WHERE TO START

Priorities

These exist between cases and within them. Some approaches to community care are in danger of sinking into dogmatism as a result of policies to 'target high need'. 'Target with what?' is the question. Some clients are beyond active therapeutic help as are some medical patients, and so care and support are the best we can offer, while others are not, but will become so if we do not intervene. If, for administrative reasons, we neglect clients in accelerating decline, then we are really saying to them: 'Sorry, your delusions are not quite florid enough; you are not hitting hard enough or often enough yet; not really convincing us with "cries for help"; not yet aggressive enough, not lonely enough or desperate enough to qualify; come back later with something more threatening'. Such approaches are bound to be more expensive in the long-run. Early attempts to prevent admission to secure accommodation, psychiatric facility or to care continue to be among the best bargains on offer to the social services and to society. Much in cognitive-behavioural practice is predicated upon such principles.

Regarding priorities within cases of multiple need, assessment decisions must be made as to the centrality of certain problems. If a job or a training place would increase self-esteem, give greater social confidence, foster new relationships, help limit association with a deviant peer group, ease family tensions, or provide a little more money which might therefore not have to be stolen, then a scheme to improve self-presentation with a view to getting one, which might otherwise look luxurious in therapeutic terms, is a good case priority.

Some priorities are 'musts'. They come in the form of statutory obligations, eviction orders, or an exasperated juvenile court hovering over an apparently unstoppable problem of school non-attendance. Others have a 'knight's move' aspect to them and require more thought.

Clients' views

It is a good general rule, even in the social services, that 'the customer knows best'. Clients usually have an intimate knowledge of their problems and are quite often in the best position to define what the priorities should be. This is not, of course, an absolute principle, and the key notion here is that of open negotiation about what needs to be done. The social worker has all the benefits and drawbacks of a more distant perspective. The two views put together are unbeatable if the compromise can be effected. Client-opinion research repeatedly underlines the need for explicitness in this area but it has proved singularly difficult to bring about in routine practice. Cognitive-behavioural approaches to assessment positively require it.

Clients' capacities

Sometimes the nature and scope of a programme are dictated by the intellectual and other personal capacities of the clients and/or others in a mediating role. Conversely, where clients have personal resources or enthusiasms which could be built upon, these too must be taken into account. In the past we have often been guilty of undue pessimism in this regard. The great revolution in training and educating people with learning difficulties and the positive outcomes of integration schemes have been built upon the close involvement of participants and painstaking work to build upon existing skills and confidence. Within the span of my own career such practices were considered unthinkable; now they are routine. Ethical issues aside for the moment, we have evidence that the more clients are taken into our confidence, and the more the pace and direction of help are the subject of explanation and negotiation, the better the results. It is what we would wish for ourselves, but the fact that it is often thought to be unworkable with others reveals something of the power of labels and categories over our thinking and behaviour.

Motivational factors

Clients tend only to come or to be referred for help when their own unaided efforts have failed. Most social workers have experience of trying to persuade families who have 'tried everything' to 'try it again – but systematically, this time'. The point is that constructive problem-solving efforts may never have been reinforced, and correcting this is an important priority. The problem is that clients who do not reinforce the efforts of staff to understand them and to help them quickly acquire the label 'unmotivated' and become the modern equivalent of the 'undeserving poor'. Psychologically speaking, there is no such thing as an 'unmotivated person'. Clients, like the rest of us at some time in our lives, often expend considerable thought and energy in pursuit of unproductive, self-defeating or anti-social aims. They are highly motivated in this regard. What we usually mean by this word is that they have not learned to want what we would like them to want. This is a matter for clarification, explanation, negotiation and persuasion, not for two-category classification. Experience of cognitive-behavioural assessment teaches one that explicit negotiation about the likely origins of problems and what might be done about them usually results in *some* level of agreement – on occasions, admittedly, at a lowest common denominator level. But even this is a place to start.

If agreement can only be reached low down towards the trivial end of problem lists, or not at all, then we may have to decide that therapeutic intervention is not indicated, and rest content doing what we must, or closing the case and not doing what we need not.

Mediators

Some behavioural programmes are dependent upon the use of *mediators*: people in the client's surroundings who can record, prompt and reinforce appropriate behaviour. The availability or otherwise of such people (whether family members, other staff, or volunteers); their willingness to co-operate in the programme; and their likely skills, are major factors in determining what the initial starting point should be. There are some cases which do not depend initially upon such helpers, for example, where the assessment reveals that a catastrophic thinking pattern ('I can feel my heart pounding, I'm going to have a stroke', or 'why does everyone always keep looking at me?') is central. In these cases cognitive-behavioural approaches based on relaxation, planning, the 're-framing' of situations and new patterns of 'self-instruction' can be used in isolation at first. However, trying out new ways of approaching worrying situations will soon become necessary and not all clients can manage this without support. In many operant schemes, having an agent, in the situation where problematic behaviour occurs, to prompt, sustain and reinforce an alternative set of responses is a vital consideration.

Goals and indicators

The question of which particular future is desirable, acceptable, fair, feasible and so on is a matter for negotiation with clients. If it turns out, as work progresses, that what is being aimed at is unlikely to represent any of these things, then the policy can always be re-assessed, one hopes without loss of professional face. Better a series of relatively short-term unequivocal, specific and monitorable goals which can be replaced as necessity demands, rather than one, protean, all-purpose, impossible-to-refute objective which allows almost any eventuality to be claimed as something resembling a success. Let me illustrate this point. I was once involved, belatedly, in a project to establish how far a purpose-built community mental health centre had achieved its primary aim of 'integrating residents into the wider community'. Too little work had been put into indicators (clear and tangible expectations, nailed to the agency's mast) and too much into the production of optimistic-sounding leaflets. When indicators *were* put in place it emerged that local residents did *not* attend the Centre's open days – only councillors and other social workers; the neighbours *did* complain about minor eccentricities of behaviour from residents; however unreasonable at a statistical level, they *did* fear for the safety of their children; and they *did* feel that while community care was a good and admirably humane policy, the siting of *this particular* facility (built before any of the surrounding houses, incidentally) was 'inappropriate'. Nevertheless, the fanciful reaction to this evaluation put forward at a meeting of the management committee was that *some* progress had been made since 'at least the local community felt able to complain'.

Now these were not irremediable problems, nor are they untypical of this field, but in clinging to vague statements of good intent and reinterpreting anything which appeared to threaten them, time was being wasted. The programme of public education which followed was based exactly upon the content of local fears and complaints and one was left with the feeling that overcoming these entirely foreseeable 'antibody responses' could well have featured in the original goals of the project. This experience has created in me a profound distrust of glossy brochures and 'mission statements' – vague and optimistic 'intentions' and 'commitments' in terse, military-sounding language, with large dots next to them to distract the eye from their hopeless lack of specificity.

Goals are points to steer by and the last thing anyone (or his or her passengers) needs when trying to steer by a point is a 'flexible' point. A flexible policy, held in shape by a series of definite points, is a different matter. Francis Bacon put his finger on this problem four hundred years ago when he observed that 'Truth arises more readily from error than confusion'.

In other words, we can learn from our mistakes so long as they are given a chance to be clearly identifiable as such and cannot be massaged into the form of half-successes.

An indicator, then, is something that reliably detects the presence of something else. If there is evidence to suggest that the disturbed behaviour of a child is caused by, or at least fluctuates in sympathy with, certain behaviours performed by other members of the family, and if these behaviours are: (i) complex, interrelated, or hard to monitor on an individual basis; (ii) suspected to be the antecedents of the child's behaviour; (iii) the logical point of intervention; or (iv) if they cluster around factors not easily observed, such as the clients' feelings for one another, then the frequency of the child's problematic behaviour can be used as the barometer of success with the family's problem. Monitoring in this type of case can be made more useful still if qualitative data – for example, self-reports about changed thought patterns and feelings – are combined with data from the first quantitative source.

Case example

In a case referred to me by a child psychiatrist, a 12-year-old boy, John Pearson, was said to be 'obsessed with fire'. The onset of the problem suggested a link with the fact that his father, a previously active and affectionate man, had suffered a serious industrial accident and was now confined to a wheelchair. His reaction to this was one of (understandable) self-pity and a preoccupation with the inadequacy of his financial compensation. The reaction of his wife was a mixture of doting and mild depression. The main hypothesis developed from the case history was that a not-in-itself very serious incident of arson (committed with a group of other boys), involving an old allotment shed, for once produced attentive responses from the family. John's married brother and sister visited the house to talk over the problem, and the father was sufficiently aroused by a visit from the police to say that he would discuss whatever was worrying his son at any time – 'you have only to ask, son'. (This had patently not been true for some time.) In this way, an otherwise random act of vandalism was powerfully reinforced.

Another more serious fire followed, this time started by the boy alone. He was charged and a supervision order was made. Then another minor fire occurred and the police made it clear to the child and parents that he was heading for secure accommodation. Actual fire-lighting ceased, but talking about fire, fireworks, fire accidents, fire engines, and the leaving of matches around in odd places, became an ever-present feature of family life, and was cited by them as the most important cause of unhappiness. A psychiatric report implicated 'family pressures' but no psychopathology.

This boy's 'obsession' with fire gained him the family's attention, jerked his mother out of a minor depressive episode, produced some fatherly behaviour, and made the boy a reputation at school as a dangerous character. Moreover, he achieved all this without actually having to light another fire and risk incarceration.

During treatment, the behaviour in parents that instigated the problem was monitored only with some difficulty. Parameters included periods of conversation between Mr and Mrs Pearson; periods of conversation not related to fire-raising topics between father and son; attempts by Mr Pearson to wash and dress himself with reducing amounts of help, and so on. This side of the analysis left out important but subtle variables; Mrs Pearson's feelings of pessimism about the future; Mr Pearson's ruminations about money and the tensions in the family when their son seemed to be pointedly withholding 'fire-talk' – 'the calm before the storm', as it was known.

It is possible to construct behavioural definitions and measures for all the subtle behaviours just mentioned, but it would have involved a mass of detail beyond even these co-operative recorders. In any case, when levels of 'fire-talk' and otherwise inexplicable periods of silence were used as indicators of the complex variables that parents called 'the atmosphere in the family', it was found that the two matched quite closely. Subjective estimates of how the week had gone, other qualitative measures concerning parental thoughts of helplessness in the face of their problems, and numerical data available on other behaviours showed that whenever the father's self-preoccupation was particularly evident, so was talk about possible incidents involving fire. It made sense then to try to deal with both sets of problems together, but to give priority to John's – the danger being that his behaviour would obtain further reinforcement from outside the family and increase his risk of custody. (A description of the methods used will be found on p. 171.) Throughout, the behaviour for which this child was referred, and associated threatening conversations about it, remained the most reliable indicators of progress; it 'stood for' a range of other complex variables.

Indicators are not 'the problem', just as failing to dress, wash, smile and converse are not depression, but a reflection of depression. The question is whether they are a reliable reflection or not. Mr Pearson could, conceivably, have sobbed into his washbasin and sat ruminating in his best suit. To rule out such effects requires a little imagination, and as wide a range of different indicators as is feasible. Indicators, therefore, are usually case-specific and are often a matter of trial and error.

EVALUATION: THE USE OF SINGLE CASE EXPERIMENTAL DESIGNS (SCEDs)

This is the point at which assessment joins evaluation, and the first task is to decide how often behaviours or indicators relevant to the problem occur prior to active intervention. This is called the *baseline stage*. It is not a measure of the problem before *any* help has been given. Baselines record the *pre-specific* or *pre-active* intervention level of a problem. They provide a standard against which the specific problem-countering policy can be assessed. Baseline data can exist in two forms: quantitative – measures of incidence of overt behaviour; or qualitative – measures of the kinds of cognitive and emotional factors we think are implicated in problems. As already proposed, the sensible approach is to combine both sets of factors into one record.

Baseline effects

Sometimes when clients set about measuring the extent of their current problems the situation improves. This so-called *baseline effect* is probably the result of focusing attention on specifics rather than generalities, and of the improvement in morale that a businesslike approach to problem-solving can bring. They are good news in therapeutic terms and a cross to bear for evaluators.

Records and recording

There is a variety of ways in which records can be kept. The graph is probably the best method since it provides information at a glance, and patterns and trends show up quite readily. However, graphs frighten some clients, and therapists need to adapt the presentation of data to suit. This said, they do provide powerful visual feedback on progress. If they are introduced in a matter-of-fact way, and explained in simple terms, they pose few insurmountable problems in the majority of cases. But if graphs or similar paper exercises are not suitable, then a little ingenuity is required. Students of mine working with youngsters with learning disabilities have used recording devices such as the 'posting' of tiddlywink counters into a moneybox, and the pasting of favourite cartoon cut-outs on to a board as recording methods. Only a few clients refuse to keep records if their purpose is explained and they are adapted to their needs and capacities. A larger problem, perhaps, is the aversion to graphs and counting felt by social work survivors of the standard British maths curriculum.

On this issue of recording, it is my experience that clients respond favourably to the following: (i) the clearly-demonstrated assumption on the social worker's part that effective helping requires careful assessment; (ii) a sympathetic but matter-of-fact approach and time spent explaining how best to keep records and what problems might arise; (iii) the social reinforcement of record-keeping; (iv) simple, well-produced pro formas with clear instructions written on them; (v) using records in front of clients and going over the data with them.

Record entries need to be made as soon as possible after the behaviour in which we are interested has occurred. Clients often try to remember numbers until a single 'totting up' session at the end of the day, but this is full of pitfalls and should be discouraged. Sometimes a recording device needs to be portable. No one is going to carry a chart around all day, and no parent is going to run downstairs at 3 a.m. to record on a wall that his or her son is out of bed for the fourth time. A variety of methods can be used, including diaries, postcards, golf-score counters, marks on sticky tape around the wrist and so on.

METHODS OF GATHERING DATA

Direct observation

This method is applicable where the problem behaviours occur at a high frequency and so a relatively short period of observation gives a good idea of current rates. It can be used only where the presence of a non-participatory observer will not be a distracting influence. This method was used in the classroom-based scheme described on p. 166, where the observer was introduced to the children simply as 'a student' (which was true).

Time sampling

Time sampling is used where it is impractical or undesirable for an observer to spend long periods of time with the client. Instead, ten 5-minute observations, for instance, can be made at intervals throughout the day, perhaps by a mediator. This method is particularly useful in residential and hospital settings, but it can deal only with high-frequency behaviours which are relatively independent of time and circumstances.

Some problems occur only at particular times or under given conditions, e.g. mealtimes, or whenever clients find themselves in situations from which it is difficult to escape without embarrassment. In these cases data need only be gathered at these points of known vulnerability.

Participant observation

Essentially the same as direct observation, this method can be used where the presence of an outsider is less intrusive if he or she joins in whatever is going on. The behaviour under review needs to be somewhat independent of observer effects, or a few dummy-runs need to be made so that the observer 'blends' into the background. A stranger with a pad sitting in a dayroom stands out like a sore thumb.

Mechanical, electronic and other aids to observation

Tape recorders, video sets, one-way screens and other such aids are increasingly available in child guidance clinics and other specialist centres. Once clients become familiar with such devices their influence becomes stable and predictable and can be allowed for. However, it is only rarely true to say that their presence is completely forgotten.

Observation by mediators

This method is very common in behavioural work. Parents, teachers, spouses, relatives and peers can all be enlisted to record the incidence of target behaviours. The method is particularly applicable to operant programmes in field settings (see Chapter 6).

Self-observation

Again, this method is very useful in field settings. The success of self-recording depends on: (i) a well-organized scheme; (ii) a clear definition of what is to be counted so that the client is in no doubt; (iii) whether the behaviours under review are of a character to make deliberate distortion likely.

It is a brave client who will report frankly on his or her own anti-social activities, and a foolhardy helper who offers an amnesty on such behaviour for recording purposes and so runs the risk of appearing to condone it (see p. 184). One alternative is to monitor the occurrence of positive (generally acceptable) behaviour which is incompatible with the problematic behaviours under review. Decisions of this kind, and decisions about whether to use mediators instead, depend largely on the amount of co-operation we can expect to receive from clients.

Self-observation is used to assess behaviours that occur largely privately – specific thought patterns, ruminations, inhibitions, feelings of panic – at low frequency and/or beyond the range of mediators. There can be a problem with cognitions in that noting when particular thoughts occur can increase their level. It is better, therefore, to use the ABC method described on p. 120 or to get the client to rate the intensity of thought patterns over a longer period. On the whole the method works well, and a client who will not co-operate with self-recording is unlikely to co-operate with the therapeutic scheme that follows.

Reliability checks

It is possible to use these different methods in combination, thus adding greatly to their reliability. Where self-reports, reports of mediators and our own observers agree substantially with each other, greater confidence can be placed in findings.

INTERPRETATION OF BASELINE DATA

All data require interpretation; only rarely will a self-evident conclusion jump out. This is especially true of the kinds of data gathered in natural settings, which are at best a compromise between rigour and relevance.

The first consideration is the length and stability of the baseline measure. The aim in baseline recording is to obtain a typical *sample* of behaviour, so recording must continue long enough for odd fluctuations and recurring patterns to be seen in context. It may be that a pattern of aggressive behaviour on Mondays, or in the presence of another particular group of people, will emerge. It may be that the last two days just happen to have been particularly difficult or particularly good, giving an artificial impression. Over a longer period such effects will show up and can give much valuable information, (Examples of SCEDs with both unstable and stable baselines can be found in Figures 5.3 and 5.4 on pp. 134 and 135). But the ideal length for a baseline depends on several different factors.

(i) Some behaviours, for instance eye-contact patterns, obsessions, or periods of detached silence in depression, are likely to occur with a *high frequency* rate, so observation over a period of two or three days will give some idea of the stable frequency. We must use our judgement here. If different things happen on different days then it may be useful to see how this affects the data. A daily time sampling approach may be the answer (see p. 131).

(ii) Where behaviours occur with *low frequency*, for example conversation in a withdrawn schizophrenic patient, enuresis, or stealing, baseline data must be collected over a longer period.

(iii) In all cases the ideal is a *stable* measure where there are no great or untypical swings in the rate of performance. This is not to say that there must be no fluctuations, just that these must be typical and so roughly cancel each other out (as in Figure 5.4), or cluster closely around the median, with only one or two exceptions well outside the range. In cases where data are very difficult to interpret, simple statistical techniques are available (see p. 252). However, except in very intractable cases where we

133

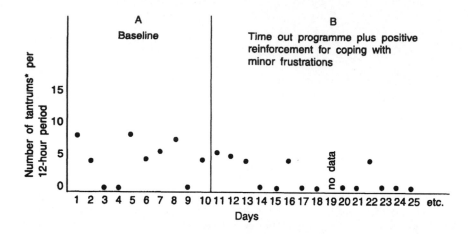

Figure 5.3 Example of an AB design with an unstable baseline: uncontrollable
temper tantrums in a 5-year-old child
* Operationally defined with parents

are grasping at straws, if we find ourselves having to do sums on ba-
seline/outcome differences it is unlikely that we are achieving much of
practical value.
(iv) Ideally, the more recorded observations of the behaviours being monitored the better. In practice this usually means the longer the baseline
period the better. However, a sensible balance has to be struck here
between therapeutic considerations and the need for careful assessment.
Although clients will sometimes suffer problems stoically for months or
years, the arrival of professional help can make further delay difficult to
bear.

Above is an example of the simplest kind of SCED, the AB design, which
makes a straightforward 'before and after' comparison. A comparison between
this example and Figure 5.4 on p. 135 should illustrate the difference between
stability and instability at the baseline stage.

SETTING TARGET LEVELS

The next stage in the assessment sequence is that of setting target levels. The
client and the social worker have to decide what would constitute a significant
improvement in the problem, remembering that in some cases it is not the
behaviour *per se* that is the problem, but the rate at which it is performed, or
the setting in which it occurs. We all lose our temper occasionally, but some

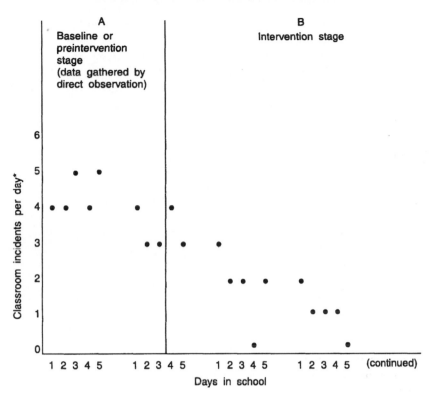

Figure 5.4 Example of an AB design with a stable baseline: baseline data from classroom management scheme for a 'disturbed' 9-year-old boy under threat of exclusion from school

* Predefined with teachers as any combination of: interfering with the work of others; causing physical pain to others; leaving his seat and failing to return within one minute of first being asked; making loud noises, or noises continuing long enough to distract other pupils.

people lose it every day and do not feel that they should try to keep it just because they are in company. It is a useful check on the usefulness of a programme, and often a spur to everyone concerned with it, if target levels are written in next to goals as soon as these have been formulated. A simple statement such as: 'Mr and Mrs A will consider that their relationship has significantly improved if rows and prolonged silences fall to half the present level', or 'David will have achieved his first target when he can dress himself unaided', will usually suffice.

We next have to decide whether the behaviours which would constitute an improvement are already *in repertoire* at any significant level (see Figure 5.1). Decisions as to which group of cognitive-behavioural approaches we are likely to select depend upon the answer to this question. We need to know whether the person whose behaviour we are seeking to change *ever* engages in behaviours *anything like* the target behaviours, whether there are *any* social situations in which self-deprecating thoughts do not occur or occur less irresistibly or less frequently. If so, then these patterns might be reinforceable. If not, or if such events are at a very low level, it makes more sense to concentrate on teaching and developing new behaviours and alternative patterns of thinking. From this distinction is drawn the twofold classification of behavioural approaches used in this book: *stimulus control* techniques (designed to change behaviour through changing the environment and the consequences it produces), and *response control* techniques (designed to alter the range, type or level of responses that clients have in their repertoire, or to equip them with completely new ones (Bandura 1969). Obviously, there are close connections between these two groupings, and many programmes will include elements from both – as when a new sequence of behaviour is first modelled and then approximate performances are positively reinforced during rehearsals.

The rest of this chapter is concerned with the various methods by which cognitive-behavioural programmes can be evaluated and in particular with further examples of single case experimental designs. This approach to evaluation is not dependent upon the use of formal behavioural techniques. So long as the user is willing to link expected outcome to behaviour in some form, then subject to the strictures put forward in Chapter 1, any method could be used.

AB DESIGNS

The reader will see from Figures 5.3 and 5.4 that the recording of the target behaviour (or some reliable indicator of it) is continued after the start of the programme designed to alter it. AB designs are a considerable advance on impressionistic case studies, but they are still quasi-experimental. That is, they offer correlational evidence of outcome; but we cannot be sure from them which of the many variables introduced into a case were the potent ones, or indeed whether the approach itself was responsible at all. It could be the therapist's own behaviour; 'placebo effects' of various kinds; particular structural elements in the programme or the passage of time (see p. 16). In the short-term, this may not appear to matter much because the main job of helping is to help, not to research psychological techniques. But in the longer-term, if we are to develop better 'recipes' for this, we need to think about sifting and refining the different ingredients of our approaches. Patterns do emerge between workers and between problem and client groups in a series of AB designs, but there is need for caution in interpreting data gathered in this way, as the following hypothetical example Figure 5.5 demonstrates.

The centre graph gives all the appearance of a successful therapeutic en-

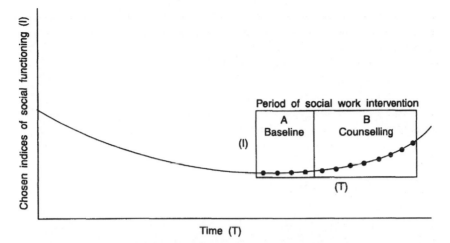

Figure 5.5 Diagram showing misleading interpretation of an AB design

counter, but the larger graph reveals a 'natural' pattern in the course of the problem, under the control of other variables.

If we happen to sample behaviour at a particularly fortuitous point in the natural development of a problem, then we can easily be misled. Although this is a hypothetical illustration, it is not a hypothetical problem. Patterns of this kind do occur. Manic-depressive illness follows a cyclical pattern, and a wide range of other problems are known to remit spontaneously. There are several things we can do to guard against such distortions in our data.

(i) We can get to know something about available research regarding the difficulties with which we are concerned. If the literature suggests that a particular problem is resistant to treatment (e.g. generalized anxiety states) yet we are managing quite respectable gains, then, with due caution, we may feel justified in concluding that this is not a quirk in the development of the problem.

(ii) We can monitor over a longer period; that is, extend the baseline period and watch for trends of this kind which are seemingly independent of what we are doing.

(iii) We can arrange follow-up contacts or visits. Clients are reassured by the prospect of these too, and they cost little.

(iv) We can look very carefully at the differences between baseline phase and intervention phase rates. The ideal is for a clear and fairly rapid distinction to emerge between the two phases. Figure 5.6, though a pleasing graph, proves little about effectiveness, whereas Figure 5.7 is rather more suggestive of it. In Figure 5.6 the 'trajectory' of the behaviours under review is already well established, and the probability is that such a well-established upward trend would continue if it represents genuine benefits for the client. In Figure 5.7 the difference between the two stages is well marked (see Appendix 1).

(v) We can employ a more sophisticated design (see below).

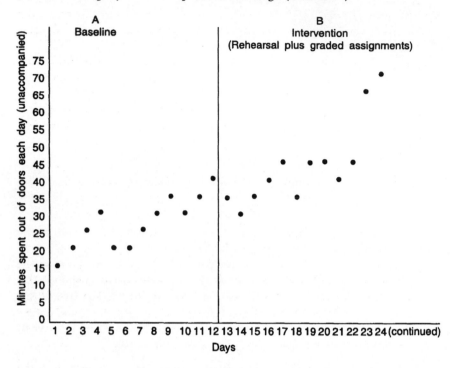

Figure 5.6 Social confidence problem in an ex-psychiatric patient

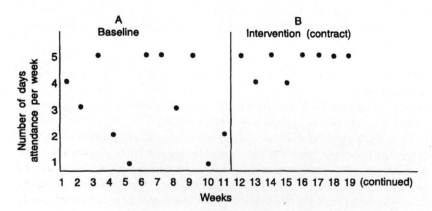

Figure 5.7 A school attendance problem

FOLLOW-UP DATA

A follow-up visit can solve many of the problems associated with simple AB designs. The fact that there is no tradition of this – even in clinical social work settings here – is something of a scandal. Is it really the case that we would rather not know? Follow-up assessment is straightforward when a particular group of problematic behaviours has been reduced to nil (or virtually nil) prior to closure, since it requires only a brief visit, a telephone call, or a prepaid letter to establish whether or not the position is still the same three months later. Similarly, when clients have experienced no great difficulties in recording items of behaviour they can be advised to continue to do this until the follow-up contact (see Figure 5.9). But not all cases fall into these categories, so another strategy is required if we are to improve upon the client's subjective impressions of change.

I have found the following approach useful.

(i) The follow-up visit is fixed in advance at the time of closure.
(ii) The client is encouraged to repeat the original measurements (some other person can do it) for a suitable period before the contact is made.
(iii) Rates at closure are compared with the average rate recorded just prior to follow-up. This is not foolproof, clients occasionally report that things have been untypically better during the pre-follow-up phase – perhaps because of the impending contact. This is particularly true of cases involving children. But then this tells us something about what is effective in controlling the behaviour in question and brief, intermittent maintenance visits might be indicated for a time. Certainly it makes little sense to squander our investment in a case for the want of them.

Figure 5.9 on p. 141 is an example of an AB design with a follow-up period built into it. The AB design with follow-up (technically ABA; see p. 141) probably represents the best compromise between evaluative rigour and therapeutic reality available to us.

BA DESIGNS

Figure 5.8 on p. 140 provides an example of a BA scheme designed to produce clear feedback on expenditure for a family with chronic financial problems. In this family, budgeting and rudimentary financial record-keeping were known to be virtually non-existent. Therefore there was no point in a detailed baseline phase. In this example we see that although the behaviours established by the budgeting programme were still in existence following the main effort to establish them, they were in gradual decline thereafter, and so some sort of 'topping-up' attention was required. In this example we are recording compliance with *means* thought to be related to the problem. The only worthwhile

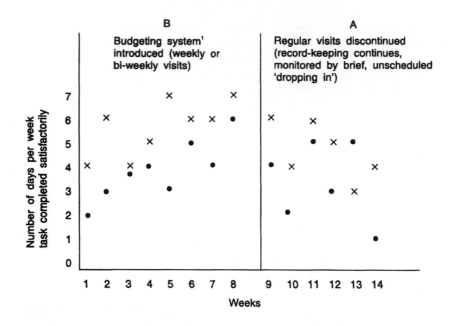

Figure 5.8 Budgetary control in a family in chronic financial difficulty
× Task involved conversion of electricity units into approximate daily costs
• Task involved keeping daily spending within budget, including payment against arrears
(separately monitored)
1 Programme consisted of simple financial record-keeping, training in electricity meter reading, plus
reinforcement for accurate records. The ultimate success of the scheme was judged by the family's financial
state (bills paid, payment books kept up to date, and so on).

outcome indicator in such a case is reduced indebtedness. In cases of anorexia, whatever the cause, target weight maintenance must be the primary indicator.

The problem with BA designs is that if the target rate falls in the A phase then we have to add a further B (intervention phase); if it does not, then we assume that learning has taken place – good news therapeutically, but we are left with no evaluation (see BAB designs, p. 148).

ABA DESIGNS

The ABA design is an advance on the simple AB approach, since it includes a complete return-to-baseline phase at the end. Figure 5.10 on p. 142 is an example from a child guidance setting. In this case the item of behaviour being measured (night-time interruptions) is an *indicator* since the social worker thought that the problem might really be a sexual and marital one. (It came with an 'oedipal problems' label on it originally.) The prevailing hypothesis

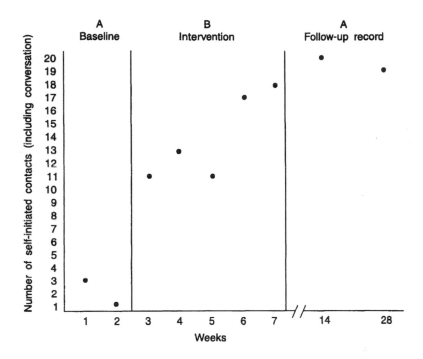

Figure 5.9 Assertion training with a withdrawn psychiatric client*
* The programme included modelling and rehearsal, graded assignments, plus a back-up reinforcement scheme.

was that mother and child were in unwitting collusion and that mother was quite pleased to have her son in the marital bed since it removed the threat of unwelcome sexual advances from her husband. The couple were eventually referred for sexual counselling but, although this was successful, the problem of the child's behaviour remained. It started as an indicator of another related problem but became a problem in its own right, requiring direct attention. The design is further complicated by the prescription of a hypnotic by the family doctor.

Whatever happens after this medical intervention (which was effective, but could not be said to have solved the problem in the longer-term) should not be used as evidence in the evaluation of the programme *per se*: this is messy, but typical. The next case example concerns a 9-year-old child causing concern to his (single) mother and to his schoolteachers because of aggressive behaviour and swearing. An operant scheme rewarding absence of this behaviour and reinforcing certain incompatible activities was used (see p. 169 and Figure 6.3).

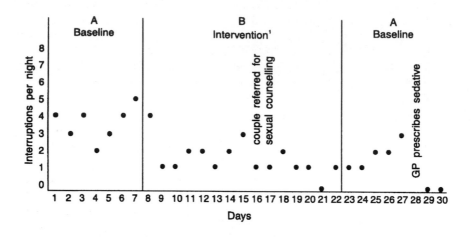

Figure 5.10 Sleep problems in a 4-year-old child
1 Reinforcement programme used model farm animals, stories and a star chart.

The ABA design has the following problems associated with it.

(i) If the B phase is exceptionally long, then some of the criticisms of the AB approach apply; that is, we can be less confident about whether it is the therapeutic input or something else that is responsible for the changes recorded.

(ii) Similarly, where a lengthy intervention phase is used, one would expect, even hope that learning would occur. In operant programmes where the therapist has tried to change the contingencies in the client's environment, confusion can arise as a result of learning effects. Let us suppose that relatives of a psychiatric patient first respond to and enquire into the content of delusional talk as usual, recording its occurrence (A phase); then, on advice, they withhold attention from delusional talk and reinforce non-delusional conversation (B phase); then they stop this programme and, under encouragement, do something close to what they always used to do; how are we to interpret the result from a case research point of view if the delusional talk remains at low level in the second A phase? Has some learning (in this case, operant conditioning) taken place? Or is this behaviour quite independent of the strategy being applied? The only answer to this question is to wait and see whether the behaviour returns. If not, then new behaviour has been acquired (see p. 146 for further details of this case). In such cases a return to baseline amounts to a reversal rather than a suspension of the programme. In this example, relatives were advised to start doing something again which they have learned not to do, that is, respond to delusional talk. This kind of reversal procedure can be useful to check whether the treatment policy is the correct one, and whether the behaviour varies regularly under its influence. But then it needs to be succeeded by a further treatment phase (ABAB; see below).

(iii) Where two different treatment methods are introduced sequentially, perhaps because of changes in the assessment, or lack of success, then specific results are easily confounded. The correct name for this type of approach is ABCA – in other words; baseline–intervention strategy 1–strategy 2–return to baseline. If a new treatment approach is introduced at the *end* of the first treatment phase, perhaps to supplement it, then this is called an ABCA design. The sequence is: baseline–treatment 1–treatments 1 and 2 combined–baseline. The example shown in Figure 5.10 is technically an ABCA design since, although sexual counselling had only just begun by the end of the first treatment phase, it might have had a rapid effect, which could have combined with the long-term effects of the initial B phase and resulted in the modest gains of the second baseline phase. The point is that in these more complicated variations of ABA the relative potency of the different approaches is very difficult to establish. Each new phase which is added could be helped along by what has gone before.

Two methods in combination, superseding one or both of these methods applied separately, can have very different effects. This is not a serious problem from the therapeutic point of view since it is the treatment 'package' which we want to evaluate. However, if we are trying to find out which type of approach is likely to be more effective – perhaps with an eye to future work – then, ideally, a separate return to baseline must follow each separate treatment phase.

ABAB DESIGNS

This is undoubtedly the most satisfactory procedure from a case evaluation point of view, although widespread application may be hindered by practical and ethical considerations. ABAB designs can be used in those cases where (i) it is possible clearly to define and separate out the target behaviour; (ii) the behaviour is likely to respond markedly to preplanned environmental changes (contingency management). Therefore the widest application of this evaluation method has been in operant work with children (see Tharp and Wetzel 1969; see also Herbert 1978).

In this sequence the problematic behaviour (or its chosen indicators) is recorded prior to intervention in the usual way (A). The main treatment programme is started (B). If this shows a positive effect it is halted for a period while monitoring continues (A). A comparison between the two phases is made; then the treatment programme is restarted (B) and further comparisons are made at the end of this phase (see Figure 5.11). Results obtained by this method are extremely reliable, since there are two points at which the behavioural effects of intervention and no intervention can be compared. This fact does away with the criticisms which, strictly speaking, can be made of AB, and (to a lesser extent) ABA designs from the case research point of view. However (the point is worth reiterating), even these comparatively simple designs represent a considerable advance on what has passed for evaluation hitherto, and in field settings they are likely to be the optimum method of evaluation.

The idea of halting a successful programme just as it is getting into gear is often viewed with misgivings, and obviously there are cases where it would be dangerous and unethical to suspend help in order to make an independent check on its efficacy. But safety considerations aside, if a particular pattern of behaviour can be seen to vary with the contingencies applied to it, then this is very well worth knowing, and treatment procedures can always be re-established. Another consideration here is the very positive 'demonstration effect' that this type of design can have (it is particularly powerful in the case described in Figure 5.11). Where parents see that the problem goes away if they stop attending to particular anti-social behaviours in their children and concentrate on others, only to reappear when they temporarily reverse these conditions, then a powerful lesson has been learned. To prevent learning factors interfering too much, suspension or reversal needs to follow quickly on the establishment of a stable trend towards improvement.

Two examples of ABAB designs are given below (see Figures 5.11 and 5.12). The first shows a clearly successful programme; the second is broadly successful, but the results are difficult to interpret. (Some of the details of these cases will be familiar to readers from earlier discussions.)

Let us concentrate for a moment on Figure 5.12 on p. 146 since it demonstrates many of the problems of an attempt at rigorous evaluation in a field setting. The reader may be able to see several compromising features. The scheme starts off well: the first baseline period is of reasonable duration considering the state of tension in the family, and is just about stable, with the rate hovering between four and eight items per day in a range from two to ten with a clustering around four and five items per day.

But the baseline shows a downward trend (regarded as untypical by the parents, and probably a demand characteristic or 'baseline effect', as discussed on p. 130). In addition, the intervention phase begins with a worsening of the problem, which continues for a while until the programme of ignoring delusional talk begins to take effect. In the second return to baseline (a reversal in this case, because parents were asked to keep a diary of the content of their daughter's delusional talk and whether it would respond to reason, and so their old practice of giving attention to these preoccupations was resumed) there is an upward trend which continued until near the end of the second A phase. Then the rate begins to fall again and so confounds somewhat the effect of restarting the programme – which produces a relatively stable and confidence-boosting downward trend.

This scheme, using parents as mediators, continued for another 46 days,

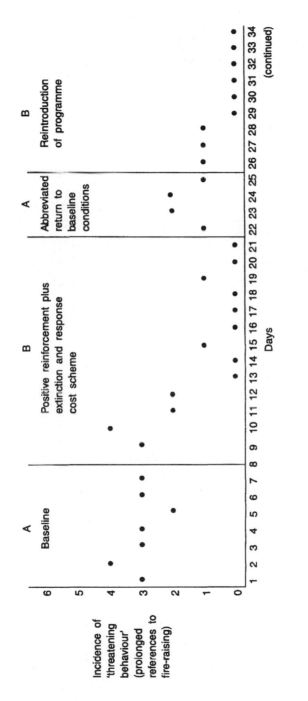

Figure 5.11 Evaluation data for contingency management scheme for coping with aggressive talk about fire by a 12-year-old boy

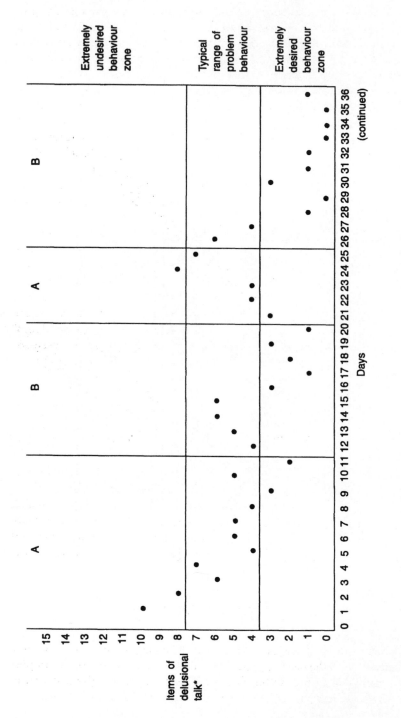

Figure 5.12 Contingency management scheme for reducing delusional talk in a 24-year-old psychiatric out-patient
* Operationally defined with relatives

during which time the incidence of delusional talk (mainly the reporting of feelings of surveillance) never rose again above two incidents per day. For 22 of these days it stood at nought. A brief follow-up at six months revealed a maintained level of improvement of roughly this order, punctuated here and there by the odd sharp increase which the mother was able to relate convincingly to various family episodes. In addition, the family and the client herself were able to report on and exemplify a number of worthwhile changes in the way in which family members related more positively to each other.

Figure 5.11 represents an arguably more complicated case (described on p. 171), but produces less complicated results. Here the return to baseline phase was abbreviated because of the tensions within the family and the not inconsiderable fire risks involved in this case. Despite the misgivings of the client's father, the 'demonstration effect' of suspending treatment was very powerful indeed. It produced a 'shot in the arm' when the family saw that the behaviour was partly under their control and not caused by some junior form of mental illness. However, the requirement that a promising treatment phase should be temporarily suspended and reversed raises ethical problems, and this design needs to be used with caution and common sense. With hindsight, and a more confident knowledge of the research literature, I now think that an ABA design would have been the best choice here. However, blanket objections to the use of such methods need to be seen in the context of the equally pressing, ethical questions regarding whether the service being provided is effective, a waste of everyone's time, or even damaging.

BAB DESIGNS

BAB designs (see overleaf) are ideal for operant work where, for various reasons, it would be unwise to delay treatment until a baseline can be established. This design can be used where target behaviours are clearly dependent on identifiable environmental contingencies, and these are subject to manipulation.

Figure 5.14 is an example of a BAB design. In this case the urgency which precluded baseline recording stemmed from the fact that the child was acquiring a reputation for being 'withdrawn' and 'troubled' among nursery school staff despite reassurances from mother and the health visitor that he was outgoing enough at home.

MULTIPLE BASELINE DESIGNS

The multiple baseline design uses each defined element of a problem as a control for the others. There are two distinct advantages with this approach: (a) it does away with the need for a suspension or reversal phase; (b) in complex cases one method at a time can be tried out. The approach is really just a series of AB designs run in a particular sequence. The procedure is as follows.

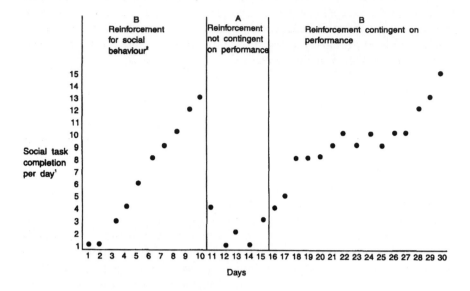

Figure 5.13 Shyness in a 4-year-old preschool child
[1] Predefined tasks (behaviour-shaping: ranging from showing interest in play of others, to solitary play nearby, to participatory play)
[2] Approval plus sweets (given by nursery staff)

First, the pre-intervention rate of each different target behaviour is recorded. When a stable rate appears in one behaviour, the treatment programme is applied first to that behaviour. During the next stage two things need to be noted: (a) the difference that intervention is making (if any) to the first target behaviour; (b) whether the base rates of the other behaviours (to which the treatment variable has not yet been applied) are changing substantially (co-varying) with the target behaviour. If not, then the programme is applied to the next behaviour, and after a suitable interval the procedures outlined above are applied again. This process continues until the scheme is in operation for all the target behaviours. Figure 5.14 on p.150 gives an example of a multiple baseline design applied to a range of disciplinary problems experienced by a single mother and her children.

Multiple baseline designs have a wide range of uses with clients who have a number of different problems. However, the approach has its drawbacks. The behaviours under investigation have to be fairly discrete; in other words, the occurrence of each must be assessed as substantially independent of the others. To the extent that the start of the first B phase produces a marked co-variance in the other base rates, the experimental principle of using the other behaviours as a control is confounded. It may be that the procedure being used is particularly potent, or – later on – that generalization is occurring. But this cannot just be assumed (however beneficial the result) and the sequence collapses into a concurrent series of AB designs – no great problem from a therapeutic point of view, little problem from a case evaluation point of view – providing that a follow-up procedure is to be used.

Baselines across settings

Another multiple measurement approach is the 'baselines across settings' design. With this, problems in different settings are baselined and the treatment variable is applied to each in sequence according to the principles outlined above.

OTHER FACTORS IN THE USE OF SCEDs

A wider range of single case evaluation procedures is available than there is space to discuss in this book. However, the main approaches likely to be applicable to routine work have now been outlined. One or two general issues remain. First, assessment and evaluation procedures of this type do not have to be used in a 'mechanical' way. The question of balance between rigour and the intrusiveness of a particular approach must always be given careful consideration. This is not to say that at the first sign of difficulty the principle of rigorous case evaluation should be abandoned in favour of some vague notion of the need for general flexibility. But, where necessary, these procedures can be changed and reconstructed, as long as due care is given to their subsequent interpretation. They are widely used in clinical social work settings in the United States in circumstances not *that* much more propitious than here.

QUALITATIVE ASSESSMENT AND EVALUATION

At various points in this chapter I have argued for a combination of quantitative and qualitative information as the sensible basis of both assessment and evaluation. When considering qualitative change, we are interested in the character and in the general social effects of new behaviour, rather than in precise changes in the rate of its occurrence. However, we must avoid the trap of seeing these different types of assessment as completely different things. An increase in the level of self-assertion, though recorded as a quantitative change, can produce notable qualitative changes – perhaps in the way that the client views him or herself, or in the enjoyment they now get out of life. Sometimes the changes produced by treatment seem (at a qualitative level) artificial or stilted because initially new behaviours are being grudgingly or mechanically performed. It should be remembered here that the availability of new sources of reinforcement produced by the behaviour can, given time, change the way these things look and feel.

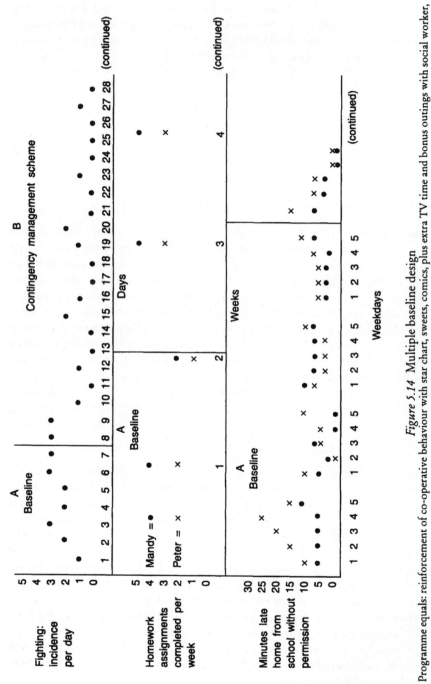

Figure 5.14 Multiple baseline design

Programme equals: reinforcement of co-operative behaviour with star chart, sweets, comics, plus extra TV time and bonus outings with social worker, determined on a sliding scale. Also agreed rates for deprivation of privileges.

As assessors we are concerned to know about the patterns of selective attention, mental imagery, beliefs, thinking styles and constructs clients have developed regarding their problems and the circumstances in which they arise. In other words, we need to know what their model of this bit of their reality looks and feels like. We have to hypothesize about their hypotheses. Here is a list of mental events on which we might concentrate such investigations.

PERCEPTION

Logically we should concern ourselves first with the kinds and classes of stimuli and events to which the client appears to respond or appears to emphasize, and those which he or she ignores, or is relatively insensitive to. Examples are: people who in the early stages of panic attacks focus on small, perhaps random visceral changes (breathing, heart-rate, swallowing saliva) and by this concentration change them, setting up the bodily equivalent of microphone feedback: the greater the cognitive attention the greater the change – the greater the emotional reaction – the greater the change – the greater risk of catastrophic thinking, and so on. This is the first function of anxiety in the absence of manifest physical or well-conditioned threat (which produce the 'hard-wired' responses referred to in Chapter 3) – to induce a state of internal hyper-vigilance to small harbingers of danger (Beck and Emery 1985). People with low self-esteem whose 'social radars' are tuned to provide early warning of rejection, for whom a knitting of the brows by another always spells disapproval and never concentration, exhibit this problem in comparable external form. These effects may be short-term (they do not necessarily feature strongly in later memories of events) but they develop a contemporary 'cognitive-processing bias' often leading to self-defeating behaviour or social paralysis. Then there are stranger people, who interpret the playful and socially undeveloped behaviour of children as 'flirtatious', so justifying their sexual arousal towards them.

Note that each of these examples contains a percept, a preferential selection of stimuli, and consequent emotional arousal and interpretation. Indeed, as we saw in Chapter 3, so intertwined and rapid are these factors that it is difficult to separate sensory, cognitive and emotional factors. The sequence is automatic, it is conditioned, *it* happens to *us*. It can even occur preconsciously, that is, without contemporary cognitive reflection, as in Dixon's (1981) concept of 'perception without awareness'. Words with sexual connotations flashed rapidly via a tachistoscope can trigger emotional reactions in subjects even when they cannot have 'registered' them, and cannot represent and recall them. Patients suffering from depression who are simultaneously presented with neutral and derogatory messages in dichotomous listening experiments tend to filter out the first and select the second; controls do not (see Eysenck and Keane 1990). Therefore an important task in cognitive-behavioural assessment is to try to establish which groups of stimuli clients are particularly sensitive to. Clients give two kinds of evidence on these points:

(i) They will admit to 'scanning for' or 'tuning into' particular stimuli. Their attention is prefocused; they are already interested in the possible presence of them.

(ii) They often describe how particular stimuli 'jumped out' at them, and acquired a sudden significance.

By getting clients to think carefully about their first inklings of a problematic episode we can gather useful information as to the internal and external stimuli they are prone to discriminate; their problems of sensitivity and insensitivity; the degree of automaticity in their links between percept, cognition, emotion and behaviour; the resistibility or otherwise of these cued sequences, and what, if anything, works to suppress, interrupt or divert attention from them.

THOUGHT PATTERNS

Here we are concerned to assess what mental images or internal 'conversations' accompany given stimulus conditions. The former seem to us like pictures, though as we saw in Chapter 2, they are probably less complete before than after we talk to ourselves or other people about them. We 'join up the experiential dots', as it were. Getting clients to describe these images gives us clues as to their interpretation of events and their fears about them.

Case illustration

I was recently consulted by a young woman about a persistent fear of vomiting in public which was ruining her social life. She turned down most invitations from friends as a consequence and if she did go out she would carry a plastic carrier bag with her to avoid the worst. What was 'the worst'? The image (it had never actually happened) was of a crowded restaurant; of her being eased into a chair at a table furthest away from the lavatory; friends looking at her, first with puzzlement as she began to gag, then with embarrassment, then with horror as she threw up over the food and covered everyone's clothing with vomit. This image was triggered by any social circumstance involving the consumption of food and was particularly prevalent if possible escape routes were blocked. Having this mental picture made things worse in that she would either concentrate on chewing and swallowing to the extent that someone would notice and ask if everything was all right, or she would over-compensate and bolt the food, which made her feel more nauseous (this case is discussed, in more detail, on pp. 214–15).

By asking clients to describe their thoughts in this way it is possible to gain an impression of the extent to which problems contain an element of catastrophic thinking, and whether their behaviour is being influenced by 'worst-case' imagery. Note how little possible control over social circumstances or sympathetic understanding from others the sufferer allows herself in the above description.

Next we are concerned with inner speech. What does the client typically say to him or herself about their circumstances and behaviour? 'What a fool I am, I shall never be able to carry this off, best get it over with quickly and get out', perhaps. We 'talk' silently to ourselves about our behaviour, we appraise our actions and what we think we must look like as if we were third parties. These commentaries have a cueing function in respect of emotion and behaviour. We have all had the experience of a sub-vocal appeal to ourselves to stay calm, and many of us will have experienced bursts of self-condemnation expressed in something like speech inside our heads. However, for some clients these self-admonishing *mantras* are there most of the time, are inhibitory, intrusive and, together with the emotions (fear, anger) which accompany them, block rational analysis and problem-solving. In this form of assessment we are concerned to know about the quality of these cognitive and emotional experiences, where they happen, how long they last and how often they occur.

BELIEFS

As a social worker in a child and family guidance clinic, I was taken by surprise by the number of referrals received featuring young children allegedly manifesting behavioural problems or developmental delays which turned out to have more to do with unrealistic parental beliefs rather than pathology, psycho- or otherwise, in the child. The belief systems of abusive parents are beginning to be taken more seriously in research and it is becoming clear that (given that child-rearing skills are not genetically endowed – though we often behave as if they were) many adults have beliefs about the supposedly malevolent intentions of babies and children that are not only exaggerated, but implausible for developmental reasons. That, for example, babies cry deliberately when parents are having a good time, or are trying to break up vulnerable relationships (see p. 50).

Beliefs are settled views of experience, and they condition us to seek information consonant with the little functional homeostases that we all expend considerable energy attempting to preserve. The chief task for the assessor is to elucidate the belief systems surrounding problems and clients' reactions to them, as a basis for comparing early descriptions with those given during and after intervention.

ATTRIBUTIONS

The most important part of the search for meaning and valency in stimuli (i.e. experience) is the establishment of cause and effect, and co-variance. We conduct 'thought experiments' to establish what reliably goes with what, and where causes might lie; for example:

> Whenever I show my disappointment about being let down over the children he claims not to have realized the importance of the situation. So what would happen if I put this beyond doubt beforehand? Would he be there, and on time? Probably not. So what does this say about my level of real influence and my and their importance in his life?

A further dimension of attribution is the *direction* of attributive judgements, that is, whether they are predominantly external – 'the bad things that happen to me are largely due to outside factors beyond by control', along a continuum to predominantly internal – 'the bad things that happen to me are mainly caused by me'. Remember that as assessors we are looking for patterns of unlikely predominance. Well-adjusted human beings are capable of blaming failures to meet deadlines on an (unappreciated) dedication and concern for quality or, in moments of vulnerability, of blaming themselves for failing to live up to the inappropriate expectations of others. The question is, do such patterns occur across a wide range of behaviour and circumstances – with delusions of omnipotence at one polarity and learned helplessness at the other?

In conducting thought experiments about our relationship with the environment we sometimes jump to conclusions on the basis of faulty or limited evidence. Many of our clients do this in an exaggerated and predictable way and such patterns give important clues as to why they act as they do, or why they fail to respond (except passively or guiltily) to oppressive circumstances. The oddest behaviour can become 'logical' (distinguish from acceptable) when we come to see it in the context of its perceived justifications. Consider this:

BOB:	There's been incidents where, say, I'm in a train going from Birmingham to Coventry with my family, and a woman got upset because I'd sat in a seat on the train that had been booked, but no one was going to be sitting on the seat. She was getting rather stuck up about it and I dragged her out of the chair and gobbed in her face. I said, 'Listen, my wife will sit wherever she wants. I'm not having you telling her where she's sitting.' My wife was carrying a baby at the time. I was rather upset about that as well, but then again it was crazy, you know, it was just over-reacting. There was no need for it. But she got up my nose and I just reacted violently, dragged her out of the chair.
PROF. BLACKBURN	(forensic psychologist, Liverpool University): How did she get up your nose?

BOB:	It was the way she was talking to me, the way she looked down at me. Just her general manner.
PROF. BLACKBURN:	How did you know she looked down at you?
BOB:	The way she was talking, like a stuck-up snob. I hated it. I ain't no different from anybody else. She might come from a posh house and a posh area, but she ain't no different from me. She got up my nose and I let her know about it and all.

(BBC Horizon Publications 1993)

Being at a safe distance from this dreadful situation allows us a cool look at it. Behavioural impulsivity is obviously present, but so is a probably very faulty pattern of interpretation. Simple observations or requests from the victim trigger powerfully negative attributions from the perpetrator, she is out to put him down and belongs to a general class of people who have oppressed him in the past.

ATTITUDES

Once the dominant concept in social psychology, and still a major field of study, particularly regarding fixed, stereotypical orientations on such issues as race and gender, the whole idea of *attitude* came under attack from an earlier generation of behaviourists as a redundant, circular, mentalistic concept (see Bem 1967). Nevertheless, it has proved to be a very resilient concept. Here is Gordon Allport's classic definition:

> An attitude is a mental or neural state of readiness, organised through experience, exerting a directive or dynamic influence upon the individual's response to all objects and situations with which it is related.

(Allport 1935)

'Attitude' (the term originally meant physical position, or spatial orientation towards something) is therefore a heuristic device for describing clusters of cognitive, affective and behavioural regularities which appear to transcend differences in contemporary stimulus conditions. They represent the sum total of yesterday's learning environments which, through memory and conditioning, influence current behaviour. They are not an infallible guide to behaviour, but the concept of attitude maps on to something real, for it would never have been adaptive in our long evolutionary history, either biologically, socially or psychologically, for humans to respond to stimuli afresh each time. Hence we develop, as it were, 'pre-taped' sets of responses for crucial sets of stimuli. Only rarely do we 'wipe' these; more often we record in new bits of consonant information and edit out bits of dissonance (see Figure 5.15). When we do not, then we tend to feel uneasy about inconsistency. This is something we learn through socialization. Rough predictability is necessary for social interaction and so we are conditioned to feel anxious when we do not display it – which is why 'but I thought you always said that . . . ?' is a somewhat threatening phrase to hear from anyone who matters.

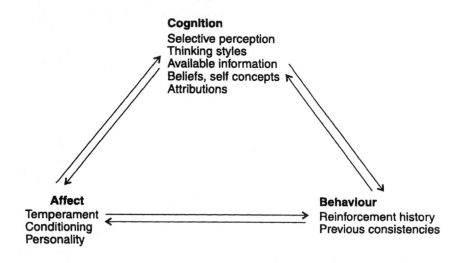

Figure 5.15 Cognition/behaviour/affect

Sometimes we catch ourselves responding to demanding stimulus-conditions and agreeing with some doubtful proposition to please others. For example: 'these people have had a hard time, why make things worse?' (I'm being tactful and kind for their good). Sometimes a feeling arises in us, anger, for example, which because of the context finds no overt expression. This too is uncomfortable unless we can say to ourselves something like, 'I hate your prejudice, but this isn't a safe place in which to say so' (I'll write a letter of complaint later). Sometimes we catch ourselves thinking along a line at odds with previous behaviour and emotional commitment: 'I'll shape him in to my point of view, he won't even notice' – 'But what about all that stuff about the value of directness and the negative effects of speaking in code that you are always going on about?' 'Well, there are *some* people, stupid people, in positions of power who don't play by the rules. They just *have* to be manipulated.' QED.

Attitudes, then, result from necessary economies of perception (knowing what best to search for in a complex field); from knowing what might give us an edge; from knowing what might lead to gratification – all under the influence of previously conditioned and reinforcing emotions.

In assessment our main task is to try to elucidate the attitudes which lie behind troublesome responses to problems, tentatively to link together specific happenings, reports of emotional reactions and patterns of thought. These may take the form of general predispositions: 'Give children an inch and they will take a mile'; 'If you are really careful you need never be caught'; 'Strong people look after you'. These will always have a previous history. Understanding problem-related attitudes provides us with therapeutic opportunities to inject controlled doses of dissonance: 'Yes, your son *obeys* you while you are around Mr Adams, but what about when you are not – and does he *respect* you for what you are trying to teach him, or does he simply fear you?' When this was said to one of my clients, for whom 'respect' was all (but by which he usually meant 'compliance') one could almost hear the crunching of mental cogwheels.

PROBLEM-SOLVING STYLES

Related to attitudes, and again based on experience, temperament and cognitive and behavioural deficits, these thinking patterns are inferable from regularly-recurring approaches to problem-solving. For example, some clients faced with multiple challenges will pick the nearest one and exhaust their energies upon it. They have learned to feel better when they are taking action, any action. Debt counsellors are often confronted by clients who have paid off an insistent but by no means crucial creditor while allowing rent and tax arrears to accumulate. Conversely, some people can be exasperating in their 'wait and see, better the devil you know' approach to decisions. Case histories often reveal lost opportunities for, on the face of it, obvious alternative courses of action which are inhibited by previously reinforced ways of approaching difficulties. Such problems are seen in an extreme form in neurosis, when a self-defeating procrastination based upon anxious and over-inclusive perusal of *all* possibilities can be a feature (see Claridge 1985; Goldberg and Huxley 1992); but no one is completely immune to such influences. New approaches can be taught but first we must deduce something about present behaviour.

CONCLUSIONS

Many of the existing assessment aids employed in behaviour modification can be adapted for the assessment of the cognitive accompaniments of behaviour. For example, clients can be asked to keep records of their thoughts in particular circumstances, in diary form, or on an ABC chart. Or, in the initial stages of assessment, they can be asked to tick various prepared statements about thinking patterns and how often they occur (see Appendix 2).

Cognitive-behavioural therapists are interested in cognitive events for two reasons: (i) to test the hypothesis that if patterns of thinking (negative self-statements, inappropriate beliefs and attributions) can be modified, then the problematic behaviour which they accompany will also change. This, as we have seen, is to assign to thoughts the role of mediating variables; (ii) to give us clues as to the type of consequences that maintain unwanted behaviour and prevent the emergence of more adaptive approaches. As with all types of assessment 'the proof of the pudding is in the eating', and we are most interested in how the client subsequently *behaves* as a result of intervention.

A good cognitive-behavioural assessment takes in three sets of factors influencing problems: cognitive patterns, emotional accompaniments and behaviour itself. Each of the helping professions has had its preferences in the past, but there is now a considerable body of research suggesting that if we neglect any one of these components, then our attempts to help will be the less effective for it.

6

STIMULUS CONTROL
(CONTINGENCY MANAGEMENT)
TECHNIQUES

The term *contingency management* is used to describe all those applications of the operant model that involve the therapist in trying to change, control or develop behaviours by altering existing patterns of eliciting stimuli and reinforcing consequences. In other words (in line with the assessment procedures discussed in Chapter 5) it is assumed that the desired behaviours are already in repertoire at some significant level, but need strengthening. That is, the client has to some extent *already learned* how to perform these behaviours, but perhaps exhibits them only in settings irrelevant to the problem under review, or very infrequently, or at only a weak level. It is on these questions that the decision whether or not to use approaches derived from operant reinforcement research rests.

Having decided that the target behaviours are in repertoire to some degree, the therapist must look next to the factors in the client's environment that are failing to elicit and maintain these behaviours or that are eliciting and maintaining undesirable responses in competition with them. This may be just a question of coming up with a rearrangement of existing contingencies – as in a case known to me, of a young man with a learning disability who was a chronic absconder from care. It was suggested that staff should occasionally supply the interesting car rides he was known to enjoy, but which currently he had only when being returned under escort (so reinforcing his running away). These were to be given *pro rata* for behaving well and (impulsivity being another of his difficulties) *not* running away.

Alternatively, it may be necessary to produce an entirely new set of contingencies, for instance: 'If there are three clear days without a single incident of fighting, William and Marion will be taken to the sports centre for one hour.'

Set out below is a summary of the range of possibilities for changing behaviour by manipulation of the contingencies that surround it (see also the summary Table 6.1, p. 191).

(i) Where the problem results mainly from an insufficiency of certain behaviour, it may be possible simply to identify and *positively reinforce* a low-level adaptive response so that it is 'amplified', performed more

159

frequently and its place in the individual's repertoire strengthened. In other words, we can work to improve the 'pay-off' for desirable behaviour. A good starting point is simply to raise the question with oneself and one's colleagues: 'what pays off for this person around here, in this setting, group, family or organization?' Answers based on observation often differ substantially from official views and intentions.

(ii) A performance may be *shaped* by the selective reinforcement of approximately similar behaviours, until they become progressively more like the fully-fledged performance desired.

(iii) Where the problem results mainly from an *excess* of unwanted behaviour, it may be possible to identify and positively reinforce a response which is *incompatible* with existing (unwanted) responses. That is, we may be able to encourage an alternative set of activities, which could eventually replace the existing behaviour, or which prevent the individual from gaining reinforcement for the unwanted behaviour.

(iv) Again, in respect of an excess of unwanted behaviour, it may be possible to apply *negative reinforcement*, so that whenever the individual stops this behaviour and performs some desirable alternative, an aversive stimulus is terminated. Here the removal of the aversive stimulus (e. g. being ignored) is made contingent upon the client refraining from undesirable behaviour and engaging in some more appropriate activity, and this serves to strengthen the alternative response.

(v) It may be possible to reduce the *frequency* of undesirable behaviour by extinction; in other words, just by removing the reinforcement currently available for it. In this way, unwanted behaviour is not encouraged by the positive consequences it brings.

(vi) In certain cases, unwanted behaviour can be eliminated by *punishing* it whenever it occurs; that is, by ensuring that an aversive consequence results from its performance. More sophisticated adaptations of this principle are available, which attach different levels of punishment to different activities. These are called *response-cost schemes* and involve the assignment of an agreed 'price' to each different pattern of unwanted behaviour, according to its seriousness. Such programmes may be useful where there is a range of different responses which the therapist is anxious to discourage in different degrees, a sort of inverted shaping approach. However, the aim here should always be to make the consequences of bad behaviour clearer. Many of our clients already inhabit unpredictably punishing environments. Response-cost schemes should aim to make controlling sanctions more predictable and rational, and, eventually, to shift the emphasis towards positive shaping (see p. 69).

(vii) Behaviour may be either encouraged or discouraged by manipulating the stimuli which *elicit* it. Thus, it may be possible to do one or more of the following: remove or reduce the effect of the environmental cues (Sds) which signal that reinforcement is available for a particular unwanted

sequence; intensify the Sds which trigger competing, desirable behaviours; intensify the cues which signal that no reinforcement will be
forthcoming for unwanted behaviour (SΔs); or remove the SΔs which
signal that no reinforcement will be available for desirable behaviour, so
that it is more likely to occur.

Items in the range of possible influences on behaviour given above are
presented separately so that each can be clearly identified. In a therapeutic
programme it is very likely that a combination of such approaches will be used.
For example, a scheme designed to extinguish unacceptable behaviour by
withdrawing attention from it is likely to be augmented by a programme of
positive reinforcement for acceptable behaviours, the aim being to shape the
individual concerned towards a more acceptable pattern of attention-getting.

SELECTION OF REINFORCERS

The popular image of reinforcement is that it involves someone in authority
dispensing artificial rewards for good behaviour – such as sweets, money or
tokens. While each of these examples could serve in some circumstances, it can
be misleading to think of reinforcement in terms of someone giving some *thing*
to someone else. Tharp and Wetzel (1969) have suggested the term 'reinforcing
event' as more appropriate to field settings, since it is often impossible to
specify exactly which part of the sequence is the potent element. Even where
something tangible is being handed over in exchange for certain behaviour, it
might well be the pleasant demeanour of the therapist or mediator that is
effective, or the client's own sense of achievement (of which the tangible
reward is merely a symbol, as when we earn stars or grades at school), or the
fact that other people see him or her receiving preferential treatment. (People
do not, after all, cancel all other engagements to dine at Oxford high tables for
the quality of the cuisine!) It is technically possible to conduct experiments to
isolate the key factor, but this is rarely worth the effort involved, and so
reinforcement often remains a 'package' of different influences presented
contingently. Therapists must use their common sense here and not respond
mechanically to clients in the interests of accuracy. Words of praise for
appropriate behaviour, which never vary in content or emphasis, quickly lose
their reinforcing power because they lack genuineness. Lack of imagination
over the selection of credible rewarding experiences is one of the commonest
reasons why programmes of this type fail.

Skinner has written interestingly on this point in his philosophical essay
Beyond Freedom and Dignity (1971). He suggests that in cases of admirable
behaviour the prestige accorded to an action is inversely proportional to the
visibility of the forces which control it. In other words, dignity, prestige and
honour are accorded to approved behaviour in direct proportion to the difficulty of identifying the reinforcement which maintains it: for instance, where

it appears to arise spontaneously; where the individual has nothing very *obvious* to gain by performing a difficult task; and where the easiest explanation is that the behaviour is 'self-motivated' and completely altruistic.

My home town newspaper recently carried an account of a young man's heroic rescue of a drowning dog from the River Avon. Since nothing much happens around here, the following week's edition contained a follow-up story where it was recounted that this individual had saved *three* other pets from a watery fate over the last eighteen months. Rationally speaking we should all have thought more of this self-appointed lifeguard and recommended him for an RSPCA medal, perhaps. But one's irresistible human reaction is: 'What is this man *doing* prowling the river bank? Just how do the dogs get in the river in the first place? What sort of person has the time for this . . .?' And, quick as a flash, our evaluation of behaviour has changed from 'brave' to 'what's in it for him?'

The practical point here is that outside the animal laboratory reinforcement is a *process*, a series of events with special meanings. What is given cannot be separated off from the manner or context of its giving. There is a tension here between technical specificity (making sure that reinforcers are given contingently and are having their intended behaviour-strengthening effects) and naturalness (taking care not to make the subject feel that he is being artificially handled and manipulated, because most of us experience this as the opposite of reinforcement). The following general points about reinforcement practices arise from this discussion.

(i) Wherever possible, reinforcement for appropriate behaviour should arise out of the setting where it is performed and should be a natural concomitant of the performance. A set of contingencies expressed like this: 'If John helps staff and refrains from aggressive outbursts, which are distracting and time-consuming to them, then they will have time to spare to help him learn to ride his moped' is usually less resented than: 'John can have 20 minutes supervised bike-riding if he refrains from aggressive behaviour and helps staff for three hours'. In the first example a causal link is made between John's uncooperative and time-consuming behaviour and what happens next. Staff have time to spare given a little help, but this is not the case if they have to spend the morning coping with John's aggressive behaviour. The consequence is a fact of life; it occurs naturally, and is less of a therapeutic device. Unless, that is, we disagree with the rationale behind it. Most of us learn early in socialization to resist controlling influences.

(ii) Where it is not possible to link naturalistic consequences to behaviour, and some more artificial scheme is introduced (as in the case of token economies in mental hospitals and secure units, or star charts displaying a record of acceptable behaviour from children), then it is important that clients appreciate both the reasoning behind the scheme and that it is a special arrangement, designed to help them gain control of their behaviour.

For example: 'As soon as Robert has achieved the specified level of school attendance, and has broken the habit of avoiding lessons he doesn't like, the daily report cards will be discontinued.' This point is particularly pertinent to the design of contracts (see p. 180), but it applies to almost all work with teenagers and adults.

(iii) Artificiality and feelings of manipulation are likely to be lessened where non-material reinforcers – such as praise, approval, affection, attention and joint activities – are a main part of the programme. Where these are unlikely to be effective, material reinforcers should still always be accompanied by them. In this way acceptable, everyday rewards acquire a reinforcement value of their own (see p. 65), and represent a basis for the subsequent fading of the artificial (that is, socially and culturally untypical) features of the scheme.

At this point it may be worth re-emphasizing that reinforcers are not special in themselves. Events or commodities become reinforcers because of the particular behaviour-strengthening effects they happen to have on the performance of a particular individual in a particular circumstance. The only sure way to find out what reinforces a sequence of behaviour is to make an educated guess: try it, and observe the effects. However, there are some general guidelines.

(i) We should try and observe the client in natural settings so that the consequences that normally follow behaviour can be determined. It may be possible then to reorganize these consequences (for example, by providing more attention for approved behaviour, and removing it from unacceptable behaviour).

(ii) We can make use of Premack's principle (1959). This states that a high-probability behaviour can be used to reinforce a low-probability behaviour when the performance of the former can be made contingent upon the performance of the latter. The assumption behind this approach is that if patient A spends 60 per cent of his day looking out of the window, then this must be at least a lowest common denominator source of reward for him. If the same patient can be induced initially to exchange one hour's access to the dayroom couch near the window for a few minutes of rehabilitation therapy, or conversation with ward staff, then a basis for shaping has been established. Premack's principle has had wide application in settings where people suffer from serious learning disabilities and in work with chronically institutionalized psychotic patients, where it is difficult to discover interests by interviewing alone. Nevertheless, it also has a wide application outside these settings – whenever it is difficult to find a specific influence to which the individual might respond (see p. 176).

(iii) Probably the commonest – and most sensible – approach to deciding what reinforcers to employ is to ask the people concerned (the client, family, friends, staff and so on) what is likely to be effective. In their work with children Tharp and Wetzel (1969) advocated the use of simple sentence-completion exercises such as: 'the person I most like to spend time with is . . .', 'the best reward costing about £2 that I can think of is . . .' or 'the thing I enjoy doing most is . . .'.

(iv) Reinforcement checklists are another method of giving an idea of what reinforcers to build into a programme. These cover a range of possible influences, from material rewards and objects to activities and the names of significant people. An example of a reinforcement checklist is to be found in Thomas (1974) (see also Hersen and Bellack 1981).

(v) Programmes can be based on generalized reinforcers (see p. 66) if nothing more specific seems likely to be effective. Attention, approval, free time, money, exchangeable tokens and so on are usually quite potent since they are a prerequisite for other kinds of reinforcement. Money or tokens have the advantage that they can be readily exchanged for other sources of reward, as well as taking into account the fact that appetites and interests change from day to day and setting to setting.

The next set of factors concerns the feasibility of using particular types of reinforcement.

(i) Reinforcement needs to be powerful enough to compete with the already-present attractions of performing unwanted behaviours. It also needs to be durable over time. In addition, some thought should be given to the question of whether one type of reinforcement will affect behaviour in different settings (for example, both inside the home and outside, where there is competition with the peer group). There is also the problem of satiation: if the programme is based on material reinforcers, or on one type of activity, it may be that after a certain number of sweets, coloured pencils and trips to the sports centre, the child will have had enough of them. Often it is better to try to elicit *types* of activity and then to vary these systematically throughout the programme.

(ii) There is little point in selecting reinforcers which will be technically difficult to present as a consequence of certain behaviour. Sometimes a token or signal of having earned a particular reward will act as a conditioned reinforcer (see p. 65) and bridge the gap between performance and ultimate reinforcement; but, generally speaking, the shorter the interval the better.

(iii) Another consideration is whether there will be someone around to act as the therapist's agent or mediator, to supervise and apply the new contingencies (see p. 127). Levels of co-operation, skill and understanding of the programme are important considerations here.

(iv) The old social work maxim 'start where the client is' applies particularly to behavioural approaches. Clients will not respond to reinforcers if these are contingent upon performances that are beyond their present capacities, or where the reinforcer on offer is simply inadequate to elicit and maintain large-scale changes of behaviour, in other words is 'not worth it' (see Figure 6.1).

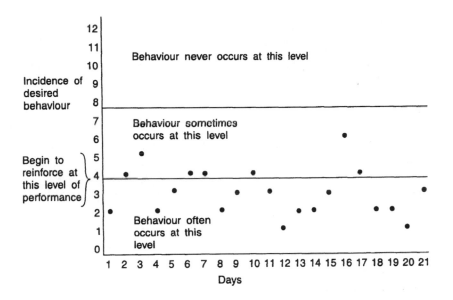

Figure 6.1 Level at which to begin a reinforcement scheme

DIFFERENTIAL REINFORCEMENT PROGRAMMES

These are probably the most widely used form of contingency management schemes and involve the setting up of a contrast between the consequences of desirable and undesirable behaviour. Behaviours that we want to strengthen are positively reinforced, and behaviours that we would like to weaken are placed on what is called an *operant extinction schedule* (wherein we arrange that no reinforcement should accompany such behaviours). To those factors can be added a third: the likelihood that in future, as a result of this clear demarcation, the client will be better able to discriminate between the two kinds of behaviour. That is, he or she will be more likely to know where, and when, each behaviour is, and is not, to be performed, as well as the likely consequences which attach to these different performances and settings.

Figure 6.1 shows the daily occurrence of a behaviour which is to be reinforced. The scatter may be divided into zones labelled as above or, alternatively, 'extremely desirable range', 'desirable range' and 'extremely

165

undesirable range'. Reinforcement should first be applied at the top end of the 'sometimes occurring' range, that is, it should be given for daily rates of 4 and above.

Case example showing the different elements of a contingency management programme

Here are some details from the case of the boy exhibiting allegedly 'disturbed behaviour' in school (hitting other children, running around the classroom, making disruptive noises), which readers will recall from p. 79. The main elements of the programme were as follows.

Extinction

In practice, this meant that disruptive behaviour (as defined above) was to be ignored by teachers whenever possible. If other pupils complained of Mark's behaviour (as they frequently did) they were told in a matter-of-fact way to ignore it if possible, as he was just 'showing off'.

Positive reinforcement

Any short period in which Mark's behaviour did *not* contain any of the disruptive features mentioned above was to be responded to as quickly as possible by the class teacher, as a useful opportunity positively to reinforce behaviours incompatible with the target behaviours. This category included: sitting still, working at an exercise, trying to read, neat work and so on. Where Mark joined in a group task – such as answering questions put to the whole group, or reciting an exercise – first the group would get the teacher's praise, and then Mark (and anyone else who came into this category) would receive a special mention for trying harder and for showing good progress.

The following reinforcers were used: physical proximity of the teacher and individual attention; praise and little displays of affection, such as a pat on the back (Mark would sometimes go through the motions of shrugging these off but undoubtedly looked for them next time); compliments on any work showing an improvement – whatever its absolute standard; ticks and initials on a card (see Figure 6.2) which was taken home to show parents and could be redeemed for small monetary rewards, or trips to the swimming baths, cinema, or hamburger restaurants with father. Limited financial aid was given to parents to establish this part of the scheme.

This classroom programme was complementary to a scheme already running at home. The daily progress card was used to link the two so that three initialled entries per day earned Mark a coloured star on his home progress chart, praise from parents, 10 minutes extra TV time per entry, plus 25p for every three entries. A bonus scheme was introduced to reinforce good weekly

PROGRESS CARD – TO BE TAKEN HOME EVERY AFTERNOON				
MON	TUE	WED	THURS	FRI
Morning	Morning ✔ *R.T.A.** ✔ *R.T.A.*	Morning	Morning	Morning
Afternoon ✔ *R.T.A.* ✔ *R.T.A.*	Afternoon ✔ *R.T.A.* ✔ *R.T.A.* ✔ *R.T.A.*	Afternoon	Afternoon	Afternoon
Mark can earn ticks for 15 minutes good behaviour in class				

* R.T.A.: Teacher's initials

Figure 6.2 A typical progress record card

averages so that, initially, four stars a week resulted in an outing with father or mother. All the rates in these various parts of the programme were gradually increased (with Mark's foreknowledge) as behaviour improved.

Other procedures

An important part of the programme was an augmented remedial reading scheme implemented by teaching staff. This was sometimes carried out by a favourite second-year teacher of Mark who did not normally have this function. This undoubtedly reduced his feelings of inadequacy and frustration in certain lessons.

Problems

The programme's weakest point was the extinction contingency for disruptive behaviour. Some behaviour was just impossible for teachers to ignore, either because of the risk of injury to other pupils, or because of the bad example set for the rest of the class. Existing approaches, such as standing outside doors, or taking notes home, had proved ineffective. Mark did not mind being put outside classroom doors as there was always plenty going on in the corridors; indeed this may have had a minor negative reinforcement effect since it put an end to classwork. Similarly, if sent home Mark would probably get a smacking from his mother, but then would be free to play on his own for the rest of the day, and mother's aversion to contact with teachers was strengthened. A further difficulty lay in persuading teachers to show interest in and affection to Mark if his *current* behaviour justified it, and not to dwell upon either what he had recently been guilty of, or upon what he might do in the near future. Early attempts were very stilted and robotic.

Time-out

A time-out from reinforcement scheme was tried, and proved to be reasonably successful by at least bridging the gap until the positive reinforcement scheme took control of Mark's behaviour. A half-empty storeroom with the door left open was used opposite the school secretary's office. A desk was placed there together with reading and writing materials. Extremely disruptive behaviour was first responded to by a special form of words, which gave Mark a clear option to sit quietly and get on with his work. If this failed he was unceremoniously removed by his teacher, without comment. This occurred on eight occasions throughout the course of the programme and the periods of absence varied from 5 to 15 minutes.

Changes were necessary at various stages of the programme. The extra TV time contingency, for example, did not work when there was nothing of interest being shown, and so playing out of doors for an extra 15 minutes was substituted as a reinforcer on these occasions.

Another problem was reported by the class teacher who, in the early stages of the case, found herself having to explain to other pupils why Mark was apparently receiving preferential treatment. She took advantage of time-out intervals to discuss with the class the idea that Mark needed everyone's help. An alternative approach might have been to involve other interested children in similar schemes, but geared to academic attainment or other individual considerations, but this idea won little favour with hard-pressed staff.

Co-operation from teaching staff increased steadily as the scheme began to pay off, and the social worker was increasingly free to concentrate on the home-based scheme, leaving the school programme to the teachers. However, there were some early problems over defining professional 'territory' and the readily available option of 'special facilities' for this child.

Follow-up of the home and school programmes at six months revealed substantial and well-maintained gains in school, and less dramatic, but still useful gains at home. However, the main achievement in this case was that Mark continued to be taught at his ordinary school and, at the time of closure, was seen, in the words of the head teacher, as 'a bit of a challenge to disciplinary skills', rather than as a 'seriously disturbed boy' in need of 'psychiatric investigation'.

This was very cost-effective exercise in multi-disciplinary co-operation resulting in a palpable degree of destigmatization, showing that behavioural change influences thoughts, appraisals and attributions, as well as the other way around.

Case examples showing use of a wider range of techniques

In the case of the young boy convicted of arson (assessment and evaluation data on pp. 128 and 145), a wider combination of techniques was used, including the following.

(i) There was positive reinforcement of activities unconnected with periods of talk about fire and fire-related 'accidents'; self-selected activities included gardening projects supervised by his father. (This new behaviour of father required considerable reinforcement from his wife at first.)

(ii) If fire talk occurred, father had instructions to come indoors at once (negative punishment: see p. 76–7).

(iii) A diary scheme: one-hour intervals without pointed fire references earned (a) pamphlets and information about agricultural and horticultural courses from the social worker; (b) visits to a local horticultural centre; (c) money to take to school. This diary was reviewed by the older brother on his visits, and outings with him (not punctuated with homilies on good behaviour) were made conditional on a rising standard of behaviour.

(iv) Extinction scheme: all talk of fire was ignored or, if it could not be ignored, it was responded to with a graded series of deprivations (see response-cost section below for further details).

(v) John was instructed that if he felt himself wanting to talk about fire he was to try to think about other things instead – outings, models, his (largely positive) concern for his parents – and if this proved unsuccessful he was to leave the room.

(vi) Targets in all schemes were gradually increased. John knew the point of this and understood that the purpose of the scheme was to build a happier family life and to keep him out of trouble – which, thanks to the persistence of his family, it did.

The next case concerns the 9-year-old son of an army non-commissioned officer referred to a child and family guidance centre as a result of aggressive and insulting behaviour towards his now-single-parent mother; his sister; occasionally towards his school teachers; and sometimes towards passers-by in the street.

The history of these problems is sad but uncomplicated. Kenneth's father was an unstable, impulsive bully to his family and there were two recorded physical assaults by him on his wife, resulting in quite serious physical injury.

Both the incidents were witnessed by the child. A social history revealed the following stages in the development of this problem:

Mother, herself from a deprived background, had initially found the 'macho' image of her husband to be both exciting and security-inducing. Their early married life was, however, punctuated by a series of disciplinary inquiries into his conduct as a soldier, and visits by the army welfare services. Charges never stuck; welfare officers were fobbed off, and a somewhat paranoid sense of triumph over 'officialdom' developed. Kenneth's childhood consisted of (a) harsh discipline from his father; (b) exposure to grossly inappropriate magazines and videos; (c) an image of manhood based on physical prowess and the domination of women. Kenneth's father left the household when Kenneth was 8 – for another woman – but continued to see him fortnightly at weekends.

From the age of 6 onwards Kenneth's behaviour had been a cause for concern to his mother and his teachers. He was aggressive to other pupils, swore at his mother, and on a few occasions when shopping he would run through the supermarket pushing trolleys into people. His general demeanour was aggressive and he liked to dress in combat gear and have his hair cropped in military style. Following the departure of his father, Kenneth's mother made a determined effort to change the behaviour of her son. At the time of her referral to the child guidance clinic she recounted that she had spoken to him at length about her embarrassment at his behaviour, tried to bribe him with expensive presents and, as a last resort, used physical punishment – all to no avail.

The approach of the social worker in this challenging case emphasized the need for consistency. Most of what had been tried before had been tried for short periods, the mother giving up and moving on to something new if an approach proved ineffective in the short-term. This had undoubtedly produced an 'immunization effect'. The differential reinforcement programme used in this case contained the following features:

(i) The identification of, and positive reinforcement of, low-probability behaviours somewhat incompatible with shouting, swearing and aggressive/embarrassing behaviour in the street. Those chosen were (a) improved school attendance; small-scale domestic tasks; regular attendance without incident at an 'after-school club'. The reinforcers used were stars signifying a build-up of credit towards significant purchases, e.g. training shoes, a construction set, football kit, plus collateral reinforcement in the form of praise and small amounts of money.

(ii) An ultra-reliable set of sanctions for adverse behaviour based on deprivation punishments, e.g. staying indoors; time-out for 15-minute intervals terminated by a believable apology; loss of television privileges; loss of credit via the star scheme outlined above.

(iii) Basic assertion training (see p. 202) and rehearsal of typical incidents with mother.

The positive reinforcement scheme worked well from the start (see Figure 6.3). A scrapbook with catalogue pictures of intended purchases was used to record clearly rates of positive behaviour. Stars could be cancelled at agreed rates for occurrences of bad behaviour. Most effort, however, was spent on rehearsing with mother her reactions to transgressions and stiffening her resolve to see each incident through. An attempt was made to enlist the help of father during his fortnightly access visits. The results were mixed with some rapid gains if he felt in the mood, some laxity resulting in setbacks in otherwise good weeks and occasional sabotage.

Further important background elements to this scheme were:

(i) Regular counselling appointments with mother, which served to boost her confidence, to remind her of the agreed view of the origins of this problem, and of her own plans for her life – currently at risk because of the behaviour of her son.

(ii) Periodic and unscheduled telephone contact to check on progress and to reinforce the need for consistency in part (ii) of the programme.

RESPONSE-COST (NEGATIVE PUNISHMENT) SCHEMES

The 'time-out' procedure described on p. 168 is one form of response cost. This technique involves the assignment of specific deprivations to different gradations of unwanted behaviour. Jehu (1967) quotes an interesting case from a residential hostel for severely delinquent boys:

> The subject was a sixteen-year-old boy named John, who severely bullied smaller boys and directed his followers to do likewise. The intimidating-aggressive behaviour paid off in that it was followed by compliance and submission from his peers. The staff found it difficult to detect and interrupt the process because the threats were often quite subtle. For instance, John had only to walk towards the television for the occupant of a choice seat to vacate it in his favour. The essence of the time-out programme was that 'when there is any reason to *suspect* that any child is being threatened, bullied or subtly intimidated, either directly or indirectly, by John or *his clique*, John is to be taken immediately to isolation', and this was expounded to the staff in some detail. After the regime had been in effect for six weeks they reported an appreciable decrease in John's aggressive behaviour.
>
> (Brown and Tyler 1968)

Case example

A different form of response cost was used in the arson case. Talk about fire, fire accidents, playing with matches and so on were at first ignored whenever possible (operant extinction) but beyond a certain level of persistence they had

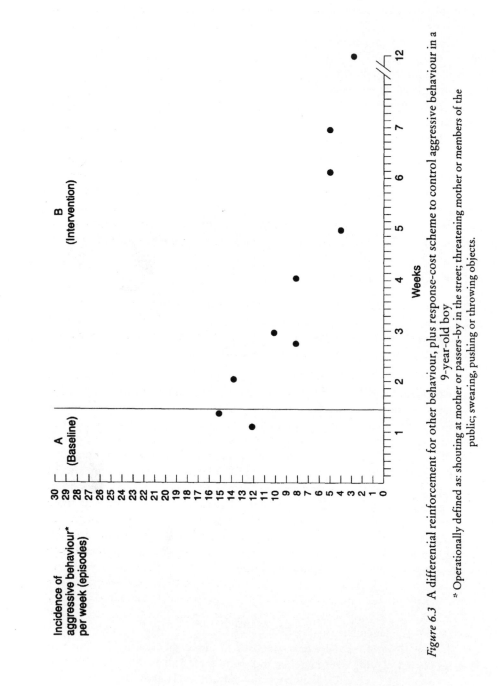

Figure 6.3 A differential reinforcement for other behaviour, plus response–cost scheme to control aggressive behaviour in a 9-year-old boy

* Operationally defined as: shouting at mother or passers-by in the street; threatening mother or members of the public; swearing, pushing or throwing objects.

to be responded to in some form. A graded series of possible responses was drawn up and given to the family. The instructions given may be paraphrased as follows.

Whenever possible parents were to ignore provocative behaviour, but not *studiously* to ignore it since this positively reinforced John's sense of control. When the point had been reached beyond which it could not be convincingly ignored, they were to issue the first warning (an agreed formula designed to give John the option of abandoning the behaviour and doing something else). If the behaviour continued, mother was instructed to take her son by the hand and lead him from the room. He was told he could return in five minutes, but that if behaviour was continued he would lose TV privileges, and an agreed sum of money allocated for him to take to school. If the behaviour still persisted he would be sent to his room for one hour. If he refused to go or reoffended at the end of this period his brother, who lived nearby, would be telephoned, and if necessary would come over and ensure that the scheme was complied with (this was only rarely necessary). Specific instructions had to be given as to how the brother should behave – in general, neutrally – since contact with him was otherwise rewarding to John. A positive reinforcement scheme was also used in this case (see p. 63), but it is doubtful whether it would have had a chance to work without the security afforded by this approach. Parents also felt more confident at being provided with an agreed and written-out formula to apply.

Such schemes sometimes founder on the problem of deciding when an agreed rule has been broken. In the early stages of the case John adapted his behaviour to the new contingencies by becoming extremely subtle in his transgressions. A single match would be left in a conspicuous place, or he would hover dramatically at the window for a few seconds, and if questioned about this would reply that he thought he had heard a police siren 'or something'. Parents were bewildered by this and had to be persuaded by the social worker to trust their own judgement (as with the residential care staff in the case described by Jehu (1967)). They were helped by another agreed formula: whenever they *suspected* John of leaving 'fire symbols' around or talking obliquely about fire, they were instructed to issue the warning described above, and to add to it in the face of John's protestations, phrases such as these – (Stage 1): 'In my opinion you are trying to irritate us with silly talk about fires – you have no need to do this'; (Stage 2): 'If we are wrong we are sorry but then since you do this kind of thing a lot we can't be blamed for any mistakes'. The response-cost scheme was then applied on the basis of parents' considered judgement as to what was occurring.

173

TOKEN ECONOMY SCHEMES

Various forms of token reinforcement systems have been applied to behavioural problems found in psychiatric, residential social work and special education settings. The results of these attempts can best be summed up as mixed, with some programmes producing worthwhile gains and others appearing to lose sight of their therapeutic intentions and becoming merely systems of day-to-day control (Birchwood *et al.* 1988). Before discussing these problems an introduction to the principles of token reinforcement is called for.

In essence, token reinforcement schemes are a group-level application of operant conditioning techniques. Schemes have the following general characteristics:

(i) An agreed list of behaviours which the staff implementing the programme would like to see strengthened – such as self-care skills, delusion-free conversation, negotiation without threat, participation in rehabilitation schemes and so on.

(ii) Tokens of predetermined value are used to reinforce these behaviours, and these are exchangeable for a range of commodities and privileges (such as access to TV, free time, and special sports equipment).

Programmes of this kind have two main effects. First, they develop and increase the frequency of behaviours likely to be useful to the client both inside, and, more importantly, outside residential settings. Second, they provide opportunities for discrimination learning in that they encourage clients to distinguish which occasions and settings are appropriate for certain types of behaviour to be performed.

The tokens themselves derive their reinforcing power from two sets of influences. First, they act as generalized reinforcers in that, though worthless in themselves, they are symbols of access to a wide range of already well established reinforcers. In other words, even if one source of reinforcement is temporarily satiated, then there are still likely to be other forms of reinforcement available. Second, and to a lesser extent, they can serve as conditioned reinforcers (see p. 65). That is, their regular association with attention, encouragement, praise and tangible rewards gives them in some circumstances an intrinsic reinforcement value.

The advantage of using tokens in place of the actual reinforcers is that they only marginally interrupt the sequences of behaviour they are designed to influence. The power of token schemes is well demonstrated by the following data (see Figure 6.4) from the psychiatric field. Note how a range of pro-social behaviours are regularly performed by this group of chronic, institutionalized patients when contingent reinforcement is available, then drop to near zero when the *same* amount of reinforcement is available – but *non-contingently* – and then return to the previous level when the token scheme is reinstated (BAB design).

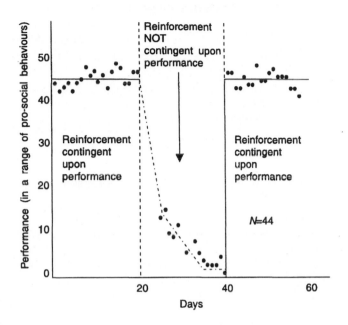

Figure 6.4 Results from a token economy scheme
Source: Ayllon and Azrin (1965). © 1965 Society for the Experimental Analysis
of Behaviour, Inc.

Problems associated with token economy systems

In an extensive review of token economy schemes at their high point, Hall and Baker (1973) took issue with Krasner's view (1968) that such programmes represent 'the most advanced type of social engineering currently in use' (leaving aside the wages system, presumably):

> It is an unfortunate fact that these forms of engineering seem especially prone to breakdown – in the engineering sense, of course. Tinkerings by psychologists, psychiatrists and others have not prevented several of these advanced social engineering projects from grinding to a halt.
>
> (Hall and Baker 1973:14)

Remarking on the 'unique sabotage potential' of these programmes, Hall and Baker identify five crucial components of token economies in institutional settings which can lead to failure. To paraphrase, four of these headings can be adapted to our purposes here:

(i) The first concerns client characteristics, with selection as the key difficulty. Where mediators have to cope with widely different types of target behaviours interfering with the emergence of these widely different problems, and markedly different intellectual capacities, then the demands on them are sometimes too great.

(ii) The mediators actually applying the reinforcement contingencies are essential to any operant reinforcement programme and may require special training – which they often do not get.

(iii) In addition, there is the need for support for staff, and a relevant question is: 'who will reinforce the reinforcers?' It is often the case that after the initial interest of setting up the programme the staff of volunteers in face-to-face contact with residents are treated as functionaries and just left to get on with it. Where this occurs, and where doubts and problems arising from the programme are not discussed, the token system becomes 'token' in another sense. This point applies equally to fieldwork programmes using mediators.

(iv) Before setting up a programme it is necessary to ensure that everyone the client is likely to come into contact with understands its principles and will agree to abide by them. There is little point in encouraging non-acrimonious discussion within the house-system of a residential school, if the metalwork and physical education teachers insist on silent obedience. Discrimination between such settings will not always look after itself and neither will the generalization of programme effects to the outside world.

USE OF PREMACK'S PRINCIPLE

Readers will recall that the definition of this approach to selective reinforcement (see p. 163) was that a high-probability behaviour could be used to reinforce a low-probability behaviour, provided that opportunities to perform the first could be made conditional upon the performance of the second. This principle is especially useful in cases where it proves difficult to find effective sources of extrinsic reinforcement – for instance, where there is nothing the client values more than the reinforcement obtained from performing a certain (high-probability) behaviour.

Case example

The following case of a 4-year-old child with one failed foster placement behind him illustrates the principle. It was hypothesized that Ian had learned three things from his chaotic first years of life: (a) adult attention is a scarce commodity; (b) if you want it you have to make a fuss and put up with the 'impurities' when you get it; and (c) when you get it, hang on to it like grim death.

Ian was placed with carefully selected foster parents but, after a short while and despite active social work support, the placement began to break down. Foster parents complained of the following behavioural problems: uncontrollable temper tantrums, with Ian resisting all comforting or diversionary tactics; excessive clinging to foster mother (this was seen initially as a transitory phase in the placement, but it did not go away as expected). Ian would hold on to foster mother for half the day, trying whenever possible to get on to her lap. Attempts to remove him resulted in violent tantrums; entering foster parents' room at night; breath-holding when frustrated.

Procedure

— The foster carers were instructed to pay special attention to Ian's occasional bouts of solitary play and whenever he seemed to be coming to the end of such a period (before he began to 'grizzle' or seek attention) one of them would invite him to come and sit nearby and hear part of a story. It was made clear to Ian that this was a reward for playing quietly.

— At the end of 5 minutes of story-telling a 'natural break' was initiated. Ian was taken back to the scene of his earlier play activities and encouraged to resume them with the reassurance that in 10 minutes or so he could come back for part two of the story. If Ian attempted to clamber back before the time assigned, he was taken firmly back to the play area. If he persisted, foster mother would leave the room, leaving the book behind. If Ian followed and refused to be taken back a 'time-out' scheme came into operation.

— A darkroom timer with buzzer was used in the early stages of this programme, and waiting for the signal for an interlude of close physical contact became a game in itself.

— Time on foster parent's lap (high-probability behaviour) was made conditional on increasingly long periods of play, or on non-attention-seeking activities (low-probability behaviour).

— Other useful behaviours, not associated with tantrums or attention-seeking, were differentially reinforced with praise or small rewards, such as Lego pieces.

Ian eventually went to his local school — not without difficulty, but with considerably less than was feared. His clinging behaviour reduced to easily manageable levels in 13 weeks of therapy (due mainly to the foster carers' grasp of the general principles of the scheme and their ability to adapt it to new circumstances). Most importantly, the programme gave foster parents a 'second wind', enabling them to continue the placement.

CONTINGENCY CONTRACTS

Contingency contracts are a very promising procedure indeed, and particularly applicable to interpersonal problems. Contingency contracts are documents that specify behaviour which the parties to a problem would like to see performed. They rest on a particular interpretation of operant theory and this needs to be taken note of before describing applications.

In many cases referred to social workers, it cannot be said that one person has the problem, or even that one person *is* the problem. Rather, difficulties lie in the conduct of relations between people. This is particularly true of family and marital or relationship difficulties. Much of our behaviour in such settings is maintained on the basis of *reciprocal reinforcement*, and this process can best be thought of as an exchange, in which behaviour from person A is elicited and reinforced on the implicit understanding that behaviour from person B will be similarly treated. Within this process will be found different 'exchange rates' for certain behaviours which are differentially valued by the parties.

In most relationships there is a tendency towards a relatively enduring balance or homeostasis maintained and controlled largely at an implicit level. Where this balance and the reciprocity which maintains it break down, as in the case of family problems or estrangement in close relationsips, then four kinds of things tend to happen.

(i) Helpful behaviours, which would normally be elicited by the everyday actions of the other party, have to be specially prompted and specifically controlled. Arguments occur about relative contributions – who has done what, what the real value of such behaviour is when weighed against the behaviours performed by others and so on. Generally speaking, people are uncomfortable in the face of breakdowns of this kind, especially since explicit prompting and aversive control rob behaviour of much of its dignity and spontaneity (see p. 161).

(ii) The balance of mutual control shifts from positive reinforcement and positive shaping towards punishment, negative reinforcement and negative shaping. Respectively: 'If you do X I shall retaliate with Y', and 'until you do A I shall keep doing B'. In other words, control of important behaviour is maintained by punishing transgressions, and by keeping 'the heat' on the other person until he or she performs actions close to those desired. This gives rise to the usual escape responses, which become increasingly sophisticated, so requiring more powerful aversive controls, so that a negative spiral develops.

(iii) In such a context a relaxation of control is often taken advantage of by the other party, and an attempt to revert to positive reinforcement is often seen as a ploy to be resisted.

(iv) When reconciliation is attempted, either internally or with the help of an outside agency, parties often start negotiations with an insistence that others must change their behaviour first. However, on the occasions when this happens the behaviour tends to receive little or no positive reinforcement for quite a time. Indeed, it is more often used to contrast previous behaviours (the 'about bloody time too' syndrome, known to social workers working with divided families).

Figure 6.5 Steve Bell, 'A useful hint'
Source: Private Eye, October 1980. Reproduced by permission of John Glashan.

These few points all add up to a view of close personal relations as a system of reciprocal reinforcement that has its own mechanisms for maintaining balance. In the same way, a gyroscope will resist small buffetings and remain stable, but a stronger force will seriously disrupt the mechanism and then equilibrium is hard to regain. This model draws on both operant and classical learning theories. When potentially useful, conflict-reducing actions are not reinforced (either positively or negatively), they are likely to recur less often. Also, when the behaviour of another person is regularly associated with punishment, this person's presence alone can eventually trigger bad feelings – irrespective of what they happen to be doing at the time.

There is good empirical evidence that relationship problems and marital problems can be overcome by direct measures to reinstitute reciprocal reinforcement. A comprehensive review of recent research in this field is to be found in Alexander *et al.* (1994).

The logical corollary of the views presented above is that the social worker seeking to improve interpersonal relations is unlikely to be successful if he or she works with just one part of this system – an estranged partner or an adolescent seriously at odds with the rest of the family. The reinforcement potential lies in the hands of people least likely to use it, and some sort of staged reduction of hostilities (my favourite analogy for use in such families is 'SALT 2' negotiations) based on the exchange model outlined above is usually the best, if not the *only* workable policy. It is in this field of family and relationship problems that contingency contracts have had their widest application. They arrange for the mutually guaranteed reinforcement of adaptive behaviours, on the basis of an agreed exchange of actions which would not otherwise be performed.

THE DESIGN OF CONTINGENCY CONTRACTS

Contingency contracts are specific written agreements about future behaviour and they are based upon two major premises.

(i) That a definite, unequivocal and publicly made commitment to a future course of action is more likely to be complied with than more implicit agreements reached about future behaviour in more casual and reflective forms of discussion – providing that the client does not feel that he or she has been unduly coerced into these decisions (Festinger 1957).

(ii) That with many interpersonal problems, the most powerful reinforcers available for adaptive behaviours lie with the person experiencing the other half of the problem. Therefore a pre-arranged and simultaneous alteration in the pattern of consequences produced by key problem-related behaviours is the best way to proceed.

The aims of these contracts are similar to those of most types of operant scheme. The behaviours under review must be accurately defined, and the future contingencies which are to apply must not be capable of misinterpretation. Specificity is all. Where definitions of problems cannot easily be reduced to items of behaviour, then a good second-best is to have an agreed list of examples to refer to, so that John's 'showing off', or father's 'put-downs' can still be accurately identified when they occur. In contract work there is an additional emphasis on negotiation between parties, and on identifying behaviours of roughly equal value to the participants so that in the presence of one, the other is much more likely to occur. In other words, considerable effort goes into striking an equal bargain, using sequences of behaviour as the medium of exchange.

Case example

Here is an example of a contingency contract (Figure 6.6) worked out between

This is a contract between Mr and Mrs Skinner and John Skinner (aged 14). It aims to increase the level of happiness enjoyed by this family by making it clear to each member what the others expect, and what consequences follow both meeting and not meeting these agreed expectations.

Mr and Mrs Skinner

Agree that if John returns home by 10.30 pm on weekdays and 11.00 pm on Saturdays, nothing will be said to him about where he has been or what he has been doing. If John is late they will ensure he forfeits time the next night.

Agree that if John stays home every Sunday evening and on one weekday, he will be allowed to attend two discos a month until 12 pm, at which time he will be collected by father.

Agree that they will give £5 pocket money per week, 50p of which will be unconditional. Sister's pocket money will be similarly worked out and no extras given.

Agree to accept politely phrased comments on their behaviour as it affects him, and to involve him more in day-to-day decisions – such as where to go out together, or what TV programmes to watch.

Every Saturday father will spend at least three hours with John engaged in an activity, away from the home if John meets the terms of this contract for one week. No mention will be made of past problems during these activities.

Parents agree to address any worries about what company John is keeping to the social worker, and will not talk to John about them for the moment.

John

Agrees that in exchange for being allowed out late he will:
(a) keep to time;
(b) forfeit double time for each 5-minute period he is late without an acceptable excuse, and 20 minutes for each 5-minute period after half an hour has elapsed past the deadline – regardless of excuses.
The time will be forfeit on the following night.

Agrees that in exchange for the privilege of being allowed to attend discos he will spend a specified time at home and will spend at least two hours of these days helping with household tasks; for instance, cleaning his bedroom, washing up, and/or gardening; and that he will telephone home before 11 pm to reassure his parents.

Agrees to forfeit money in up to 50p units if he fails to:
(a) help around the house as defined;
(b) telephone to reassure parents or is spiteful to his sister (by social worker's definition).

Agrees that in exchange for being consulted, and having his views listened to, he will try hard to keep his temper, stop swearing at home and leave the room rather than shout at his parents. Failure to co-operate as defined by social worker means loss of one evening out.

In exchange for going out alone with father, John agrees to:
(a) stop provoking his sister into rows;
(b) listen to the points father makes, providing they are within the terms of this document.

In exchange for the privilege of being allowed to choose his own friends, John agrees to call to see social worker briefly once per week after school by appointment, and will be prepared to discuss his activities and their possible consequences.

There will be a fortnightly family meeting with social worker to discuss disputes and any problems arising from the use of this contract.

Signed ....   Signed ....

Date ....

Figure 6.6 Contract (Skinner family)

a 14-year-old 'skinhead' boy who was referred to social services by the police and his parents. The three main problems were: (a) a risk of his committing further offences (property theft, damage to public property, assault); (b) his increasing estrangement from his family – father having threatened to evict him several times; (c) a real and continuing risk of violence between father and son (mother described their behaviour as a 'love–hate relationship' but rejection was undoubtedly in the ascendancy at the time of referral).

This contract was abandoned after eight weeks of successful operation. It did not solve every aspect of the family's problems; father continued to idealize his own childhood and draw unfair comparisons between the somewhat anti-social views of John and his gang and his own golden youth. Nor was it possible directly to influence John's behaviour outside the home. However, no further offences were committed over the next eighteen months and the parents thought that this was at least partly because John spent more time at home and had less interest in 'shocking' his family in retaliation for what he saw as their unreasonable treatment of him. This is speculative; what the contract achieved without question was an effective truce between the warring factions, the rules of which, as the contract was faded out, became part of their normal day-to-day behaviour. Three general things can be said about contracts such as this:

(i) They work best when potential solutions to problems lie substantially within the gift of the parties directly involved. That is, where each of the protagonists genuinely possesses the power to alter things for the other(s) and satisfy them to some degree. There is little point in trying to produce an internal settlement in a dispute maintained largely by outside pressures.

(ii) It is far better to agree relatively easily and substantially on something small, than with difficulty and partially on something grand. The results of flying diplomacy may look good on paper and produce lots of hand-shakes and *bonhomie*, but the shooting often starts again before the presidential jet (or, in this case, the departmental Vauxhall) has landed back at base. As with other types of behavioural schemes, the all-important task of the early stages of contact with the clients is to provide a positive experience of problem-solving. A contract must prove its worth in the short-term or it will not usually get a chance to prove itself in the long-term. Clients rarely refuse absolutely to negotiate about behaviour, but are more concerned to establish a reasonable level of behaviour, and to negotiate exchanges of positive behaviours at what they see as a reasonable 'price', measured by the effort involved against the rewards received.

(iii) Contracts should be focused on interpersonal 'flashpoints', that is, upon regularly recurring 'set piece' patterns of discord. In the example above, the most important gain was in removing the nightly row (and sometimes fist fights) with father who would wait up to interrogate his son. John knew this, and so delayed his return home according to 'may as well be hung for a sheep as for a lamb' principles.

Figure 6.6 gives an example of a contingency contract which meets most of the general criteria of good practice. Here is an example of one which does not (Figure 6.7). The reader is invited to identify its many flaws. I am grateful to my friend and colleague Barbara Hudson for supplying the raw material for this example.

Between 15-year-old Peter Harris and Mr and Mrs Harris, in order to improve the atmosphere in the home.

Conditions

1 Peter agrees that every weekday he will do three hours' homework in order to make up for lost time.

In exchange for this, on Saturday he will receive enough pocket money for the whole week.

2 He further agrees to improve himself, will try to be good, and will be friendly to his parents at all times.

He will then receive the privilege of going out to the cinema once a week on a day to be determined by his parents.

3 Peter further agrees to help his mother with the housework and shopping when she wishes it.

In exchange, Peter will then receive the privilege of spending Saturday as he wishes – until 8 pm, and subject to his father's approval of his plans.

4 Peter agrees that in weekly school tests he will get at least a B and will behave in such a way as to earn this grade.

Parents will encourage this in every way possible.

Failure to keep to this contract If Peter does not keep to his side of the bargain on one of these points he loses all his privileges for a week, and in severe cases he will also be punished in a way to be determined by his father.

Figure 6.7 Contract (Harris family)

Jokes suffer badly from having to be explained, but could you count the following faults?

(a) General one-sidedness of the contract (all clauses).
(b) Vagueness of terminology (clauses 2 and 4).
(c) Rewards sometimes precede the performance of required task (clause 1).
(d) Reinforcement not contingent on specific performances (clause 1).
(e) Hopelessly high levels for target behaviours (clauses 1 and 4).
(f) Parental vetoes available (clause 3).

(g) Some required behaviours are beyond the control of the signatories (clause 4).

(h) Neither positive nor negative consequences follow immediately and invariably upon given performances (clauses 1, 3 and 5).

(i) The contract has 'limited liability' clauses: 'when she wishes'; 'subject to father's approval'.

(j) The contract contains long-term punishment clauses likely to discourage positive responses ('failure' clause).

As if this were not enough, there are other kinds of errors associated with the use of contracts (see Figure 6.8).[1]

Between Mr and Mrs Parkinson and Billy (aged 14)

Billy agrees to stay out only until 1 am on weekdays and 3 am on Saturdays and Sundays.	Providing Mr and Mrs Parkinson will give up asking the whereabouts of the cat.
Billy agrees to reduce his spending on alcohol to £25 per week.	Providing Mr and Mrs Parkinson supply a new sheath knife of Billy's choice for each complete week in which this target is met.
Billy agrees not to mug citizens above pensionable age unless strongly provoked.	In exchange, Mr and Mrs Parkinson agree to provide money for Billy's karate classes.
Billy agrees to visit his social worker at least once per calendar month for ongoing discussions about his attitude.	Providing Mr and Mrs Parkinson refrain from telephoning about care proceedings and stop asking Billy to attend school.

Signed.. Signed...

Figure 6.8 Contract (Parkinson family)

Less exaggerated versions of the foregoing have, not without some justification, brought the idea of contracts, and social workers in general, into considerable disrepute:

> Social workers have drawn up an amazing contract giving pretty 14-year-old Justine Carter freedom to stay out ALL NIGHT . . . 'I begged the social worker for assistance (said Mrs Carter) and a contract is what I got . . . I signed it to keep the peace but I certainly didn't agree with it.'
>
> (*Daily Mirror* 1978)

The technical principle of starting with small reductions in problematic behaviour and working gradually from there is a good one. After all, coming in at midnight is better than coming in at 3 am. However, by agreeing to a staged reduction in dangerous behaviour, social workers in the case publicized above fell into the trap of appearing to condone it. In such cases, arguments that the client would probably be doing something worse were it not for the written agreement do little to allay public consternation.

In less controversial cases of this general type, the best approach is to have the practical necessity for a policy of reducing problematic behaviour in stages discussed by as many of those on whom it will impinge as possible. This may include the clients' families, other agency staff, or potential complainants such as school authorities or the police. Some kind of mandate from interested parties is the only way in which social workers can be justified in using contracts which can give the *appearance* of licensing potentially harmful, or anti-social behaviour.

NEGOTIATING CONTINGENCY CONTRACTS

'The medium is the message' so far as the actual process of negotiating contracts is concerned. The social worker, insofar as he or she has the ability to conduct open and honest negotiations and to reduce conflict by compromise, will serve as a model for the other participants. This will be so whether they are aware of the fact or not. There is, therefore, an opportunity here to go beyond negotiated truces between clients, or *détente* between client and social worker. The process of drawing up a contract can itself serve as a device for teaching and demonstrating the skills of non-aggressive self-assertion, or the skills involved in repairing damaged relationships. Indeed, unless some kind of learning and generalization does occur, the contract has fulfilled only a limited function.

Here is a list of further points to keep in mind when trying to produce a workable contract:

(i) For a contract to be worthy of the name there must be some degree of equality between the parties to it. Legal contracts may be set aside where the relative powers held by the signatories are deemed to be grossly unequal – as in the case of a desperate tenant who signs an agreement which purports to exclude him 'consentingly' from his rights under the law.

There are similar ethical dangers with behavioural contracts, where an anticipation of coercion or loss of privilege can produce the same kind of sham voluntarism. This is a particular danger where the social worker has a 'captive' client population – as in some residential establishments (see Chapter 8).

(ii) If a contract is to work well, then all parties must see clearly that they will get something out of it. The benefits of keeping to the contract must be worth the 'costs' of the change in behaviour that this requires. It is vital, therefore, that the negotiator checks out thoroughly the balance of value to the respective parties.

(iii) The worker must not be afraid to offer to renegotiate contracts where they are plainly not doing their job satisfactorily. In this way agreements can be adapted to changing circumstances, and clients can be given further practice at defending their points of view in a reasonable manner. There are, of course, dangers in constant renegotiation, but in general a series of definite if short-lived agreements is better than staggering on with one over-distended and complicated version of the original.

(iv) Wherever possible the contract should be couched in positive terms, or at least contain a balance of benefits and sanctions. That is, it should be clearly stated that from now on *this* pleasant consequence can be relied upon to follow *that* particular behavioural sequence; rather than arranging solely for unpleasant consequences to operate *unless* X behaves in a particular way – this can mean that the non-performance of one sequence of behaviour results in the other party having to withhold adaptive behaviour.

(v) Once substantial agreement has been reached, a draft should be produced and used as a basis for further discussion. Ideally the final document should be typewritten, logically set out, and written in plain language. Each of the signatories should have his or her own copy.

(vi) It is a good idea to fix in advance a regular series of meetings to review the operation of the contract. This makes it less likely that parties will withdraw unilaterally following a dispute.

(vii) Contracts cover most of what we do in our daily lives outside the home – in employment, and in our commercial relations. However, when they are brought in to regulate aspects of family life, they have an artificial feel. We prefer the rules by which we govern ourselves in this setting to be implicit rather than explicit. To some extent this is also the case with social worker/client relationships, though there are fewer definite expectations here. Given the force of this cultural norm, it is very important that the purely *temporary* nature of contracts should be underlined. As soon as sufficient stability has been achieved, and the main contract terms are implicitly rather than explicitly observed, the rigid terms of the agreement can be phased out clause by clause. A good indicator of when to do this is provided when the clients start to apply the principle of non-acrimonious negotiation to aspects of behaviour other than those covered by the original document.

(viii) Contracts fail for three main reasons: (a) the terms are not specific enough and are interpreted differently by the various parties, leading to early disappointment; (b) new behaviour is insufficiently reinforced and/or there is too great a time lag between performance and the counter-response supposedly guaranteed by the contract; (c) there is insufficient supervision of the operation of the contract by the social worker in the early stages.

Contracts can also be used to define more clearly the relations between social worker and client (Sheldon 1980). They are not a panacea; neither are they always an end in themselves. Often their main function is to provide a dependable structure within which long overdue consideration can be given to how long-standing problems have their daily effect through *contemporary* behaviour.

Case example

The Smith contract (originally a referral for child behaviour problems) was an extremely simple one. The couple concerned had identified two key difficulties, which were really two markedly different styles of handling conflict: 'clearing the air' by having a row was the preference of the husband, whereas complete social withdrawal was the reaction of the wife (based, incidentally, on her childhood experiences of parental clashes). Both disliked the other's behaviour in this regard and contracted (a) to limit their own response; (b) to practise resolving conflicts through discussions governed by preset rules (for example, Mrs S would not refuse to discuss problems if husband agreed to do so calmly). The baseline rates of threatening behaviour from Mr Smith and protracted silences from Mrs Smith clustered around twelve items per week. After thirteen weeks during which the contract was used these fell to four incidents per week – with noteworthy positive effects on the management of their young child.

OPERANT EXTINCTION TECHNIQUES

Extinction is a process most often used in combination with other contingency management techniques, but with simple unidimensional problems it can work well on its own. Overleaf (Figure 6.9) is an example of its use in a common problem – excessive crying in children. Although infant crying is an everyday occurrence for most parents, where it occurs to excess – and on top of other problems and frustrations – it can be a trigger factor in child abuse.

APPROACHES BASED ON NEGATIVE REINFORCEMENT

The therapeutic application of negative reinforcement principles (see p. 63–4) is called *avoidance training*. Clients are taught to make responses which terminate pre-existing aversive influences. For example, in a social skills group of my experience, adolescents with a reputation for truancy and disruptiveness in the classroom were taught to reduce teacher disapproval and anxiety by admitting that they could not understand a given point, by apologizing for

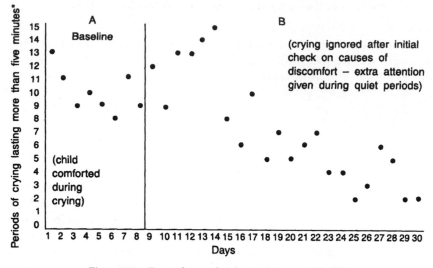

Figure 6.9 Excessive crying in a one-year-old child
*Medical examination showed no physical cause.

disruptive behaviour and so on. Whether such schemes work, or descend into parody, will depend upon the willingness of adults to forget what happened yesterday and seize a good opportunity when it is handed to them.

Negative reinforcement is usually just one of a number of factors in contingency management programmes. The concept itself is more useful in explaining why maladaptive behaviours are performed in the first place. Many are an easy means of escape from aversive circumstances – such as when a low achiever at school plays truant to escape criticism and the daily evidence of his ineptitude, or when someone takes a tranquillizer to 'switch off' or at least 'turn down' what appear to be the constant demands of children. In such cases the therapist has the option of trying to remove the cause of the negative reinforcement (by trying to obtain a more sympathetic approach from the teacher in the first case, or a behavioural scheme to change the behaviour of the children in the second).

SATIATION

Satiation schemes are based on the simple principle that while certain consequences reinforce behaviour, a flood of the same objects, or constant exposure to the same series of events, will remove their reinforcement value. (Think of a laboratory rat who gets a cageful of food pellets every time he presses his lever!) Thus, it may be possible to eliminate ritualistic behaviour by having the client go through his ritual so many times that its reinforcement value is lost.

SHAPING, FADING, CHAINING, PROMPTING

These procedures are grouped together partly because they have been dealt with elsewhere in the book and partly because they are all really sub-techniques rather than full-blown strategies. This means that they are more likely to be used as features of a more comprehensive programme than in their own right.

Shaping

Shaping (see p. 69) was a feature of the two main contingency management case examples used in this chapter (p. 166 and p. 169), and involves the reinforcement of successive approximations of the finally desired performance. It is therefore a major feature of most contingency management programmes. In Figure 5.4, better and better approximations of non-disruptive classroom behaviour and higher and gently higher compliance rates were required before reinforcement occurred.

Fading

Fading (see p. 70) involves the standard shifting of control from stimuli occurring in one setting to those which occur in another. It is a vitally important dimension of behaviour modification in residential settings, where the recently acquired behaviours will eventually have to be performed under somewhat different circumstances. Bringing responses under the control of variables likely to be found in the outside world, by fading out 'artificial' reinforcers and introducing the more naturally occurring variety, is therefore likely to be a powerful factor in determining long-term results of the pro-gramme. In the case example on p. 166, monetary support for the outings used to reinforce adaptive behaviour was reduced by stages, as parents began to think it worthwhile to budget for these themselves. Similarly, the daily report card was faded by being brought home at less frequent intervals, eventually to be replaced by a more generally phrased note of weekly progress.

Chaining

Chaining occurs when complex performances are broken down into their component parts and each stage in the sequence positively reinforced. The reinforcer then becomes the discriminative stimulus that cues the next stage in the sequence. A variant of this approach, *backward chaining*, is widely used in teaching basic skills to clients with learning disabilities. For example, in the case of dressing, the procedure is to start with the garment already in place; one arm is removed from the sleeve, and then physically guided back into the sleeve. This prompt can eventually be faded and the next stage, putting on the coat from the 'two-sleeves empty' position, can be attempted, and so on until the person has learned the whole sequence. With backward chaining the positive reinforcement of having the coat on (together with any additional praise) is fairly immediate to start with, becoming conditional on a longer chain as progress is made with the task.

Prompting

Prompting is a series of discriminative stimuli which indicate that a certain behaviour is now appropriate or that, if performed, it will be reinforced. The example of backward chaining above included prompting. Prompts were also used in the case of the socially unconfident client described on p. 121, and usually took the form of gestures and facial expressions to cue verbal responses and eye-to-eye contact. Prompts can be faded as soon as the behaviour is brought under control of other, naturally occurring, situational cues.

ATTENTION TO DISCRIMINATIVE STIMULI

Behaviour can also be changed by the therapist manipulating the naturally occurring discriminative stimuli which elicit it. In the case of the difficult foster child (p. 176), foster parents eventually became very skilled in spotting situations that were likely to give rise to attention-seeking behaviour, and would do their best to remove these or divert the child's attention elsewhere.

Changing the environment of cues and consequences in which problematic behaviour occurs, or which blocks the emergence of adaptive sequences, is an essential ingredient of all the behaviour therapies, and is perfectly consistent with the inclusion of cognitive reappraisal elements.

Thinking clearly about what sort of life she wanted to have, about what could reasonably be expected of a 14-year-old and about the need to remedy a learning history for which she was in part responsible, helped the parent in the case on p. 169 to maintain control over her son's home environment and conduct when in her company. Largely cognitive, 'remote control' approaches are unlikely to work with other than already well-motivated clients, which species is in short supply in the social work field.

A larger problem lies in the vague ethical queasiness which many workers have over the issue of pointed, as opposed to general, background forms of taking control of problems (see Chapter 8). Yet however well-intentioned, to do nothing, or nothing much, in the face of problems usually means abandoning clients to the less benign and more forceful contingencies responsible for their problems in the first place.

Table 6.1 Summary of contingency management techniques

Techniques	Main features	Application
Contingency management	A compendium approach using all appropriate reinforcement, extinction and punishment applications. The environment is changed so as to support useful behaviours and ignore or discourage unwanted behaviour.	Used to increase the frequency, strength of adaptive behaviours by providing contrasting consequences for the two. Wide range of applications: child behaviour problems, learning disability where behaviour problems block social acceptability, or any setting where some control can be gained over the consequences of behaviour.
Positive reinforcement	A consequence is provided which increases the likelihood that a given behaviour will be performed. Immediacy of reinforcement is an important factor.	Used to increase desirable behaviour. Behaviours incompatible with problematic behaviours can also be reinforced. The technique of choice in a wide range of social work programmes, it is important that the behaviour to be reinforced should occasionally occur at reasonable strength, since this is otherwise a labour-intensive approach.
Token economy systems and points systems	Tokens (generalized reinforcers) are given for pro-social behaviours and are exchangeable for a variety of goods, privileges, access to activities and so on.	Used mainly in residential and hospital settings particularly chronic wards of psychiatric hospitals (but increasing application in community schools).
Use of Premack's principle	High-probability behaviours are made conditional on some performance of low-probability behaviours.	Used where it is difficult to specify reinforcers in the usual way. Increasing levels of low-probability behaviours are usually sought in exchange for opportunities to perform high-probability behaviours.
Contingency contracts	An exchange of equally valued behaviours (which each party would like to see more of) is negotiated. The performance of one	Used in interpersonal problems – marital, work and relationship problems, conflict between parents and children.

Table 6.1   continued

	item is contingent upon the performance of an item from the other.	
Operant extinction	Removing available reinforcement from a response.	Used for attention-seeking behaviours, usually in combination with the positive reinforcement of incompatible behaviours.
Negative reinforcement	Aversive stimulation is maintained until desired behaviour is performed and then terminated.	Mainly used as a feature of broader contingency management programmes.
Punishment	A known aversive stimulus is presented on contingency and reduces the frequency or intensity with which a behaviour is performed.	Can be used as a suppressant of behaviours likely to interfere with programmes based on positive reinforcement. Punishment has the disadvantage that it strongly encourages escape and avoidance behaviours.
Satiation	Such an excess of reinforcing stimuli is provided that their reinforcing power is lost.	Used for low-level addictions, hoarding, and so on.
Shaping	Control of behaviour is shifted from one stimulus to another which resembles it fairly closely.	Used by the therapist to build on behaviours similar to those already in repertoire, and gradually change them, so that they more closely resemble the performance required.
Fading	Therapist-supplied reinforcement is gradually withdrawn to bring new behaviour under the control of naturally occurring (non-artificial) sources of reinforcement.	An essential feature of all reinforcement programmes. Especially important in residential work prior to discharge.
Over-learning and over-correction	This involves the intensive and over-rehearsal of an adaptive correction behaviour well beyond the level normally required. Aids clear discrimination.	Used (for example) as a special feature in programmes with enuretics. On the attainment of complete dryness, the client is encouraged to drink before bedtime, so that inhibiting responses are well-learned.

Table 6.1 continued

Attention to discriminative stimuli	The cues suspected to be eliciting behaviour are removed, or acted upon at an early state.	Should be a feature of all behavioural programmes. Particularly useful when problematic behaviour is known to occur predictably in given settings or situations.

7

RESPONSE CONTROL
TECHNIQUES

In the previous chapter attention was drawn to techniques that exert influence through specific alterations to the client's environment, such as changing the contingencies which surround him or her – producing new cues and new consequences which affect behaviour. Now we turn to a set of approaches which focus on the nature of the responses produced within a given set of contingencies, rather than to the stimuli themselves. These *response control* techniques (Bandura 1969) are directed towards the production, by direct teaching, of new and more adaptive motor, verbal, emotional and cognitive responses. In other words, they seek to change what a person does, feels and thinks in response to the environment within which problems arise.

Let us begin, as before, by locating ourselves on the assessment diagram, Figure 5.1 on p. 116. Response control techniques are mainly used where the answer to the question: 'are target behaviours already in repertoire at any significant level?' is 'no'. That is, when clients have either: (a) never learned to perform the types of response which it is thought are needed to solve their problems; or (b) where such responses have been learned in the past, but are now lost – as with certain psychiatric conditions and the associated effects of institutionalization; or (c) where, for whatever reason, the behaviours occur very infrequently or at a low level, and operant shaping is likely to be too labour-intensive an approach.

There are also occasions where responses are in excess – as in the case of aggressiveness, where either the therapist is unable to gain sufficient control over the contingencies supporting this behaviour, or the problem stems from behavioural deficits (the client never having learned how else to respond). These *prepotent* responses can also be brought under control by the teaching of new behaviours which are incompatible with the old (see p. 195).

Sometimes problematic behaviour is under the control of variables to which the therapist does not have ready access – for instance, when the client is influenced by his peer group, or when problems occur at work. Here, although ideally it is the contingencies supporting the problem which should be modified, any help given has to concentrate on assisting the client to modify these conditions for him or herself. Although it makes sense to attack the problem of bullying at school, or exploitation at work, by trying to change the behaviour of the bullies and the exploiters, this is quite often impossible, and so we are left with the option of changing the client's own responses so that bullying and exploitation become less reinforcing for those who engage in them.

The research evidence for each of the techniques listed in the summarizing Table 7.5 (p. 230) has already been reviewed (see Chapter 3). Reference to this foregoing material will be made as necessary, but this chapter will concentrate mainly on the practical application of these findings.

MODELLING AND SOCIAL SKILL TRAINING

Modelling is a technique that could easily be included in the social worker's repertoire of therapeutic methods. Arguments have already been put forward about the dangers of relying exclusively on the interpretation of problems and verbal descriptions of what needs to be done about them, and then expecting the client to come up with the new behaviours while his or her environment obligingly supports these new efforts. Modelling approaches are a way of bridging the gap between an understanding of what needs to be done and possessing the skills to do it.

Some authors draw a distinction between modelling and social skill training. While this is technically correct, because modelling theories attempt to explain how new responses are developed through observation alone, in most therapeutic programmes modelling is used in conjunction with rehearsal and selective feedback on performance. Also, since social workers are mainly concerned with deficits in the problem-solving performances of clients, the distinction between the two approaches virtually disappears.

STAGES IN MODELLING

When modelling is used in the way suggested above, with feedback and appropriate reinforcement, the process normally passes through the following stages.

(i) Identifying specific problems resulting from gaps in the client's behavioural repertoire, and deciding what new behaviours could be developed to fill these.

(ii) Dividing the target responses into their component parts (for example: coming into a room full of people; deciding who to stand next to and what to say; introducing oneself; getting in on the conversation; and so forth).

(iii) Identifying with the client any patterns in their thinking which may encourage misinterpretation of the motives of others and/or avoidance responses, e.g. 'people are looking at me because they can tell I don't belong here'.

(iv) Demonstrating to the client what a competent performance looks like; repeating any problematic parts of the sequence or going through it slowly and deliberately; emphasizing options and decision points.

(v) Encouraging the client to perform simple sequences, with the social worker shaping and correcting these as required.

(vi) Developing more complex performances by chaining together different sequences.

(vii) Paying attention to any problems of discrimination; that is, identifying any difficulties the client may have in knowing whether a certain piece of behaviour is appropriate for a given setting.

(viii) Gradually introducing difficulties likely to be found in real life as the client becomes more able to cope with these (for instance, not getting an immediate answer when trying to make new friends).

(ix) Gradual fading of artificially strong or explicit reinforcements.

(x) Supervising practice, or practical assignments on which the client reports back (for example, getting the client to initiate three short conversations or to ask for clarification from an official).

MODELLING TO REDUCE FEARS

Modelling can also be used to reduce maladaptive fear reactions (as in the case of animal or insect phobias). These, though trivial-sounding, can be crippling to people who avoid all the places where, say, spiders or dogs *might* be found, that is, just about everywhere.

The aim here is to present the client with a clear picture of someone coping reasonably well with the circumstances they fear. The learning components of such an approach could include any of the following. (a) Through watching and experiencing the usual emotions, the client's fear eventually subsides since nothing terrible happens. This is known as vicarious extinction and is a kind of exposure therapy (see below). (b) The client may learn new things about the feared objects or circumstances, or about how to handle them – in other words that dogs do not usually bite if approached confidently, that they usually respond to affection, and so on. Or in the case of fears about a social performance, the client can learn that there are 'tricks of the trade'. (c) Through 'imagining along' with the modelled performance, clients' expectations of themselves may change; they may repeatedly imagine themselves coping with such a situation so, in future, thinking about the stimulus conditions may not trigger such powerful emotional reactions and thoughts of escape (see discussion of perceived self-efficacy on p. 95).

OPTIMUM CONDITIONS FOR MODELLING

From the foregoing discussion and the previous section on the theoretical basis of modelling, the reader will have seen that attention needs to be paid to four different components if new learning is to occur efficiently:

(i) Characteristics of the modelled performance.
(ii) Cognitive components – how the client *interprets* the situations in which difficulties typically arise.
(iii) Characteristics of the matching response.
(iv) Feedback and reinforcement characteristics.

Taking each of these in turn, the ideal model is someone who can easily capture the client's attention and who has credibility in his or her eyes. This last point has little to do with formal authority. To the members of an intermediate treatment group the person with the highest status may be the toughest-sounding kid, and the worker will be wise to make use of this fact. Credibility in rehearsals is an important consideration and staff concerned in such programmes need to take precautions to ensure it. First, they can make sure that their own performances are not 'wooden', by practising beforehand, and not modelling embarrassment. Next, and again without going 'over the top', they can make sure that their performances include appropriate emotional expression.

Particularly in the early stages of modelling, the therapist is trying to teach coping skills, not mastery – which the client may conclude is beyond reach. The ideal performance is one of relaxed competency. It is also important to vary the models demonstrating coping skills so that the client is not left with stereotyped responses and can learn from a range of different styles. In this way learning is more likely to generalize.

Where complex tasks are being demonstrated, it may be useful to 'talk through' the performance so that the observers can see what features the model is attending to, and what forms the basis of his or her decision about how to behave next. If clients do the same, this may help them to remember what sequence follows the last: 'Right, here I go, the door's open so I don't bother to knock, several people are looking at me, that's fine ... smile ... wave to the only person I know ... now look expectant ... someone's coming over ... now for my name ...'.

The performance characteristics of the client need only a brief comment, since the things to pay attention to here are much the same as with any type of behavioural or cognitive-behavioural programme. First, the performance must be broken down into manageable stages. If the client feels more anxious as a result of participating in the programme, then a key element (lessening anxiety and engendering feelings of confidence) has been lost. Similarly, the worker must be ready to prompt new behaviour and then to reinforce approximations of it, *as* they are performed – not just at the end – because it may not be worth the wait.

The setting in which the programme is used is also important. No male teenager is going to practise less aggressive behaviour (which he may initially regard as 'cissy') if he thinks that his brother may enter the room at any moment. Few parents will care to practise handling their child differently, if their own parents (who may think such skills genetically endowed) can hear everything in the next room. Other people need to be either fully involved or completely excluded. A feeling of security is important, so that cultural norms about pretending, and practising things which, by all accounts, should some-how already have been learned, are not too seriously violated.

Feedback on approximate performances should always be couched in posi-tive terms. The concept of *shaping* (see p. 69) covers what is necessary here. Clients who already associate certain kinds of social behaviour with fear and embarrassment will be very sensitive to criticism, even where this is implicit. Elaborate explanations are best avoided. Showing clients what is meant, and prompting them by a re-enactment of the same, or a similar sequence, is much more effective.

The ultimate aim of any modelling programme is to bring newly acquired responses under the control of naturally-occurring reinforcers and of self-reinforcement. Attention and praise are often sufficient, particularly if the client accepts the need to develop new skills as likely to make life easier.

Closed circuit television is an ideal medium for modelling new behaviours. Using portable equipment (which now costs about the same as six wasted visits by a social worker), it is possible to produce lively, believable performances, which are intrinsically interesting to observers. Sequences can be 'frozen', re-run, played without sound to concentrate attention on the non-verbal element, or run without the picture to achieve the opposite effect. Here are some examples.

Case examples demonstrating the use of modelling techniques

Example 1

It was noted by social workers that patients in an acute psychiatric unit due for discharge, normally treated as individual cases, held a number of fears and concerns in common. It was therefore decided to bring together these clients in groups, further to define their misgivings and to rehearse with them ways of coping with these problems. The misgivings identified in preliminary discussions were as follows:

(i) What to say to people about an unexplained period of absence in psychia-tric hospital?
(ii) How to deal with the stilted behaviour of family and friends.
(iii) How to approach and try to make reparation to family members who may have suffered as a result of the client's mental illness.
(iv) How to overcome the fear of stigmatization at work, or by neighbours.
(v) How to prevent future relapse by seeking help early on.

(vi) How to deal with practical and financial matters.

Assessment

Discussion of these fears or problems in the group (n=7) suggested the following commonalities and/or deficits:

(i) Stigmatization: beliefs that people would somehow be able to tell that they had suffered an acute psychiatric episode just by looking at them; that in varying degrees they had somehow contributed to their illnesses, and that the illnesses were something to be ashamed of.

(ii) Trepidation regarding suggestions by staff that they might seize the initiative, be *direct* with relatives and friends and *ask* for help and understanding during rehabilitation.

(iii) A feeling of potential loss of control that would prevent them from seeking help to prevent relapse plus an associated view that they would not wish to waste their general practitioners' time with 'trivial' worries.

(iv) Lack of information on income support, housing matters and so forth.

Procedure

Eight sessions were scheduled, four within the first fortnight, then once per week, with a post-discharge meeting to review progress. The elements of the programme were as follows:

(i) A discussion of the nature, prevalence and known causes of relevant types of mental disorder focusing on its widespread nature, that is, the various mixtures of biological and stress factors known to create vulnerability. A psychiatrist was present to underline lack of culpability among the patients themselves. The most interesting discussions concerned matters of cause and effect and how it is possible for us to muddle them when feeling low or anxious, e.g. that in some cases where florid symptoms had created family problems and led to temporary estrangement, this was a product of illness and fear, not of deliberate intent or incompetent behaviour on their part. Two positive factors were identified in these sessions: (a) how much better for patients to be given information about mental illness directly and systematically, rather than in *ad hoc* ward encounters; (b) a feeling of relief that others had had similar experiences to their own.

(ii) Role play sessions based on common fears, e.g. meeting a neighbour who would say: 'well hello, haven't seen you around for some time, hear you've had a bit of trouble?' Or a rather busy GP figure who was to be induced into listening more carefully to the patient's fears and needs by a direct appeal based on these. Or a sticky encounter with over-solicitous relatives using the special calming voices reserved for people with psychiatric histories. Or 'earthing' a strange 'atmosphere' at work by an honest appeal

199

for help while settling back in. These sessions were made palatable by staff taking the lead initially and by trying to engender a humorous atmosphere by using exaggerated character roles (these faded to something more realistic later). The focus of these sessions was on basic assertion skills for difficult or stressful encounters: being direct but not over-forthright or aggressive; explaining feelings (the most difficult); making specific and unequivocal requests for help and support (see also p. 202).

(iii) Homework or outside assignments. Towards the end of the programme clients and staff negotiated first mildly challenging tasks (going in twos and threes to a local arts centre to enquire about activities and obtain leaflets); telephoning a friend or relative, or making an appointment with a doctor, the money advice centre, the social services department or a housing action group. Attendance remained high throughout the programme. The evaluation cited the importance of being *shown* how to do things rather than spoken to, and the importance of trying to take control of potentially threatening circumstances by planning and rehearsal (see also Trower *et al.* 1977).

Example 2

Paula Douglas had spent five of her 26 years in mental hospitals and psychiatric clinics of various kinds. She was diagnosed as schizophrenic and described as 'shy', 'withdrawn', 'self-preoccupied' and as being 'somewhat bizarre in her behaviour'. She avoided the centre of rooms as if they were mined; constantly hung her head; shuffled around the house; neglected dress and personal hygiene; and spent whole days in her room reading, refusing to eat, or to speak to anyone. This case was referred to social services for 'after-care' following discharge from a psychiatric unit and the failure of a course of rehabilitation therapy.

Assessment

Initially grudging conversation between Paula and the social worker revealed that she knew that her behaviour 'put people off', but that she was too shy to do much about it alone. She felt very conspicuous when confronted with new people or situations, and was ashamed of her psychiatric history.

It was decided not to delve further into the historical background of this problem, but to identify clearly one or two behavioural deficits, and try to remedy them.

Procedure

First, the view was put to Paula that people could only think her 'mad' if her behaviour put this idea into their heads. She found the notion that 'mad is as mad does' interesting, and a series of training sessions was set up with the explicit intention of showing her how to behave in the type of circumstances she found difficult.

Two basic items of behaviour capable of being built on later were selected: (i) walking confidently into a room and introducing herself to a visitor; (ii) giving non-verbal reinforcement to other people during a conversation, as a means of conveying interest and understanding, and so counteracting Paula's usually rather vacant appearance.

These two classes of behaviour were broken into their component parts and repeatedly modelled by two students. The students played counter-roles and also offered constructive criticism on each other's performance. The sessions became increasingly friendly and light hearted and always ended in a period of conversation about novels and various other cultural pursuits, known to interest the client.

After seven half-hour sessions Paula had mastered walking into rooms, and her mother was introduced into the programme. They were encouraged both to look for, and reinforce, behaviours of a similar kind throughout the rest of the day.

Believable, non-verbal signals of understanding were harder to establish. Paula's performance approximated to that of the modellers only vaguely and mechanically, and the initial programme had to be slowed down and rethought. Maintaining eye contact was discovered to be a primary problem and this was selectively reinforced with approval, initially by getting her to look at foreheads if she couldn't manage or hold eye-to-eye gazing. When low levels of eye contact had been established, Paula's other non-verbal behaviour improved substantially.

By the end of the students' placement, Paula had two new pieces of behaviour which she did not possess before, and her family showed increasing tolerance towards her, and an increasing interest in what else she might be capable of. She was eventually able to attend evening classes at a local technical college.

Conclusion

Modelling is a well-researched and effective technique for developing new behaviours and reducing the anxieties that often attach to inadequate social performance. One variant of it, social skills training, aims both to remedy particular deficits and to add other general-purpose skills to the client's repertoire. These techniques are being applied across a range of client groups and can be used in combination with other approaches to help with a range of different problems.

ASSERTION TRAINING

Assertion training is a widely used behavioural technique, based on a combination of modelling, rehearsal and operant reinforcement approaches. Its purpose is to teach people how to stand up for themselves without being aggressive. Since social workers, more than other professional groups, deal with the weak, the powerless and the put-upon, this technique has particular relevance for us. However, it would be naive indeed if, as a result of our interest in behaviour therapy, we came to see these states as entirely due to behavioural or psychological deficiencies. In their extreme form they are structural in origin, a corollary of the way society works. Such factors are unlikely to yield before anything but a concentrated political effort in which social workers, like any other citizens, are entitled to join. However, further down the scale there is much that can be done at an individual level. Not all oppression is due to the macro-effects of the political system; a broad range of everyday misery and oppression is psychological in origin. To a considerable extent, exploitation depends on the expectations held by the exploiter (that he will be successful), and on the compliant behaviour of the 'exploitee'. Social psychology has much to tell us about the effects of these behaviourally induced factors – as demonstrated by Milgram's (1974) dramatic conformity experiments and by a legion of studies where the verbal content presented to an audience is held constant, but the style, expression and behaviour of the performers are varied to produce markedly different audience reactions (Cohen 1964).

Assertion training can be carried out with individuals and groups and is relevant to a wide range of interpersonal problems. The approach has been well researched and a number of comparative and controlled studies exist, testifying to its effectiveness (McFall and Lillesand 1971; McFall and Marston 1970). It can be used both to increase assertion skills and to reduce aggressiveness in favour of assertiveness. However, before we proceed further we need a definition of assertiveness:

> Assertion involves direct expression of one's feelings, preferences, needs, or opinions in a manner that is neither threatening nor punishing toward another person. In addition, assertion does not involve an excessive amount of anxiety or fear. Contrary to popular opinion, assertion is not primarily a way to get what one wants, nor is it a way of controlling or subtly manipulating others. Assertion is the direct communication of one's needs, wants, and opinions without punishing, threatening, or putting down the other person.
>
> (Galassi and Galassi 1977:3)

I hope the foregoing has convinced the reader that assertiveness is a reasonable aim: that it enables others to know better where they stand with us; that it ensures clear messages about intentions, desires and opinions; above all, that such a style of behaviour is likely to condition the behaviour of others towards us. An appropriately assertive style also produces important internal effects. That is, we are likely to think and feel differently about ourselves as a result of behaving assertively. By letting other people see, through our behaviour, that we expect to be treated as a person of worth, we are also likely to affect our own evaluation of ourselves and what we are capable of. Here, then, is an example of a behavioural technique which follows research into the relationship between attitudes and behaviour (Cohen 1964), and suggests that the best way to improve self-esteem is to demonstrate and train clients in behaviour that signals a clear expectation of reasonable treatment.

Turning now to the training schemes themselves, assertion training programmes are likely to contain combinations of the following approaches.

(i) Assessment: problems are often confined to particular situations or settings (such as work or relationships) and no extra or special assessment is required. But in cases where there is a general inadequacy – as in the case of excessively shy or withdrawn clients – an assessment schedule such as the one reproduced in Figure 7.1 will give a better idea of the extent of the problem.

(ii) Discrimination training procedures: these can be used to teach the client to discriminate accurately between assertiveness, false compliance and aggression.

(iii) A modelling and rehearsal component: this is usually included so that the client is *shown* in a step-by-step fashion how to behave with different degrees of assertiveness, in different kinds of situation. The client will then rehearse and attempt to perform these behaviours him or herself, receiving positively couched feedback on successive approximations.

(iv) Attention needs also to be paid to the grading of tasks and assignments given, so that clients experience success rather than confirming their worst fears about themselves.

(v) A desensitization component: as with other modelling techniques, a major aim of an assertion training scheme is progressively to remove the fear that is associated with certain behaviour. This is usually done through gradually exposing the client to such situations, but in some cases extra help with relaxation may be required (see p. 228).

(vi) Generalization: active steps must be taken to ensure that therapeutic gains generalize to the everyday experiences and problems of the client. The best way of achieving this is to vary the format of the programme and give the client experience in progressively more realistic settings.

Now let us look at each of these items in more detail.

Assessment

To start with, the client can be asked to complete a schedule (see Figure 7.1 and Rathus 1970). He or she does this as fully as possible, adapting the headings to

Persons

Behaviours	Friends of the same sex	Friends of the opposite sex	Intimate relations, that is, spouse, boyfriend, girlfriend	Parents, in-laws, and other family members	Children	Authority figures, such as bosses, doctors, teachers	Business contacts, sales-staff, or waiters	Workmates, colleagues, and subordinates
Expressing positive feelings Give compliments								
Receive compliments								
Make requests, for instance ask for favours or help								
Express liking, love and affection						■	■	
Start and maintain conversations								
Self-affirmation Stand up for your legitimate rights								
Refuse requests								
Express personal opinions including disagreement								
Expressing negative feelings Express justified annoyance and displeasure								
Express justified anger								

Figure 7.1 Asserion self-assessment checklist

Source: Adapted from Galassi and Galassi (1977), by permission of The Human Sciences Press. Copyright © 1977.

particular circumstances, noting feelings and anxieties at the time of each incident, and the practical effects of a given pattern of behaviour. Also, when it would have been appropriate to behave as suggested in the chart, but he or she did not, note can be taken of what the consequences were.

Discrimination training

Some clients have difficulty in distinguishing between suitably assertive behaviour, aggressive behaviour and falsely compliant behaviour. They may see all kinds of outspokenness as nasty, or as 'asking for trouble', and may rationalize compliancy into just a question of 'good manners'. Usually, however, people know what they would like to be able to say and do (as evidenced by the familiar internal dialogues and self-chidings that go on *after* the occasion has passed by). In these cases, discrimination training is used partly to clarify the different types of behaviours, and partly to provide opportunities for helpful candour. Table 7.1 outlines the main difference between the three kinds of behaviours.

To start with, Table 7.2 gives a simple example of behaviours which the reader might like to categorize in line with Table 7.1 (answers are given at the bottom of the table).

Table 7.1 Key differences between non-assertive, assertive and aggressive behaviour

Non-assertiveness	Complying with illegitimate requests. Agreeing with opinions you don't share. Avoiding people because they may ask you to do things and you find it difficult to say 'no'. Failing to express your own opinions. Failing to make requests or to ask favours of others. Avoiding forthright statements – giving mixed, vague or confused messages.
Aggressiveness	Expressing strong feelings but for your own benefit. Dominating conversation with threats and demands, and adopting a behavioural style that is dominating, punishing and demeaning to other people. Giving no consideration to the other person's rights, needs or feelings. Possibly resorting to verbal abuse and often making an attempt to humiliate the other person. Failing to acknowledge, or act upon, the other person's point of view. Adopting a threatening bodily stance, with eye contact overlong and glaring, and gestures which appear to be the forerunners of physical attack.
Assertiveness	Expressing feelings directly, but without accompanying threats. Politely refusing unreasonable requests.

Making reasonable requests.

Expressing opinions, while not automatically agreeing with those of others.

Standing up for your own rights and needs, and making clear your wants, while making no attempt to impinge those of others.

Performing these behaviours without undue fear or anxiety.

Being relaxed when asking for what is reasonable or legitimately due.

Expressing anger and affection as appropriate.

Maintaining appropriate eye contact.

Matching body posture to mood.

Table 7.2 Simple assertiveness discrimination exercise*

Your spouse or friend arrives late and the meal you have prepared is spoiled. You feel annoyed.

You say:

Response		*Tick one*
(1)	Hello, have you been busy? You must be hungry, what can I get you to eat?	(a) assertive (b) non-assertive (c) aggressive
(2)	I hope you have a good explanation, I've been waiting for an hour and the meal I made is spoiled now.	(a) assertive (b) non-assertive (c) aggressive
(3)	I wonder you bothered to come home at all, where the hell have you been? This is the last time I ever cook for you. You're just too inconsiderate to bother with.	(a) assertive (b) non-assertive (c) aggressive

Answers

(1) (b) non-assertive: feelings are being disguised and there is a pretence that nothing of importance has happened.

(2) (a) assertive: feelings are duly expressed about the inconvenience caused and the consequences of it are spelled out (dinner is spoiled) but there is an opportunity to explain.

(3) (c) aggressive: sarcasm, threats and denunciation are used and there is also a reference to general failings.

---

* With a little practice it is easy to think up situations where an assertive response is required, and then to identify its aggressive and non-aggressive alternatives.

MODELLING APPROPRIATE NON-VERBAL BEHAVIOUR

The principles of modelling and the verbal component of assertive behaviour have already been covered (see p. 195), and so here we shall concentrate on the non-verbal factors that make up a successful performance. Particular attention should be paid to the following.

(i) Stance and posture: it is difficult for clients to begin to make an assertive response unless they face the person they are to address. If seated, leaning forward slightly demonstrates interest, concern and lack of fear.

(ii) Eye contact: if the client finds prolonged eye contact difficult, he or she should be persuaded to practise it at a distance and gradually move closer to the other person for increasingly long periods of time. Another way of beginning is to get the client to focus on some other part of the face and progress gradually towards eye–eye contact (as in the case example on p. 200). Eye contact – conveying sincerity and lack of fear – is an important characteristic of assertive behaviour.

(iii) Facial expression: the client can practise this alone in front of a mirror. Using this method (or closed circuit TV if available and appropriate) will teach clients the difference between what they feel like inside and *think* they are conveying, and what they actually *look* like. Sometimes the difference is marked.

(iv) Use of gestures: confident but not exaggerated hand gestures do much for a social performance. These must not be aggressive – as striking the palm of the hand is, for instance – for the key point, as with facial expression, is that gestures should be congruous with other behaviour. This is a matter of practice and appropriate feedback from the therapist.

(v) Voice level and tone: it is not uncommon to meet clients with loud voices who think it unlikely that they can be heard, and clients with quiet voices who think themselves perfectly audible to anyone *really* interested in listening. Tape recorders are a useful way of dealing with this problem, as the client can hear, and try to improve upon playbacks. In addition to an appropriate voice level, appropriate inflection adds conviction to a performance.

(vi) Accent: many people are afraid to speak up because they are ashamed of their accents. This is particularly true in Britain, where accent and dialect carry strong social class connotations. A little 'cognitive restructuring' is required here. Express the view that the important consideration is whether a person speaks clearly and can get his or her meaning across.

REINFORCEMENT PROCEDURES

As with the other techniques discussed in this chapter, the key principles involved in application are: simple tasks to begin with; a clearly modelled performance which is believable without being elaborate; reinforcement for usefully approximate matching-responses, together with helpful feedback to help the client improve. The programme then proceeds in step-by-step fashion to the point where real-life assignments are possible. Before the client undertakes complex assignments or tries out his new skills in situations which really matter, it may be useful to equip him or her with a range of responses for dealing with rebuffs and unexpected reactions: the principle of 'immunization'.

DESENSITIZATION FACTORS IN ASSERTION TRAINING

Another reason why people feel unable to assert themselves is that they fear the emotional and behavioural consequences of so doing. Therefore, it may be useful to try to analyse with the client exactly what he or she *expects* to happen as a result of self-assertion and to point out any inconsistencies or exaggerations in these beliefs. Often clients believe that their condition of lack of social competence is inborn, or is an unalterably-fixed part of their personality. While this is not so, a lifelong experience of kowtowing to other people is not easily set aside. Fear and anxiety will be partly conditioned through previous bad experiences, and any escape or avoidance responses which reduce this fear will have been negatively reinforced. Alternative ways of reducing anxiety must be employed.

This reduction of anxiety is partly handled through the therapist's arrangement of a gradual progression from simple to demanding tasks. Such a procedure not only aids the acquisition of new responses, but also acts as a kind of desensitization therapy (see p. 227), the client feeling increasingly relaxed as the performance improves, and a new, benign association is gradually built up. However, care must be taken to ensure that clients do not get out of their depth too quickly, with the result that the old, vicious circle is reinstated.

Once the new assertive responses have been learned, they may be regularly reinforced in place of avoidance behaviour, since their deployment will reduce both anxiety and the often-reported sensation of having feelings 'bottled up'. These assignments are best preplanned with the client under the following headings: thoughts, fears, relaxation, monitoring the performance, consequences.

Case example

Assertion training was used with Mr Thomas. He felt unable to do any of the following.

  (i) Refuse unreasonable requests from his less conscientious workmates to do their work after finishing his own.
 (ii) Refuse overtime when he had other plans.
(iii) Compliment his wife in any way.

(iv) Initiate sexual intercourse.

(v) Speak up when it was his turn at the bar, in a meeting, or in a group of friends.

(vi) Check his change in shops, or ask for clarification from shop assistants when buying something.

The problems that occurred at home were dealt with by a contract (see p. 180), and the work-related items became the main focus of work since they caused frustration which the client was apt to take out on his wife.

Procedure

Progress was very halting to begin with, but when the scheme was transferred to a meeting room at the social services office, and an agreement made not to discuss the details of the programme with his wife, things improved dramatically. Typical problem-sequences were analysed and re-enacted with the aid of a student, with the emphasis on how to talk to the foreman when fixing which days in the week would be available for overtime. Key phrases were written up on charts and Mr Thomas made his own notes for later study. In the initial stages considerable praise was required for quite small gains. Mr Thomas's first assignment was to accompany the therapist to a local tobacconist, buy cigarettes and check his change in front of the shopkeeper (not being able to do this, despite having previously been given short change, seemed to be of symbolic importance to him). He achieved it first go, but with considerable blushing. Some help was given with relaxation to overcome this (see p. 229), and after a while conversation about the weather and so forth was included in the assignment, without further difficulties. Mr Thomas tackled his foreman after five weeks (seven sessions), and on his own initiative mentioned to his workmates (who were apparently sitting around doing little or nothing) that he would not help them later if they got behind with their work. The main positive effect of this programme was on the marital relationship, since Mr Thomas came home on time, as planned, and was a much less frustrated and angry person.

GROUP APPLICATIONS

There are many advantages to carrying out assertion training in groups. To begin with, the client realizes that his or hers is not a unique or isolated problem. Group training also provides opportunities to practise new responses in front of an understanding audience of fellow sufferers – an audience, moreover, well aware of all the tricks of self-deception which excessively shy people make use of: 'I didn't really mind going along with them.' In addition, trainees at different stages can learn from each other, and may be encouraged by the progress of other group members. Additionally, the range of feedback the client is able to receive on his attempts to be assertive is much greater. Against this must be balanced the fact that having a number of clients together, each perhaps with subtly different problems, perhaps inclined to criticize rather than to facilitate, and perhaps inclined to reinforce each other's avoidance behaviour, could lead to the sessions becoming a club for the socially disabled. Everything depends upon selection; the establishment of clear rules for group behaviour, and the balance the leader is able to strike between the encouragement of individuals and the control of the group as a whole. Alberti and Emmons (1970) report on experiments suggestive of the following conclusions: two therapists (ideally of different sexes) are better than one; frequent sessions are best (they suggest twice-weekly sessions of one-and-a-half hours each as an ideal). The enthusiasm of these authors is supported elsewhere by research into the effectiveness of this technique. Absenteeism and drop-out rates are generally very low, given the emotional demands made by this method.

DECISIONS ABOUT ASSERTIVENESS

I can think of few worse fates than being surrounded by people constantly and reflexively asserting their needs, wants and preferences – even if not directly at my expense – when no one is set to deprive them of anything. The important point to stress throughout training is that an assertive reaction is an *option*. Sometimes relationships can be improved by one party deliberately *refraining* from forthrightness in conditions where the other person knows full well that he or she has no right to expect an extra helping of tolerance or forbearance. Through assertion training we are really extending the clients' choices of available responses, so that they know they can assert themselves when they choose and when it matters – that is, when they are too often called upon to deny their true feelings or to bear more than their fair share of the emotional costs of living in harmony with other people.

SELF-MANAGEMENT AND SELF-CONTROL TECHNIQUES

The cognitive-behavioural field has recently witnessed an upsurge of interest in self-help programmes of various kinds over the last decade or so. Some of the theoretical reasons for this interest have already been reviewed: the development of social learning and other cognitive-mediational theories of behaviour, for example. In addition, as more people have begun to apply behavioural principles in their work, the field has opened up to include settings far removed from laboratory and clinic-based programmes. The practical problems posed by this are clearly identified in this quotation:

> How can you ensure that desired behaviors will occur at times and in
> places where you can neither prompt nor reinforce the behavior? How

can you get someone to do something – over there, in some other time or place – when you cannot intervene over there in that setting?

(Risley 1977:71)

An alternative to the use of mediators (for there are many settings inaccessible to them, too), and to reliance on generalization-effects to cover behaviour in natural settings, is to teach behavioural principles to the client and enlist his or her help in administering a suitable programme. Anything which promises to extend the range of behavioural methods is an attractive proposition, but, once again, caution is necessary. A principal ingredient of 'traditional' behavioural approaches has been the attempt to control contingencies in the client's environment directly. Might not the effect of leaving this complicated task to the client be that we are led down the primrose path towards ill-designed and sloppily monitored programmes – as other disciplines have been before us?

There are three possible safeguards against this possibility. The first is that behavioural self-control programmes tend to be monitored and evaluated rather more carefully than other kinds of self-help approaches. The second comes from a corresponding emphasis on the concreteness and specificity of the assignments given to the client, so that he or she is in no doubt as to how to respond. The third stems from the level of training given to clients in the procedures they are to apply to themselves and the amount of time given to rehearsal. It follows, then, that these are likely to be demanding programmes for clients, and so they are probably best reserved for people who express a clear desire to change, but who perhaps do not know how best to go about it, or for people who have hitherto been unwilling to pay the price of change, but may make the effort if a stage-by-stage approach is adopted. Alternatively, in marginal cases, it may be possible to design small-scale pilot programmes which give an experience of success and opportunities for reinforcement and shaping.

The general aims of self-control programmes are to teach clients about the environmental factors that influence behaviour, and to widen the range of appropriate responses which they can make in the face of these.

Here, in more detail, is the range of approaches that can be used in such programmes.

(i) The client can be taught about eliciting stimuli (Sds) which may 'trigger' unwanted behaviour. These may be identifiable if the client fills out an ABC chart (see p. 122), especially if he or she is encouraged to keep a record of the thoughts occurring prior to the performance of unwanted behaviour.

(ii) Clients can be taught about the particular contingencies affecting them, with a view to changing these, or substituting more appropriate responses. For example, connections can be made between a client's excessive desire to please, her tendency to volunteer for extra work and the hurtful criticism which she receives when, inevitably, she fails to meet the quota.

(iii) New associations between activities and places, which provoke fear and avoidance in the client at present, can be built up by the selective use of positive images. Some people hardly ever allow themselves pleasant reveries – 'laurelizing' I call these psychologically necessary episodes of self-congratulation.

(iv) Where external reinforcement for adaptive behaviour is weak or unavailable, clients can be taught how to reinforce themselves, following agreed or pre-rehearsed procedures.

(v) Cognitive techniques are available, which seek to change clients' expectations about the efficacy of their own behaviour and its likely outcome (see p. 213).

Here is an example which relates particularly to items (i), (ii) and (iii) above. The instructions set out below were used with a group of chronic night-time worriers and insomniacs:

(a) Lie down, intending to go to sleep *only* when you are sleepy.

(b) Do not use your bed for anything except sleep, that is, do not read, watch television, eat or worry in bed. Sexual activity is the only exception to this rule. On such occasions the instructions are to be followed afterwards when you intend to go to sleep.

(c) If you find yourself unable to go to sleep, get up and go into another room. Stay up as long as you wish and then return to the bedroom to sleep. Although we do not want you to watch the clock, we want you to get out of bed if you do not fall asleep *quickly*. Remember the goal is to associate your bed with falling asleep quickly. If you are in bed more than ten minutes without falling asleep and have not gotten up, you are not following this instruction.

(d) If you still cannot fall asleep, repeat step (c). Do this as often as necessary throughout the night.

(e) Set your alarm to get up at the same time every morning, irrespective of how much sleep you get during the night. This will help your body acquire a consistent sleep rhythm.

(f) Do not sleep during the day.

(Bootzin 1977:189)

Programmes of this type have also been used to control compulsive eating. In these cases the client may eat as often as he or she likes, but only at the table – which must be properly set. As soon as the meal or snack is finished, the table must be cleared and everything put away. Set meal times must be observed, however many snacks have been taken. This sort of scheme does away with absent-minded nibbling, and with any self-deception about how much food has actually been consumed. In time it introduces a new set of discriminative stimuli (table, knife and fork, set mealtimes and so on), and eventually establishes a new set of associations – eating at particular times of day rather than at idle moments, and eating in particular places.

The principle used in both the previous examples is that of teaching the client how to reprogramme the environment so that it gives maximum support for adaptive behaviours.

Another method of building up, or maintaining, a low-probability behaviour is to train the client to reinforce him or herself. In some cases this can be done with the aid of a contract or schedule which specifies certain rewards for the completion of approximate tasks. Later, self-administered material reinforcers are faded in favour of rewarding self-statements or mental images and associations. Here clients are given as much practice as possible in visualizing themselves obtaining control over certain behaviour or situations – say, being introduced to someone attractive and holding his or her attention during the subsequent conversation. We all like to imagine ourselves performing well from time to time. In self-reinforcement this is brought under control, so that scenes are imagined contingent upon an adaptive sequence of behaviour. Walter Mitty-type fantasies are to be avoided: the aim is to get the client to visualize a pleasant but *believable* scene as a consequence of having performed the target behaviour. This also produces a new association between these behaviours and the pleasant sensation of mental self-congratulation. (Cognitive procedures of this kind are discussed more fully below.)

A critical factor in self-control programmes is the level of monitoring by the therapist. There is little point in giving the client a list of instructions and leaving him to get on with it. Time limits should be set on all homework assignments and the client's levels of achievement noted, and appropriately reinforced by praise, references to progress, and to the new options open to the client as a result of his efforts. Clients also report that they visualize the social worker's likely reaction to their behaviour as they perform it, and the more cues to appropriate behaviour of this kind there are the better. This depends upon very clear instructions to the client from the worker, and on time spent rehearsing what the client's reactions to setback and obstacles should be.

Both the nature of the job, and the well-established concern of social workers to involve clients as fully as possible in decisions regarding their treatment, mean that they should quickly feel at home with this kind of approach. In addition, there is a growing empirical literature suggestive of the fact that full participation by clients greatly affects outcome.

THE COGNITIVE COMPONENTS OF THERAPY

This is the new frontier, but there has been a considerable amount of experimentation already, and there are emerging trends worth reporting (see Meichenbaum 1974, 1977; Scott 1989; BABCP 1993).

The aim of cognitive-behavioural procedures is to modify the following:

(i) Negatively selective perceptions.

 (ii) Irrational thoughts and thinking styles.
(iii) Self-talk and 'internal dialogues'.
(iv) Catastrophic imagery associated with particular behaviours and settings.
 (v) Maladaptive emotional reactions – to the extent that these are cued and maintained by thought patterns and thinking styles.
(vi) Deficits in self-reinforcement.

The main theoretical assumption here is that maladaptive cognitive events (interpretations, attributions, beliefs) trigger maladaptive emotional reactions and behaviour, and that it is possible to alter this by changing the cognitive events that mediate stimulus–response connections. A representation of this model is given in Figure 7.2 on p. 216.

There may be occasions when cognitive events themselves are the target of modification – as in the case of obsessive thoughts and ruminations, and accompanying images relating to future disasters; conditions found in psychotic disorders, cases of clinical depression and of obsessive-compulsive neurosis. Also, and at a less intense level, cognitive events become the target of modification where thoughts and images about failure inhibit social performances which the client might otherwise carry out reasonably well. However, in most cases we are interested to hypothesize about relations between cognitive and motor behaviour because we want to influence the latter – to change what people do; and here it must be noted that directly changing what people do often changes the accompanying thoughts and feelings. Therefore, in my view, the sensible approach in cognitive-behavioural therapy is to experiment with it carefully, as a more explicit, additional dimension of conventional programmes.

Case example

Readers are referred to p. 152 for the basic details of this case. It featured a young woman with a persistent fear of vomiting in public which in her terms was 'ruining her life'. The first stage in assessment revealed details to warm the cockles of any psychoanalyst's heart, viz.: a curious mixture of mollycoddling and strictness from Calvinist parents; a desire on their part that she should fulfil all the ambitions sacrificed by them for her sake, and be grateful. She volunteered that she 'had had to swallow so much' in her life (!). A more prosaic version of the aetiology of this problem was that anxiety and unpredictability were a feature of her childhood and adolescence and that her determination to 'do the right thing' carried with it physiological consequences, mediated by anxiety and maintained by 'catastrophic thinking'.

The treatment programme was an amalgam of cognitive techniques and gentle exposure methods with the following main elements:

— A plain explanation as to how anxiety (as a mild version of the fight/flight mechanism) causes drying of the mouth, constriction of the larynx and tension in the stomach – all incompatible with the easy swallowing and digestion of food.

— A concentration on the fact that her *preparations* to obviate a minor risk (vomiting in public) were the major part of her problem. Her worst fear had never been realized.

— A brief introduction to the principles of relaxation therapy (see p. 229) accompanied by increasingly challenging food-swallowing exercises (iced water to begin with) in gradually more demanding circumstances, e.g. sitting near people in the canteen rather than with them (see desensitization on p. 227).

— Reality testing: singling out one or two friends and confiding in them about her problem. Contrary to her expectations they were more than willing to help in the above exercises.

— Assertion training: learning how to take control of where she sat while consuming food; in whose company; dealing with enquiries about her difficulties over food; excusing herself; explaining herself on her return and so forth.

This mixed programme of cognitive reappraisal and desensitization began to show results in three weecks, the client then taking it over and extending it herself. Interestingly, though originally a difficulty over swallowing food in public, the resolution of this had much wider consequences for the client's social life and sense of well-being.

The main cognitive techniques most directly relevant to social work are: (i) self-instructional training; (ii) stress inoculation training; (iii) cognitive restructuring; (iv) covert conditioning approaches; (v) thought-stopping procedures. Each of these methods is discussed in more detail below, but it should be remembered that this is not an exhaustive list, and that the trend is towards combinations of methods and generalized practice.

SELF-INSTRUCTIONAL TRAINING

A major premiss of self-instructional training is that what we say to ourselves – that is, the content of our 'internal dialogues' – cues, shapes and maintains our overt behaviour. The Russian psychologists Vygotsky (1962) and Luria (1961) suggested that this important relationship between language, thought and behaviour develops in three stages during socialization. In early childhood, behaviour is controlled mainly by the speech of others (particularly adults). During the next stage, the child begins to use his or her own developing speech to regulate behaviour (as in the play commentaries of young children). Finally, this function is assumed by the cognitive accompaniments of speech, and speech 'goes inside'. It is these sequences of cognitive cues to behaviour that we seek to influence.

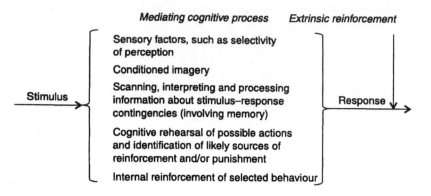

Figure 7.2 A cognitive-mediational view of behaviour

In this view, behavioural excesses and deficits can result from inadequacies in cognitive controls over behaviour (lack of self-governing responses in the first case; lack of self-encouraging responses in the second). A second proposition is that it is possible to remedy these deficits by teaching clients to reprogramme their responses with the aid of appropriate *self-statements*. Meichenbaum (1977) refers humorously to this approach as 'teaching clients to talk to themselves'.

In problems resulting from impulsiveness, clients are instructed to interrupt the sequence of behavioural and cognitive events that leads to, say, an aggressive reaction, by deliberately thinking, or saying aloud a prerehearsed statement, and/or visualizing a series of images which are incompatible with the behaviour they are about to embark upon. The emphasis in self-instructional training is on coping skills, which the client brings into operation in situations which they find difficult. These coping skills are maintained by cognitive cues, reinforcing images and by covertly or overtly recited instructions, covering each step in the sequence. These techniques are, therefore, often combined with social skills training and modelling approaches (as in the case described next).

Case example

This programme was designed to help control paranoid ideas in a 34-year-old ex-psychiatric patient living in a hostel. The client (also under treatment for chronic mutism and social withdrawal) complained initially that noises coming from other rooms seemed excessively loud, that there was more laughter to be heard than before and that she felt much of this was directed at her. She also listened intently to silences because she felt people had lowered their voices so that she could not hear. The hostel staff knew of nothing unusual in the behaviour of the other residents.

Procedure

The seemingly irrational beliefs were the first focus, and the inconsistencies in the client's account were confronted directly. These were that Laura felt people were talking about her both when they were behaving noisily and when they were quiet – it was pointed out repeatedly that she couldn't win with this belief. The idea that she was a person likely to excite this constant level of interest was discussed. The client was asked to think about her own interest in other individuals and whether this could ever be concentrated on one person for twenty-four hours. The client, grudgingly, thought not, and when pressed she laughed (an infrequent response) and admitted that it would he boring. What then was so especially interesting about her? Her answer was that she looked strange and didn't talk to anyone – which was true to some extent.

The client was then shown videotapes of herself from early on in treatment, when she looked dishevelled and had a kind of 'Old English sheepdog' haircut, covering her eyes. These pictures were then compared with more up-to-date tapes, showing a considerable improvement in self-presentation. Next the client was reminded of the effort she was making (weekly sessions, homework assignments, letter writing, and exercises in reading aloud). Wasn't she trying very hard to overcome her difficulties and become more sociable? Did all this effort count for so little? Had she not reported that other residents and staff answered her when she forced herself to greet them? The following self-instruction sequence was also agreed and the client was taught to review it, item by item, whenever she felt her ideas of reference returning.

(i) Steady now, six deep breaths, it's only because I'm on my own and paying too much attention to what is going on outside my room that I am reading things into those noises that are not really there. Everyone does it from time to time, I do it too much.

(ii) I think people are talking about me because I don't have much to do with them. This may happen occasionally but definitely not all the time and among so many different people.

(iii) I am trying very hard to overcome my shyness but I am not ready to cope with talking to other people yet – one day I will be, that is my aim, and that is why I am working on these problems.

(iv) I look better now than I have ever looked, and I intend to go on looking after myself in future. This is one problem I am on top of.

(v) Right, I agree that this is all off the point and not worth worrying about. I have better things to do – like one of my homework exercises ... (client instructed to repeat reading exercise).

217

Laura first read from these typewritten instructions, and eventually memorized parts of them.

Use of imagery

Laura found that relaxing, and deliberately engaging in a favourite fantasy (pony trekking, or grooming a horse meticulously stage by stage), were more effective than homework exercises as an activity to follow after going through her instructions. Two further images were made use of. First, a visualization based on videotape recordings was used, comparing her appearance and verbal skill level of nine months ago with today. This image was used whenever she felt unduly conspicuous or had thoughts about derogatory comments by other people. Second, she was offered an image of the therapist praising her for the effort she was putting into her work, reminding her of the progress already made. In seven weeks the ideas of reference disappeared, although they occasionally reappeared when under considerable stress – when she was asked to telephone. In addition she had abandoned a grisly self-punishing ritual of repeatedly sticking pins into her arm as atonement for whatever her neighbours were supposed to he criticizing her for.

STRESS INOCULATION TRAINING AND SELF-INSTRUCTION

These techniques involve therapists in rehearsing coping skills with clients, preparatory to entering into a stressful situation. They are used mainly in programmes designed to combat maladaptive fear and phobias, where research is suggesting that rapid exposure to the threatening stimulus – with the client remaining in the stressful conditions using prerehearsed coping mechanisms – is a faster and more effective treatment approach with many clients than desensitization (Marks 1971, 1975; Beck et al. 1985). Orne (1965) introduced the concept of *immunization* in his discussion of the importance of changing the beliefs of clients about their ability to cope with stress given appropriate rehearsal, an emphasis that should remind readers (see p. 95) of Bandura's theories regarding the importance of modifying efficacy and outcome expectations (Bandura 1977). Table 7.3 shows a typical schedule of self-instruction, which came into operation after appropriate rehearsal with the therapist of the different elements in the process of confronting a particular stress.

A further consideration when using self-statements in this way is the voice clients use to talk to themselves. We are all familiar with the 'sound' of our parent's voice inside our heads admonishing us, and with the experience of 'hearing' ourselves praised and having our views supported by figures noted for their sanity and intelligence (I always use Lord Soper). Here is an example of what stress and panic feel like from the inside:

As I stand talking to the audience, I hope that my mind and voice will

Table 7.3 Self-statements

Preparing for a stressor	What is it you have to do? You can develop a plan to deal with it. Just think about what you can do about it. That's better than getting anxious. No negative self-statements; just think rationally. Don't worry: worry won't help anything. Maybe what you think is anxiety is eagerness to confront the stressor.
Confronting and handling a stressor	Just psych yourself up – you can meet this challenge. You can convince yourself to do it. You can reason your fear away. One step at a time: you can handle the situation. Don't think about fear; just think about what you have to do. Stay relevant. This anxiety is what the doctor said you would feel. It's a reminder to use your coping exercises. Relax, you're in control. Take a slow deep breath.
Coping with the feeling of being overwhelmed	When fear comes, just pause. Keep the focus on the present; what is it you have to do? Label your fear from 0 to 10 and watch it change. You should expect your fear to rise. Don't try to eliminate fear totally; just keep it manageable.
Reinforcing self-statements	It worked; you did it. Wait until you tell your therapist (or group) about this. It wasn't as bad as you expected. Your damn ideas – that's the problem. When you control them, you control your fear. It's getting better each time you use the procedures. You can be pleased with the progress you're making. You did it!

Source: Meichenbaum (1974)

function properly, that I won't lose my balance and everything else will function. But then my heart starts to pound, I feel pressure build up in my chest as though I'm ready to explode, my tongue feels thick and heavy, my mind feels foggy and then goes blank. I can't remember what I have just said or what I am supposed to say. Then I start to choke. I can barely push the words out. My body is swaying; my hands tremble. I start to sweat and I am ready to topple off the platform. I feel terrified and I think that I will probably disgrace myself.

(Beck and Emery 1985:3–4)

COGNITIVE RESTRUCTURING

The reader has already been shown an attempt to correct a disabling belief by confronting the client with arguments about its illogicality (see p. 217). Techniques of this kind depend very much on the pioneering work of cognitive therapists, such as Beck (1970), and more particularly, on the rational-emotive approach of Albert Ellis (1977, 1979). The main theoretical assumption in this approach is that beliefs, apart from being situation-specific, cognitive and emotional accompaniments to behaviour, are themselves organized into systems, which have a durable effect on behaviour across a *range* of settings. The logical corollary of this is that if we can correct these faulty beliefs, or faulty thinking styles, then we can change problematic behaviour. The cognitive notion of *thinking style* is quite close to the behavioural notion of *learning history*, that is, the sum total of learning experiences which the individual is known to have undergone. It is easy to see how a particularly disjointed learning history, resulting from perverse or depressing childhood and family experiences, educational failures and so forth, can lead to a pervasively negative view of the world which, by the usual procedure of the self-fulfilling prophecy, is regularly confirmed. Ellis has noted several unnatural patterns of thinking, such as 'awfulizing' – believing that it is *awful* not always to meet targets – or the belief that surrounding circumstances are always part of a mischievous conspiracy against one's aims. Readers could probably add to such a list from their own experience. For purposes of illustration, I offer the 'Eeyore syndrome':

> 'Sometimes,' said Eeyore, 'when people have quite finished taking a person's house, there are one or two bits which they don't want and are rather glad for the person to take back, if you know what I mean. So I thought if we just went – '
> 'Come on,' said Christopher Robin, and off they hurried, and in a very little time they got to the corner of the field by the side of the pine-wood, where Eeyore's house wasn't any longer.
> 'There!' said Eeyore. 'Not a stick of it left! Of course, I've still got all this snow to do what I like with. One mustn't complain.'
>
> (Milne 1928:11)

Marzillier, in a very useful research review, summarized the aims and methods of the cognitive therapies as follows:

> Thus both Beck and Ellis regard change in fundamental cognitive structures and beliefs as the ultimate goal of therapy. Beck *et al.* (1978) describe the aims of therapy as 'to identify, reality-test and correct maladaptive, distorted conceptualizations and the dysfunctional beliefs (schemes) underlying these cognitions'; and Ellis (1977) sees therapy as needing to produce a 'profound cognitive and philosophic change in

clients' basic assumptions, especially their absolutistic, demanding, masturbatory, irrational ways of viewing themselves, others and the world'.

(Marzillier 1980:251)

The main approach in attempts to change irrational belief systems is clearly
to identify and exemplify such patterns for the client; to rehearse with him or
her alternative views of reality, and alternatives to negative self-statements.
This can be augmented with practice in different styles of thinking (as discussed
on p. 156), cued by predecided self-statements, and maintained by self-
instruction schedules and appropriate self-reinforcement. Here is an example
of a cognitive therapist trying by very direct means to render a client more
aware of the automatic and illogical nature of her thoughts about the past and
the future. Such a direct focus has been unusual in most forms of social
casework (family therapy is a possible exception) because of the status we have
always accorded to the 'feelings over facts' principle of the psychoanalytic
model (Hollis 1964).

THERAPIST:	Why do you want to end your life?
PATIENT:	Without Raymond, I am nothing . . . I can't be happy without Raymond . . . But I can't save our marriage.
THERAPIST:	What has your marriage been like?
PATIENT:	It has been miserable from the very beginning . . . Raymond has always been unfaithful . . . I have hardly seen him in the past five years.
THERAPIST:	You say that you can't be happy without Raymond . . . Have you found yourself happy when you are with Raymond?
PATIENT:	No, we fight all the time and I feel worse.
THERAPIST:	You say you are nothing without Raymond. Before you met Raymond, did you feel you were nothing?
PATIENT:	No, I felt I was somebody.
THERAPIST:	If you were somebody before you knew Raymond, why do you need him to be somebody now?
PATIENT:	[puzzled] Hmmm . . .

(Beck 1976:289–90)

To such challenges to irrationality must be added practice in alternative
ways of *behaving*, since, as we have seen, extrinsic reinforcement for alternative
behaviours is likely to affect thinking patterns – or at least to give weight to
discussions about their effects. Similarly, the evaluation of such programmes
should include a behavioural indicator (see p. 127) if we are to avoid the old
problem of working with purely subjective data.

One further word of caution. Certain well-established, and presumably functional, delusional patterns in psychiatric cases are unlikely to yield to anything; and excessive demands in therapeutic programmes could constitute exactly the kind of 'expressed emotion' conditions known to cause relapse. Nevertheless, with less extreme cases, good results are being recorded across a range of problems and client groups (Ellis 1979). Stern (1978), for example, combines cognitive restructuring techniques with positive self-statements, social skills training and a simple differential reinforcement programme managed by the husband of the client, in a case of mild depression. (But note that in unsupervised settings and in cases of any severity, safety – best secured by adequate anti-depressant medication – is of paramount importance.)

COVERT CONDITIONING APPROACHES

Counter-conditioning techniques (the application of stronger, incompatible stimuli to weaken maladaptive conditioned responses) predate cognitive approaches, and their application is reviewed on p. 223. Covert counter-conditioning (which relies upon the same principles but uses *images* rather than overt stimuli) is discussed here so that it can be seen for what it is – a cognitive technique.

Covert conditioning techniques are of two kinds. First, there are the *positive* techniques, where the clients are trained to visualize themselves coping well with a particular fear-provoking circumstance and receiving reinforcement. Alternatively, they can be trained to imagine a prerehearsed scene which they find pleasant, and to relax while under stress. Training usually takes the form of just clarifying the image, with practice at summoning this on cue, and then visualizing the circumstance that arouses the fear reaction and countering this with the positive image. Practice *in vivo* usually follows reported competence with this technique. An interesting development of this approach involves the training of problematically sexually deviant clients (for example, convicted sex-offenders) in image-switching during masturbation. At the point of no return, the deviant image – for instance of a child – is replaced by some other suitable, adaptively erotic scene, so that orgasm is paired repeatedly with this, and it eventually acquires reinforcing properties of its own (see Laws and O'Neill 1981). Such approaches have a place in wider behavioural programmes concentrating on the stimulus-conditions in which the behaviour is more likely to occur.

Second, *covert sensitization* procedures may be employed. These techniques use punishing and negatively reinforcing images to develop avoidance responses. They are applied to maladaptive behaviours, such as dependence on alcohol or drugs, and over-eating. The client is trained first to summon up punishing images to accompany visualization of the behaviour he wishes to remove: being sick over a friend after a drink in a bar, for example, or being caught engaging in some dubious practice by someone he regards highly. The next stage is for the client to terminate these aversive scenes by ceasing to perform the target behaviour. Adaptive and relief-providing responses can then be visualized and are negatively reinforced. Research evidence suggests that covert sensitization is more likely to be effective in changing very specific behaviours (Kazdin and Smith 1979), and, generally speaking, results are mixed.

THOUGHT-STOPPING

Thought-stopping techniques have been employed by therapists of many different persuasions over the years. They may be used to control obsessive thoughts and ruminations, or as a method of controlling the self-presentation of images used in some of the cognitive approaches reviewed above. The usual procedure is to get the client to close his eyes and summon up a clear and detailed image of what it is that troubles or obsesses him, and then for the therapist to shout 'stop!' The client opens his eyes immediately. He then practises this for himself, first aloud and then sub-vocally. Alternatives reviewed by Tryan (1979) in her useful article include the use of thick elastic bands around the wrist, which can be stretched and released on cue, and deliberate counting backwards from ten followed by relaxation. The aim of these little devices is to interrupt the unwanted sequence of thoughts. Again, the research evidence on their effectiveness is mixed. Also, because thought-stopping techniques are usually employed in combination with other methods, it is difficult to obtain an independent measure of their potency. Positive results are, however, reported by Hays and Waddell (1976) and Gambrill (1977).

TECHNIQUES FOR REDUCING ANXIETY AND AVOIDANCE

The behavioural therapies have always been best known for the success of the work done on phobias, and on less severe, irrational fears and anxiety states (see Beck and Emery 1985). There are a number of techniques which can be used in the face of such difficulties, and each of these is now discussed in turn. (Notes on the theoretical origins of these approaches are contained in Chapter 3.)

Positive counter-conditioning

The principle here is to 'break up' maladaptive conditioned associations (for example, fear of everyday events, objects or animals) by introducing a new response which is incompatible with, and stronger than, the existing problematic response. This is Wolpe's principle of 'reciprocal inhibition' (Wolpe 1958), which states that if we pair a response capable of inhibiting anxiety with the anxiety-provoking stimulus, it can be used to weaken the conditional association between that stimulus and anxiety. This approach makes use of the simple fact that it is impossible to feel both anxious and relaxed at the same time, and by pairing the two responses the client can, loosely speaking, 'unlearn' their fear reaction. It will also be seen that assertion training has a counter-conditioning component to it.

Case example

Angela was brought into care for reasons of neglect punctuated by physical abuse. The precipitating circumstances were that her father arrived home drunk one night and found her grizzling over having her hair washed before going to bed. He grabbed her and thrust her head into the sink, turning on a hot water geyser and scalding her head and neck. Following discharge from hospital she went to live in a children's home before being fostered. Here several understandable problems developed which caused concern for her health and were increasingly cited as obstacles to placement: she refused to have dressings changed without a fight; she refused to have her hair washed, or medication applied to her neck; in any situation where she was not in control, e.g. over choice of food or size of helping, she became aggressive – on one occasion threatening staff with a carving knife.

The theme of control = safety here was very evident and the counter-conditioning programme used acknowledged this in general terms while focusing on specific instances of anxiety.

Procedure

— Circumstances or events were predescribed in respect of their purpose, and she was allowed to stay in charge of the speed of these (e.g. dressing changes), building in little breaks as she wished. Staff were encouraged to break down these episodes into more manageable 'chunks', and to talk out loud about what they were doing, to involve her in the task, e.g. holding dressings and bottles, carrying out similar practices on dolls at the same time. Time-consuming, but resulting in far fewer episodes of distress and aggression.

— Water toys were purchased, including a rather expensive boat, and she was left to play with these. She found her own way to the water and washing was gradually faded in. The association of pleasure, in the face of retention of control, became incompatible with fear and anxiety.

Rapid exposure therapy

Exposure is used in the treatment of panic and profound fears and is derived from respondent extinction research (see p. 60). A phobia is a powerful, conditioned fear reaction to objects, animals, people or just about any other environmental circumstance. Clients experience powerful physical reactions to particular stimuli, and, even if they know that their fears are illogical, are unable to control them. Phobias are largely *learned* reactions and obey the principles of classical conditioning. However, they are often maintained by negative reinforcement —maladaptive escape and avoidance responses being strengthened by the relief they bring. Phobias also generalize to circumstances which resemble the original stimulus conditions. The case described on p. 57 is of a typical agoraphobia; this, together with social phobias (fear of people and groups), is the type of reaction most often met with in social work.

For years the established treatment for these problems was systematic desensitization: slow exposure to threatening stimuli accompanied by induced relaxation based on counter-conditioning principles (Wolpe 1958). This was the first of the behavioural approaches to establish itself in the therapeutic repertoire. However, recent research investigating the relative part played by each of the ingredients of systematic desensitization, plus the results of increasing experimentation in clinical settings with rapid exposure methods, have resulted in a considerable rationalization in this field (Marks 1975, 1978). In his very readable book, Stern (1978) suggests that instead of viewing rapid exposure and systematic desensitization as two separate techniques they should, for practical purposes, be thought of as a continuum – from slow exposure to rapid exposure. Although it is now reasonable to suggest that rapid exposure to the feared stimulus is the treatment of choice in phobias, this is a little like suggesting that a large injection of money is the best approach to poverty. It may be a good idea but it is not very feasible. The client may be staunchly unwilling to confront his or her worst fear, however much encouragement and support is given to him or her. This leaves us having to work for an optimal solution. The problem remains, that is, getting clients to confront their worst fears *as quickly as possible* after due preparation, and helping them to stay there until the anxiety subsides. It is important to explain to clients that their fears will subside, however powerful the anxiety.

Where the client will not co-operate with a rapid exposure approach, slow exposure is indicated, and to the extent that induced relaxation aids this process, we are left with a useful role for some form of systematic desensitization.

Procedure in exposure therapy

(i) Preparation for rapid exposure is most important and may involve the therapist in using other techniques such as modelling and rehearsal. First, the causes of phobias (see p. 60) should be reviewed with the client. I am not suggesting here that an academic discussion should be entered into, but that some basic principles arising out of the social worker's investigation of the problem should be simply outlined. It is usually helpful for the client to grasp the ideas behind what is being proposed and to register that the method being employed is the result of considerable research and practical experimentation, not just a therapeutic whim. This is not just to impress him or her, but because (as when medical procedures are necessary) stress is easier to bear when we understand its origins, can estimate its likely duration, can assess the limits of its effects on us and can have some actual control over it.

(ii) The next stage involves the mapping out of a treatment rationale which is acceptable to the client. Generally speaking, the fewer the number of steps before the client confronts the stimulus conditions usually avoided the better. Against this must be weighed the risk of premature withdrawal from a session found too overwhelming.

Clients do not usually experience difficulty in describing the various stages of fear-intensity and avoidance which given conditions produce, and a short hierarchy of these can be drawn up, as in Figure 7.3.

(iii) There are many things that can be done to equip the client for coping with stress. Reassurances can be given about the relatively short-term nature of anxiety; worst fears and irrational expectations can be confronted and analysed, clients can be encouraged to imagine themselves taking steps to cope with anxiety or they can be encouraged to 'reality-test' some of their fears. Reassurances can also be given that the therapist will stay with the client and help him or her to remain in contact with the feared circumstances as long as necessary. Alternatively, relatives or friends can be trained as mediators and can help in this way. Rehearsal sessions can be started where the procedure is modelled by the therapist and then by the client.

1	2	3
Touching the dustbin lid until it no longer produces feelings of strong anxiety	Sorting through the dustbin to retrieve specific items placed there by the therapist. Gloves worn.	Establishing prolonged contact with the lavatory bowl without gloves or other protective clothing.

Figure 7.3 Stages in the treatment of an excessive fear of dirt and germs

These methods aside, programmes of this type depend greatly on a relationship of trust between client and therapist; an approach characterized by supportive firmness in the face of fear, and by a clear commitment from clients that they will not abandon the session before the anxiety has subsided. Homework assignments can be designed to cover the period between sessions, and Stern (1978) rightly lays great stress on the importance of these behaviour-maintenance measures. Here is his description of a treatment session involving a man with a profound fear of travelling on public transport:

During the first session of *in vivo* exposure to buses he had several short bursts of panic and grabbed the therapist's arm tightly. He also cried out 'help', 'help', to the surprise of fellow passengers. The therapist told him: 'Keep seated and eventually the panic attack will pass. Nothing terrible will happen to you. Whatever happens don't run off the bus now or you will find it very difficult in future to overcome this.' Then as the patient calmed down and looked reassured: 'That was very good. I'm glad you didn't run away during the panic attack. This shows you can cope if you try hard.'

(Stern 1978:252)

Rapid exposure techniques *necessarily* create great anxiety in clients, and without being too dramatic about it, simple precautions are needed to ensure that people with heart ailments or respiratory problems do not attempt resolutions of this type. The best method of ensuring this is to discuss prospective cases with the GP or psychiatrist, and enlist medical co-operation at the assessment stage. Such referrals are particularly important in the treatment of panic disorder, where clients often harbour irrational beliefs about ever-increasing heart rates, strokes or collapse into mental illness. Here, a sympathetic medical consultation can be part of the reality-testing features of the programme.

Slow exposure and systematic desensitization

There are two kinds of systematic desensitization: *in vivo* (live practice); and *imaginal*, a cognitive approach using the same principles, but in imaginary form. Both forms have the same three main therapeutic ingredients: (i) a graded hierarchy of anxiety-producing stimuli; (ii) a relatively slow rate of progression through the stages of this hierarchy, the pace being dictated by a considerable lowering of anxiety before the next item is approached; (iii) a counter-conditioning element in the form of deep muscular relaxation. This was always an effective technique (Bandura 1969; Bergin and Garfield 1986), and rapid exposure methods are only coming to supersede it on the grounds that they are more efficient, more parsimonious and also produce very reliable results. Tests of the various elements of systematic desensitization, to see what components are the really potent ones and which could usefully be pruned away, suggest that the relaxation element, and the idea of a smooth progression through an incremental hierarchy, are less important than was previously thought (Cooke 1968).

Such research leaves us having to make three separate decisions about three essentially separate techniques.

(i) Will the client co-operate with the rapid exposure approach? (This decision should be based on a judgement of his or her *capabilities* as much as on expressed intentions.)

(ii) What is the optimum rate of progression towards the fear-provoking

227

stimulus in this client's case (remembering that he or she must remain in contact with it for some time)?

(iii) Will relaxation exercises serve as a coping technique to help the client through the process of exposure?

The first point has already been covered. Turning to the second, it is important to emphasize that the rules of slow exposure are somewhat different from those of desensitization. In the latter approach, the idea was to *slide* gently along the hierarchy, keeping anxiety to a minimum and counteracting its effects in little steps. In slow exposure, the production of some anxiety is deliberate; it is the fact that the client remains in contact with the fear-provoking stimulus until its effects subside that is the active ingredient. An illustration may help to clarify this (see Table 7.4).

Table 7.4 Contact with fear-provoking stimuli

17	Stand alone on footbridge for 10 minutes	*High anxiety and*
16	Stand alone on footbridge for 3 minutes	*avoidance*
15	Stand near footbridge for 10 minutes	
14	Stand near footbridge for 3 minutes	
13	Stand 100 yards from footbridge	
12	Walk to town (unaccompanied)	
11	Walk to edge of town (accompanied)	
10	Walk to shops	
9	Cross the road	
8	Walk 20 yards down road	
7	Stand on pavement	
6	Stand at front gate	
5	Clean windows	
4	Put out washing	
3	Stand in garden	
2	Stand on front step	*Low anxiety and*
1	Stand in porch	*avoidance*

In the case of the agoraphobic client from Chapter 3 an extended hierarchy was constructed – she would not have continued confrontation of her anxiety-provoking circumstances.

She was taught progressive relaxation and deep breathing during these assignments (see below) and spent several sessions on each item, sometimes accompanied by the social worker, and sometimes deliberately not. If the next step looked too large, the progression from one to the other could be bridged by spending longer completing the task. The procedure was labour-intensive and in fact this client never did make it across the footbridge during the course of the programme. She said firmly that she could easily go to town another way, so that it was not a real problem. However, she reported on follow-up that she had at last conquered this fear. Following a row with her husband, she had felt particularly determined about the issue and had marched to the bridge and stood trembling on it for 10 minutes: amateur counter-conditioning, but very effective.

Relaxation therapy

The reasons for considering this technique separately have already been given. It has specific uses for clients who have high background levels of anxiety, who suffer migraine attacks or frequent tension headaches. In addition it may be used as a technique to cope with temporary or situation-specific stress, and has a place as an adjunct to the cognitive procedures outlined above.

Procedure

(i) First the client is taught about the nature of anxiety, that it is a *bodily* phenomenon developed for useful purposes, and that it can be brought under conscious control to a considerable extent.

(ii) Next the client is taught to distinguish clearly between muscular contraction and relaxation. The procedure is that he or she first tenses then completely relaxes each muscle, working in sequence from toes upwards to the forehead muscle.

(iii) Instruction is given in deep breathing, so that a slow, deep respiration with an emphasis on the out-breath can be produced on cue.

(iv) The client may also be encouraged to imagine pleasant or peaceful scenes and with practice should be able to use these images to induce relaxation.

(v) Relaxation training is usually given with the client sitting in a comfortable chair and practice is necessary if the client is to learn to relax while going about his or her everyday business.

(vi) In imaginal desensitization, items from a prepared hierarchy of threatening items are introduced one by one; while the client is in a relaxed state, he imagines himself coping with these in a step-by-step fashion.

(vii) Relaxation tapes are widely available and clients can use these at home as an adjunct to treatment.

Biofeedback devices

Biofeedback instruments amplify internal organic events and levels, such as heart rate, blood pressure and skin resistance, so that to some extent they can be brought under conscious control. Behavioural management techniques exist for heart disorders such as tachycardia; also for hypertension and migraine. The device most relevant to social work is the Galvanic Skin Response (GSR) meter which gives an index of arousal (anxiety) by detecting small changes in the electrical resistance of the skin. Changes in skin resistance are part of a

Table 7.5 Summary of main response control techniques

Technique	Main features	Application
Modelling	Demonstration of key elements in behaviours likely to prove useful to client. Usually coupled with positive feedback on successive approximations from client.	Used for learning deficits of all kinds plus vicarious extinction of fears and phobias.
Social skills training	As above, but with extra emphasis on rehearsing social and conversational skills and deciding on which occasions a given performance is appropriate.	Used for withdrawn and unconfident clients; people with learning disabilities; psychiatric patients; children; and in work with delinquents where such deficits can be implicated in offending.
Assertion training	As 'modelling' above, but with extra emphasis on fears associated with assertiveness, and on discriminating between assertive and aggressive responses.	Used with excessively shy or withdrawn individuals. Often used in groups and as an adjunct to wide programmes.
Self-management techniques	Designed to teach coping skills. Emphasis on helping clients to develop techniques to relabel their experiences and change expectations of personal efficacy and the likely outcome of their behaviours. Also teaches clients to obtain environmental support for new responses by changing contingencies.	Used in a wide range of personal problems, especially with deficits and avoidance behaviours resulting from these.
Cognitive approaches	Means of identifying the personal constructs applied to self and to problems and making appropriate changes in these. Emphasis on use of positive self-statements and self-reinforcement to maintain new responses.	Useful for wide range of performance difficulties. Particularly applicable to relatively unstructured field settings. Can be used in conjunction with other behavioural programmes.

Table 7.5 continued

Positive counter-conditioning	The introduction of a response capable of inhibiting anxiety to weaken conditioned anxiety reactions.	Used in the treatment of specific fears and anxieties.
Exposure therapy	Controlled but rapid exposure to threatening stimuli maintained until anxiety extinguished.	Can be used to control excessive fears, panic attacks and phobias in co-operative clients.
Slow exposure	Gradual exposure to hierarchy of threatening stimuli, initially to the accompaniment of muscular relaxation (systematic desensitization).	Used to control excessive fears and phobias where clients are unable to co-operate with rapid exposure. (Muscular relaxation component can be used independently to overcome stress reactions.)
Biofeedback	Use of electronic instruments to amplify and display data from bodily processes such as heart rate, galvanic skin response and blood pressure, with a view to bringing these under conscious control.	Can be used in desensitization therapy but more often employed in the treatment of stress reactions and stress-related illness.

conditioned response, arising from the body's tendency to prepare to combat threat by rapid heat loss. This is a sort of 'pre-sweating' response, and part of the fight/flight reaction described on p. 101. Some of these machines are portable and can be worn like a hearing aid. They emit a tone, which the user attempts to reduce by whatever means he or she chooses – muscle relaxation, slower breathing, thinking of something else or whatever. Such devices are cheap, costing about as much as two ineffective visits by a social worker.

This chapter has covered both predominantly behavioural techniques pointing out their cognitive components, and predominantly cognitive approaches, where opportunities for rehearsal and reinforcement are likely to add to their efficiency.

231

8

ETHICAL CONSIDERATIONS

It is a curious fact that any form of therapy with 'behaviour' or 'behavioural' in its title seems to attract more critical attention from philosophers, lawyers and journalists than any other type of psychological help in the extensive present-day repertoire – no matter how silly or ill-conceived, and no matter what its track record in empirical research. There are two main reasons for this interest: (a) behaviour therapy is a visible process; what is done is uniquely open to inspection and criticism. Its methods are not mysterious; nor are they passed on by means of long apprenticeships with attendant initiation ceremonies; nor do the subtleties of the approaches evaporate when exposed to the lens of a video camera; (b) behavioural methods work well; they have practical, tangible effects, and anything that succeeds in changing people raises questions. Change for good or ill? Whose idea of change? By what right are people being changed? In this sense, the critical clamour that has greeted the development of the behaviour therapies, and which irritates many *aficionados* should really be regarded as a mark of respect. If these were not potent methods, no one would bother. But while the use of methods with a behavioural component certainly does give rise to ethical questions, these are not, by and large, issues qualitatively different from those that could be raised about any type of therapeutic endeavour. It is the success of these approaches that draws the fire of critics; the fact that the target is in full view which makes it so tempting.

In this chapter I would like to try and categorize, and respond to, the commonly raised objections to the use of a cognitive-behavioural approach by social workers, as well as discussing one or two worries of my own.

THE QUESTION OF CONTROL

It is above all the idea of the *control* of human behaviour that raises the ethical hackles of social workers. Partly this is a sentimental reaction, made on behalf of clients who have more than enough controls in their lives as it is, but in part it may just be what Leon Festinger (1957) has called 'dissonance reduction'. Let me begin with this point. The worst accusation that can be made about social workers, in their own book, is that they are mere 'agents of social control'. This view (advanced mainly by social scientists from the touchlines) usually produces only blanket denials, and social workers have tried hard to get the charge dropped altogether. A more constructive approach would be to set about discriminating between those types of social control which we might well be *pleased* to be identified with: the supervision of offenders as an alternative to prison, securing treatment for mentally ill people who constitute a danger to themselves and others, protecting the rights of children by controlling those who threaten them.

There are two powerful fallacies at work here.

(i) The idea that social work (or for that matter psychological intervention in general) is such a powerful medium of change that, even in the face of determined resistance, *great* moral restraint is required in its application, lest people be induced into socially convenient conformity.

(ii) The idea that social workers and other therapists introduce controls and liberty-endangering influences where none existed before.

In the light of the empirical research which shows how difficult it is to produce worthwhile gains over control-group rates and make them stick, 'dare we use the CBT method, Dr Karloff?' considerations (point (i) above) could be seen as a case of advanced self-flattery – hence my earlier point about dissonance reduction. Furthermore, apart from certain important exceptions (cases where substantial amounts of material aid are, or might be thought to be, dependent upon compliance, or certain residential settings where clients are literally 'captive', or dependent upon staff for the meeting of their basic needs), the scales are heavily loaded *against* the would-be influencer. (Alan Sillitoe's novel *The Loneliness of the Long Distance Runner* (1959) shows this beautifully.) In reality, clients who are not persuaded of the need for help have many ways of avoiding it. I shall return to the exceptions cited later.

Next, I would like to argue a more general point, namely, that concern about the occasional unwanted side-effects of therapeutic good intent needs to be balanced by an equal concern that the 'goods' should be delivered to clients as needed, or wanted and as agreed, within reasonable time limits. I know from my own experiences as chairman of a complaints tribunal that the issue of *not* getting services constitutes the overwhelming body of concern among service users. The following comment from Bandura, although addressed primarily to the fainthearted among psychotherapists, has a wider relevance:

> Discussions of the moral implications of behavioral control almost always emphasize the Machiavellian role of change agents and the self-protective manoeuvers of controlees. The fact that most people enter treatment only as a last resort, hoping to modify patterns of behavior that are seriously distressful to themselves or to others, is frequently overlooked. To the extent that therapists engage in moral agonizing, they should fret more about their own limited effectiveness in helping persons

willing to undergo hardships to achieve desired changes, rather than in fantasizing about their potential powers. The tendency to exaggerate the power of behavioral control by psychological methods alone, irrespective of willing co-operation by the client, and the failure to recognize the reciprocal nature of interpersonal control, obscures both the ethical issues and the nature of social influence processes.

(Bandura 1969:85)

As for the second fallacy, about exercising control where none existed before, the standard behaviourist line should already be familiar: that we are each bombarded daily by countless controlling influences and that to see control as a game of billiards where only one influence at a time operates is indeed to take a naive and mechanistic view of human behaviour. It is more sensible to see the therapist as entering and (if he or she is lucky) *possibly* affecting an already active field or network of contingencies. Bandura again:

All behavior is inevitably controlled, and the operation of psychological laws cannot be suspended by romantic conceptions of human behavior, any more than indignant rejection of the law of gravity as antihumanistic can stop people from falling.

(Bandura 1969:85)

In which case, given that lots of things are already happening, deciding *not* to intervene (if the law allows) is an influential decision just as much as intervening is. The decision not to intervene, or excessive procrastination about the issues raised by intervention, means that the behaviour of the individuals concerned is governed by forces which we have decided *not* to try to control; not to replace with other, hopefully more benign influences; and which we have not taught the client how better to control for him or herself. Sometimes it is right, or judicious, or necessary, to stay out of a case, but this should be recognized as to some extent an abandonment of the client to other controls, and not as a simple decision not to seek control. There are no real vacuums in social life and some influence or other will prevail. Therapeutic 'sins of commission' must therefore be weighed carefully against equally damning 'sins of omission'. The child abuse field has been reduced itself to a state of 'frozen watchfulness' by public criticism over too much or too little action. One can now discern similarities between the 'defensive medicine' practised in the United States and the 'defensive social work' now taking hold here. Social workers, too, respond to contingencies (largely punishment, in our case) and not always constructively.

Case example

Jane Campbell, aged 12, was referred by a child psychiatrist. Her problem (apparently) was soiling and smearing faeces on the walls of her bedroom. A

234

physical examination had revealed no organic problems and early interviews produced blank denials that anything was wrong. The psychiatrist suspected unspecified 'problems in the family'. An interview with the family (parents, Jane and a 5-year-old sister) produced a series of shoulder-shrugging responses to questions about how they all got on together. Separate interviews with Jane produced similar expressions of polite surprise. Her story was that she just couldn't help soiling and 'didn't know what came over her' to make her smear. She was punished physically by her parents, as well as by being sent to her room, having toys taken away, and being prevented from watching TV. She considered this 'fair'.

Enquiries outside the home gave quite a different picture. Jane was regarded as a model pupil at her school, was a keen member of various school clubs, a girl guide, and a regular and enthusiastic attender at Sunday school. She was described by all outside sources as polite, helpful, keen and mature beyond her years.

Baseline recording revealed an average four-times-a-week rate of soiling, but after that the case had to proceed very much on a 'hit and miss' basis. A therapeutic scheme was devised directed purely at the soiling and smearing. The main components of this were: (a) a differential reinforcement programme withdrawing attention from soiling in case this was maintaining it, with clear periods being reinforced by praise, trips to the cinema, swimming baths and so on; (b) a response–cost scheme: Jane was to clean up her own mess and remain in her room for 30 minutes following a soiling incident; (c) polite prompts about visiting the lavatory were given at the danger times identified in the baseline records.

For two weeks the scheme worked well and the soiling rate fell to one incident in the first week and two in the second. In the third it shot up to seven and stayed there for another three weeks. 'The worst ever', parents reported.

At about this time I was telephoned by a very secretive-sounding Mr Campbell, who asked to see me 'in strictest confidence'. He came into the office as if being pursued by secret policemen and told the following story. The couple had been having severe marital difficulties for the past few years – following an affair between Mr Campbell and a female employee at work, which his wife had found out about. He described a catalogue of rows, badgerings and humiliations, the latter extending into the sexual sphere, his wife having apparently developed an appetite for degrading him as prelude to very occasional sex. Mr Campbell described himself as a prisoner unable to leave because of what might happen to Jane. The child had always been close to him and, in his view, was now being used to punish him. Mrs Campbell apparently took great pleasure in punishing her and deeply resented the time she spent alone with her father. Mrs Campbell had followed them on two occasions, and had made references to her husband's 'unfatherly and unmanly interest' in the child – no evidence of sexual abuse was ever forthcoming. It also transpired that Mrs Campbell had been using, and illicitly extending, the behaviour modification scheme to make her daughter's life a misery from the moment when she saw it begin to work. Furthermore, beatings had continued in clandestine fashion alongside the scheme, as had depriving Jane of the things she valued most – her girl guide and youth club activities. Everyone in the family had been sworn to secrecy, but Mr Campbell felt now that he had to tell someone. He then tried to swear me to secrecy with the warning: 'She'll kill me if she finds out I've been here'.

I had already explained to Mr Campbell that while I could be discreet, I could not meet his request for complete confidentiality as this implied an infringement of the rights of his daughter. He returned to work in trepidation. A private interview with Jane was arranged at school where she tearfully repeated her father's stories of cruelty at the hands of her mother – amplified by the behaviour modification scheme, which mother had been using as an excuse to punish her further. Jane expressed the wish to live away from home, and as soon as possible. A lengthy and very stormy family interview followed where the whole story was uncovered.

Jane was brought into care and, with some difficulty, provided with a place at a boarding school, which she enjoyed and did well at. (The 'difficulty' arose from trying to explain to the education authority that this was a normal child in a maladjusted family, not the reverse, and therefore that a placement in a normal educational setting was required, not something 'special'.) Mr and Mrs Campbell were referred to the National Marriage Guidance Council for help, but decided to split up after one interview. This they did with considerable acrimony. Mrs Campbell went to live with her mother, and took her younger daughter with her. Mr Campbell found a flat and lived alone. He saw Jane frequently and their good relationship was maintained, but Jane refused to go and live with him, preferring the security she already had.

The lessons in this case for me were as follows. (a) That any therapeutic device can be used for good or ill, but that behavioural approaches, with their requirement for control over rewarding and punishing consequences, perhaps need special care when they are being used to change the behaviour of those in inferior power positions. (b) Things are not always what they seem, nor are the people referred as 'the client' necessarily the right targets of change. (c) It is possible to be fooled, as I certainly was here; however much we prefer to see them as the victims of circumstances, clients and others involved in cases do lie sometimes. Mr and Mrs Campbell certainly needed help. They were offered it, by the psychiatrist, by me and by the National Marriage Guidance Council, but, except for a brief foray with the latter organization, they refused to take up the offers. Mrs Campbell's goal was nothing less than the complete degradation of her husband, who had been unfaithful to her and (in her eyes) had held her up to ridicule. Her chosen means of achieving this were by exploiting her husband's rather weak character and tormenting the person closest to him – his daughter – while he was forced to watch. For a time the behavioural programme helped her to do this on a 'scientific' basis – ostensibly for the child's own good. I could argue here that 'at least the scheme brought everything out into the open', had the reader not already been sternly cautioned against the dangers of *ex post facto* reinterpretations of objectives in an earlier chapter.

PSYCHOLOGICAL TECHNIQUES: THEIR USES AND ABUSES

Whenever therapeutic regimes go sour, the argument is put forward that the techniques are themselves morally neutral, but are abused by the people who apply them. This argument can be used to justify all sorts of dubious practices – from indiscriminate arms sales to the development of germ-warfare facilities. As an argument it is technically correct (water can be used for drinking and for drowning people in), but morally it is unconvincing. A different ethical standard needs to be applied. That is, does a particular 'technology' do anything to *encourage* wrongdoing – to make it easier, or more tempting? Our concern here is the degree to which problems are structured into a given approach. Are the contingencies constituted by the approach, taking into account the settings in which it is likely to be used, more likely to shape behaviour towards good rather than evil, or the reverse?

If serious problems do arise from the use of a particular approach, then we need to examine the extent to which these problems are regularly accompanying factors; effects which cluster around this particular type of programme or setting. For example, if behaviour modification schemes used in juvenile detention centres were regularly to be abused across the range of such settings, and were held by the inmates to be repressive, then it would be pointless and naive to argue simply that these approaches need not be so applied. The key question would be, do such measures lend themselves to abuse by giving the seal of scientific respectability to what is really crude coercion and maltreatment? We also need to examine to what extent the approach concentrates power without safeguard, almost as a necessary condition of its effective operation. If it does, then it may be unsafe in *any* hands and a regularly recurring pattern of abuse in different settings would confirm this as a serious problem.

Let us try now to measure behavioural and cognitive-behavioural methods, as generally practised, against this little template of moral sufficiency. Showing up clearly on the plus side is the fact that they contain their own inbuilt safeguards against hard-to-detect wrongdoing. These techniques are largely activity-based; they centre on the client doing things differently, or more or less often. It is therefore very hard to explain away either the aims or the results of cognitive-behavioural therapy in obscure or euphemistic terminology. Both ends and means are open to inspection – which is certainly not true of many other therapeutic approaches. Thus, whether a particularly objectionable 'means' is a regularly accompanying feature of programmes directed to particular problems, or to a particular client group, is open to scrutiny. Similarly, to the extent that the 'ends' being pursued are couched in behavioural terms, they will be less equivocal and less likely to be interpreted differently by the clients, the therapist, and by other interested parties.

The behavioural therapies have a large and vigorously pursued literature testifying to their humane and tangibly effective application across a wide range of problems. Therefore we are permitted to see that these approaches have occasionally been misused. However, in many of the reports of misuse, one retains a strong impression that the manifest intention of those in charge was to control, punish and subjugate those in their power rather than to help them. The idea of behaviour therapy is brought in later, as a weak justification for this ill-treatment. This was undoubtedly the case in the Staffordshire Social Services 'pindown' scandal (Levy and Kahan 1991) where staff were found guilty of using punishments, deprivation and isolation. I was approached by the inquiry panel to check out how reasonable were the claims of staff to have been using 'behaviour modification' techniques – when in fact the avowed justification for this dubious regime was a warped version of psychoanalytically based 'regression therapy'. My reply was that they were doing so only in the sense that General Pinochet's secret police might claim, on conviction of human rights offences, of having merely been employing the procedures of negative reinforcement. The observation by Mrs Bottomley, Minister of State for Health, that the problem of uncontrollable children might be solved by the recruitment of 'Street-wise' grannies into the social services (monitored, no doubt, by a new street-wise Grandparent Quality Council) fails to convince, since children who manage to burst through every containing facility the State can provide are rarely the product of 'street-naive' family backgrounds. The ethical point is that the more difficult and dangerous and uncontainable children become, the less likely they are to encounter mainstream, qualified, professional help and the more likely they are to be tidied away into special units where few of us would care to work. The technical issues raised in this book boil down to a more fundamental human truth:

> Those to whom evil is done
> Do evil in return.
> (W.H. Auden, 'September 1st 1939')

Nevertheless, behavioural methods have gained a reputation from *somewhere* for over-detachment. Perhaps the sometimes rather cool reactions of professionally secure and legitimate therapists to such malpractices has helped to reinforce this image? Consider this chilling historical example:

Cotter (1967), in his report of the uses of operant conditioning techniques in a Vietnamese hospital, found that after twenty electro-convulsive shock treatments delivered as negative reinforcement, there were still non-responders. He found that three days' total starvation produced a 100 per cent response rate. Perhaps even these patients wouldn't have responded if they had known that discharge to the community was, for them, work in an Army-defended farm, surrounded by the Viet-Cong!

(Hall and Baker 1973:255)

In making a judgement about the extent to which behaviourism encourages this sort of thing, we have to begin by weighing the tremendous good achieved by the application of these procedures against reported cases of actual harm. From this total we must then subtract some constant based on the human propensity for wickedness – with or without behaviour therapy to use as a justification for this. What remains is down to us, and requires the very closest consideration.

In arguing this, I am aware that there are genuine moral problems in trying to decide what is contingency management, what legitimate control and what illegitimate coercion. In fact, there is no clear line of demarcation separating response–cost programmes from coercion, which is why anything behavioural is regularly linked in the media with *Clockwork Orange* fantasies and with brainwashing. It is silly just to deny any connection. To take an extreme case again: certain of the techniques used by the Chinese and North Koreans on captured American prisoners in the early 1950s would be, at a technical level, recognizable to most behaviourists. They were used, of course, in the context of dire threats, either explicitly made or implicitly ever-present, and the victims knew of – and in some cases had already experienced – serious maltreatment (Farber *et al.* 1966). Nevertheless the theoretical root principles (principally negative reinforcement) so misused then are greatly amplified versions of the ones described in this book for other, better purposes.

A system for discouraging aggressive behaviour among the pupils at a community school by assigning 'costs' to this behaviour (no privileges, home visits, access to recreational facilities and so forth) is a form of coercion, albeit for a desirable purpose. The decisions about such programmes have to be made on utilitarian lines. To what extent do the rights of other people not to be physically abused require this sort of well-intentioned action?

Two further points can be added to those made above. First, critics should ask to what extent clients are expected to *learn* something from a therapeutic programme. Our ethical concern should increase the more the scheme is used just as a device for controlling behaviour. A good test of this issue is whether the main controlling features of a programme are faded, for individuals or for groups, once unwanted behaviour is brought under influence. In addition, critics should ask to what extent the behaviour of clients is being positively shaped, so that it is brought under the control of the usual, socially acceptable stimuli. If no attempt is made to do these things, then the staff in charge must, in reality, have little confidence that their scheme is anything other than an artificial mechanism, the effects of which will not generalize to more natural settings, or circumstances where different and less easily manipulated contingencies operate.

It is possible, however, to conceive of a behavioural approach being used to 'clear the ground' for another type of therapeutic or educational emphasis – for example, by removing disruptive or interfering behaviour that is preventing new learning (see the dramatic example provided by Bucher and Lovaas (1968), and the case example on p. 79). But, once again, the acid test is whether obviously and continuously troublesome behaviours are eventually brought under the control of this second treatment approach, or whether behaviour generated by this treatment successfully displaces harmful or anti-social behaviour.

A further point to be made is that the greater the emphasis on punishment, response–cost and negative reinforcement, the more closely we need to look at a programme with ethics as our main concern. At some stage, and ideally on a concurrent basis, new behaviours need to be taught, and potentially useful responses reinforced and shaped. If this stage is long delayed, or occupies only a minor role in the scheme, then, generally speaking, the scheme is more to do with control than therapy. Here is a case example which shows some of the difficulties of distinguishing between these two aims.

Case example

Mrs Brown, a 74-year-old widow and resident of an old persons' home, kept coming into the senior care assistant's office at awkward times and staying there for lengthy periods. Baseline recording showed this to occur on average eight times a day. Her visits interrupted meetings, report-writing, interviews with other residents and relatives and so on. Furthermore, Mrs Brown was getting herself something of a reputation. Other residents would sometimes shout and jeer when they saw her taking one of her trips to the office, and on one occasion a junior member of staff had to be formally reprimanded for returning her to the dayroom rather roughly.

An investigation of what occurred when Mrs Brown came into the office revealed: (a) that she would repeatedly ask the same question about her relatives (she had none locally and she received no visits); (b) that most staff would repeatedly discuss the position with her and then escort her back to the dayroom. Occasionally they would remonstrate with her for repeated interruptions.

The following programme was devised, on the assumption that it would be better for all concerned if Mrs Brown limited her visits to the office, and also that the behaviour was probably being reinforced with attention that was legitimately available to her in other forms. Staff were therefore advised to respond politely, but briefly, to Mrs Brown's interruptions on the first occasion before lunch, and on the first occasion after lunch. On every other occasion Mrs Brown was to be asked to return to the dayroom, and five minutes later a staff member would attend to her. So far the programme was designed mainly to control behaviour for the sake of hard-pressed staff. However, in addition to this part of the scheme, Mrs Brown was to be regularly approached by staff in the dayroom to talk about matters of concern to her – writing a letter to a friend living some distance away, for instance, or talking about old times. Eventually this regular contact was augmented with a school-girl volunteer, and the problem of interruptions disappeared.

This latter part of the programme was more directed to Mrs Brown's own needs and balanced the earlier concern to run the home with reasonable efficiency for the good of all the residents. This was not a minor problem, though it is possible to imagine guides to staff development suggesting that such problems should somehow never arise in the first place. Staff and residents were exasperated by Mrs Brown's behaviour, and to leave the matter as it was would simply have reinforced her stigmatized status as an 'odd person'. Although based on technical principles (reinforcement) I believe that this was an ethical procedure in that significant benefit accrued to the client.

The issue of control is not easily resolved and the two aims can be much more jumbled up together than in the example cited above – as in probation work, or work in secure treatment units. For many of its recommended approaches behaviour therapy requires a fair degree of control over events. The way in which this tension between therapy and control is managed is at the crux of many of the ethical decisions we need to make, though they are by no means peculiar to the individual methods under consideration here. Another version of the same problem is examined below.

MOTIVATIONAL ISSUES

A frequently reported criticism of behavioural approaches is that they only work well with 'motivated clients'. When an opponent of this view gives examples from operant work with chronically institutionalized mental patients, then the charge is usually amended to one of 'repression of the helpless'. What can be said about this issue of motivation and control?

Let us begin by analysing just what is meant by the statement: 'behavioural approaches only work with the well motivated'. The implication here is that there are lots of other therapeutic strategies which work very well with 'the unmotivated' (that is to say, with people who, through fear, habit or reasoning, decide that they want little or nothing to do with therapy and therapists). This is nonsense. Whether people decide to co-operate or not depends in the last analysis on their weighing up the benefits and the costs of co-operating against the benefits and the costs of not co-operating. Or – remembering classical conditioning – it can depend on what they associate with the things on offer and the way they are being offered. For many stigmatized and oppressed groups 'help' has come to equal control because that has been their experience. Acknowledgement of this, sincerity of purpose and the full involvement of clients in the helping processes on offer are the only factors likely to weaken this association. Potential clients may lack information on, or may misunderstand, many things about what is being offered. They may over-value the benefits of the status quo, or fear an alternative future. Attempts can be made to correct these misapprehensions, when that is what they are. We can influence, persuade, entice, reinforce, shape, beg or cajole the client into co-operation. But if at the end of this he or she still stands firmly against the idea then there is little that can or should be done on the therapeutic front. The idea that by some subtle and hard-to-write-down method of verbal 'hypnosis' clients can be 'wooed out' of their recalcitrance is hard to take seriously.

It is the business of social workers and others to lay down clear views and guidelines for clients, and to enhance, within reason, the attractiveness of the solutions they are putting forward, and to work to modify the environmental contingencies which may be maintaining the status quo. When these approaches have been tried, but the attempt to build a useful relationship has failed, then the social worker has probably done all that he or she can. If society through legislation or the agency through its regulations insists on continuing contact then it is important that no one should misunderstand, or be able to misconstrue, the nature and purpose of this enforced contact. In many cases of juvenile delinquency, where courts grant supervision orders attaching social workers to clients, what is done will be just that – the client and the people with whom he lives or associates will be *supervised*, looked over, watched; they will have their activities monitored and assessed. In many cases, sadly, nothing else is possible, and the wider community has its rights too. The danger lies in the distinctions between these two different kinds of social work becoming blurred, both in the thinking and doings of social workers and their clients, and in the view of a society only too willing to salve its conscience by always seeing the need for inspection as an opportunity for something 'more constructive' – in other words, therapy. Sometimes, when people decide they have nothing to lose by co-operating, there is such an opportunity, and sometimes there is not. By pretending that there almost *always* is (reports to magistrates' courts are usually optimistic on this point) social workers are making four different mistakes.

(i) They are giving to the community a greatly exaggerated view of their unaided powers of influence, and the expectations to match.

(ii) They are putting the profession time and again in the position of having to excuse itself for things over which (were it not for the point made in (i)) it could not reasonably be expected to have control. (No one likes a moaner, still less a moaner who blames his patron for giving him the commissions asked for.)

(iii) By failing to discriminate accurately those occasions when mainly inspection or supervision rather than mainly therapy is required (or is feasible), they are bringing about a considerable waste of resources. This means that social workers are tied up for longer periods of time than may be necessary, and that resources are channelled into providing quasi-therapeutic services when they could be better used to finance diversionary schemes and improvements in social policy.

(iv) By blurring issues of therapy and control or even therapy and punishment, social workers are sometimes a party to the infliction of greater distress. There is a certain dignity in being punished for acknowledged wrong-doing, which is lacking in regimes that are an unholy mixture of therapy and unacknowledged punishment. In other words, sometimes the things done in the name of helping are more painful and degrading than the things done in the name of retribution, where the individual is held to be responsible for his or her actions. This is different from 'entirely to blame for his actions', hence the concept of mitigation.

The effect of all this is not to decry therapeutic endeavour – quite the reverse – it should, ideally, be seen as a special benefit. It is, after all, difficult to do, taxing on both parties, something that demands time, energy, great skill and scarce resources, and therefore something that has ideally to be done *with* people and not *to* them. It is, therefore, something that would benefit from a little isolation from our other activities. I am not arguing here for a return to the bad old days of preciousness about therapy, when it was practised by an elite who did little else and who regarded fuel bills and bad housing as epiphenomena. I am arguing for greater discrimination about who gets therapy (in other words, those who can be persuaded to and who want to and can use it) and for equal, if different, energies to be spent on other worthwhile activities. People have a right not to be 'helped' and this important principle has always had a distinguished body of advocates:

> The only purpose for which power can be rightfully exercised over any member of a civilized community, against his will, is to prevent harm to others. His own good, either physical or moral, is not a sufficient warrant. He cannot rightfully be compelled to do or forbear because it will be better for him to do so, because it will make him happier, because, in the opinions of others, to do so would be wise, or even right. There are good reasons for remonstrating with him, or persuading him, or entreating him, but not for compelling him, or visiting him with any evil in case he do otherwise. To justify that, the conduct from which it is desired to deter him must be calculated to produce evil to someone else. The only part of the conduct of any one, for which he is answerable to society, is that which concerns others. In the part which merely concerns himself, his independence is, of right, absolute.
>
> (Mill, J.S. 1859:73)

This is a much tougher view to hold now than in 1859. In complex indus-trialized societies, people are much more interconnected and interdependent, and with the arrival of the mass media the line between 'evil to oneself' and 'evil to others' is much harder to draw. Is the contemporary glue sniffer harming only himself by his habit, or do his actions contaminate others nearby?

In any case, Mill put forward many exceptions to his rule, for instance, children, the insane and the mentally infirm – and some of these categories demand, but at times defy, close definition. However, although this principle of not doing things to people to 'help' them if they do not themselves wish it is hedged around by all sorts of marginal cases, and has been nibbled away at the edges by bevies of philosophers, it stands nevertheless as a profound truth, a clearly visible light by which to steer ourselves. There may be all sorts of short-term justifications for changing course from it, but in the longer-term I believe that we do so at our peril.

Therapy should always be on offer where we have some knowledge and experience to back up our expectations of a positive result, or where, with the client's informed consent, we are conducting a genuine experiment. But it should be something for which clients have to 'sign up'. There should always be a contractual phase to it; a period of explicit negotiation about purposes and desired outcome. Where this is not possible (as in extremes of psychological infirmity, or in the case of very young children) we must be guided by those who care for the individual, make the best judgements we can and try to render ourselves as publicly accountable as possible. Outside this category, where no contract can be agreed either explicitly or implicitly, then the persons concerned are not clients in the strict sense of the word (the very notion of a compulsory *client* is paradoxical, as is the use of the term 'customer', or 'service user' in child protection, or statutory mental health cases). They may still be people we need to see, or people that we have been put 'in charge of', and they may still (we would hope) be treated with an exemplary kindliness and concern. But we must not delude ourselves that we can help everyone, either with cognitive-behavioural approaches or with any other approach.

This said, it is a dangerous thing to see freedom and ethical purity as virtues which flourish only when there is an apparent absence of control. An absence of proper control in the case discussed on pp. 234–7 simply allowed Mrs Campbell free rein to persecute her daughter.

THE SPECIAL CASE OF INSTITUTIONAL AND RESIDENTIAL TREATMENT

Any ethical concerns we have about the use of behavioural approaches in general are likely to be multiplied when we consider their use in residential settings – particularly in closed or secure units. Much excellent work has been in these fields, but together with the penal field in the US, they have, in the past, been the setting for the most disturbing examples of misuse.

My own view is that the field of residential social work offers special opportunities for the application of behavioural techniques, but that, alongside these, special safeguards are required. First the opportunities, which derive from these settings:

(i) Behaviour therapy is a labour-intensive method, particularly at the outset; therefore, to have staff and clients together in the same locale is a distinct advantage. The residential social worker does not have to wait until the next visit to see that things are not going according to plan.

(ii) The arrangement of consequences is a key part of the behaviour therapist's function – either as part of an operant programme, or to provide background encouragement for modelling and other 'response-control' activities. Many field-based programmes fail because reinforcement or 'consequation' do not follow immediately on the performance of particular behaviour. In residential work – despite the many pressures on staff – having clients in close proximity ensures that this can be done more easily. Therefore more complex and demanding programmes can be mounted in these settings.

(iii) Given that the necessary expertise exists, *in situ* supervision is easier to arrange. Staff can more readily gain access to the person in charge of the project. This is a major problem in field settings where access is limited and often delayed. Now that basic courses are more readily available, the next urgent priority – if we take our own theories about the importance of support for new behaviours seriously – is the setting up of supervision facilities for relative newcomers to the discipline. Residential social work is by no means immune to the administrative problems this poses, but the record of certain residential programmes in providing supervision for junior staff makes the situation look rather more hopeful.

Now for the problems.

(i) Residential settings provide opportunities for considerably greater control over the behaviour of clients than elsewhere in social work. As suggested above, such opportunities can be used for good or ill. However, in line with our previous discussion about 'structured-in' problems, we need to decide whether these exist to any great extent in the application of behavioural techniques in this type of setting. My own view is that a number of 'built-in' problems do exist, and that – while they are not insurmountable – they always need to be guarded against. The first of these is the tendency of institutions to try and take short cuts with residents, to try and rub the awkward corners off them, and to socialize them into the ways of the institution. This process of institutionalization (Goffman 1968) is not usually any individual's specific intention; it happens because of the problems thrown up by having a large group of individuals, with their awkward individual needs, living in the same space. So individuality is sacrificed sometimes, just to keep the place ticking over. To this problem can be added our experience of what happens when the real therapeutic goals of a residential agency get subverted by the interests of administrative neatness, order, 'discipline', 'target-maintenance' and so on. Add to this covert 'risk management' (making sure, above all things and whatever the 'mission statement' says, that the department's name stays out of the newspapers) and we have a well-prepared seedbed for therapeutic tyranny. It need not occur; it usually doesn't; but the conditions are just right.

When behavioural techniques are used in settings which show a tendency to have these problems, they can very easily come to be misused – particularly at face-to-face staff levels. We must expect this: it has happened with psychotropic drugs and ECT in mental hospitals, and with the 'remission for good behaviour' system in prisons. Misuse in this context has three main effects. (a) It provides a detailed, scientific means of ensuring conformity for conformity's sake. Unless care is taken clients can be systematically shaped into institutional behaviour, rather than into patterns of behaviours likely to be of use in the outside world. (b) Institutional control can easily be dressed up as harsh therapeutic necessity. (c) Where residents can see no distinction between behavioural control for internal, institutional reasons, and behavioural control for good, individual, therapeutic reasons, the system is brought readily into disrepute. Although its main requirements may be met so as to obtain rewards and privileges, these behaviours will not become a permanent part of the individual's repertoire because, as we have seen, people *interpret* stimuli, though they may respond to them in the short-term. Token economy schemes in residential centres for delinquents are often paid lip-service to, but any influence such schemes might have is more than countermanded by the contingencies which apply in the underlife of the institution. It is just possible that new habits may be acquired and reinforced under such circumstances, but rather unlikely. More powerful controls lie with the peer group and, unless the treatment scheme has gained respect or toleration at this level, it has little chance of success in the longer-term.

(ii) The way out of some of these difficulties is not always as straightforward as it sometimes is in fieldwork settings. The obvious solution of obtaining the 'free consent' of clients who are on the receiving end of a regime needs a second look. First, what is 'free' or 'informed' consent? For any semblance of a contractual relationship between parties to exist, there has to be some semblance of equality between them. The danger is that, given the considerable disparity in actual, taken-for-granted power that exists between staff and clients, compliance can easily be mistaken for consent. Where co-operation with a therapeutic regime is – or could be thought by the client to be – linked to his standing or security, to the meeting of his need for food, shelter, human contact, affection, approval and stimulation, then a 'free choice' is virtually impossible. An unconstrained choice probably does not exist in nature anyway, and we would be fools not to make our therapeutic programmes attractive just in case anyone joined in for the wrong reasons. Perhaps the best we can do here is to argue for an absence of deliberate sanctions surrounding the decision whether to participate or not.

Here are my own suggestions. (a) Where tangible rewards and inducement are used they must always be over and above basic civilized provision. (b) Where possible, behavioural programmes should be modular rather than all-embracing schemes which encompass every aspect of the client's life and rob him or her of any 'breathing space'. The latter are a technical temptation in residential settings because of the 'captive, audience effect' referred to above, but are ethically dangerous. (c) Clients should have to commit themselves formally to behaviour-change programmes in some way, knowing clearly and by established reputation that they need not do so, and that basic residential and/or educational facilities are theirs by right anyway. This point needs to be explained carefully. It may be that, on occasions, such precautions make programmes more attractive because entry to them is not required or automatic. (d) Time should be spent in explaining the purposes behind the scheme and, where feasible, residents should have a hand in managing them themselves.

Worthwhile progress has been made over the last few years in handing back power to the users of services – in children's homes, homes for elderly people and hostels for the mentally ill, so that it is now more usual than not to see people, who would once have been disqualified by their client status, with seats on management committees for the facilities in which they reside. In the main, it is social workers who have ensured this.

Where clients take part in setting targets for themselves and their peers, these are more likely to be met. There is no reason why, given appropriate technical advice, these bodies should not be encouraged to play a part in designing therapeutic programmes too. Where this happens there is less likelihood that schemes become identified solely with staff interests and complied with for the wrong reasons.

(iii) However, operant schemes in residential work, where a wide array of contingencies is managed solely by staff, can easily come to reinforce feelings of 'them and us' in the recipients. Contingencies imposed as an external force are not necessarily learnt from. Understanding is vitally important, not only at an ethical level, but at a technical level too. Some behaviour therapists have in the past been guilty of using their subjects for what looks more like advanced human puppetry than therapy. Where clients understand in detail what they are being encouraged to do and why (other considerations suspended), results tend to be superior, both at the acquisition and the generalization stage.

The present trend, discernible in residential work, away from the use of operant schemes in isolation towards combinations of methods, including cognitive approaches, social skills training and problem-solving courses, is to be warmly welcomed. (A recent review of social work effectiveness research by Macdonald and Sheldon (1992) confirms this trend.) There is far less chance that schemes of this type, which have an educational rather than a controlling emphasis, will become distorted by the pressures of communal life.

But what of those clients and patients who are ill equipped to make any choices about participating in therapy and have no trusted relatives to act on their behalf? It may be that we sometimes under-estimate the decision-making ability of our clients, whether they are children or long-stay psychiatric patients, and could try harder to win genuine consent and co-operation. One of the most interesting unlooked-for findings of a recent research project to gauge the reactions of discharged psychiatric patients to a local authority community care scheme was the richness of opinion and testimony coming from respondents supposed to lack insight into their condition (Macdonald and Sheldon, forthcoming). But having said this, we are still faced with clients who for one reason or another cannot be fully involved in the helping process. The only possible answer here is that *someone* has to decide for them, lest the 'sins of omission' points made on p. 234 are to apply. The only possible criteria for evaluating such decisions are: whether they are reasonable; whether they are publicly made; whether they are made after due consultation with other interested parties; whether the therapist would be happy if in similar circum- stances similar decisions were made about a member of his or her own family in similar circumstances (an acid test); whether they have the effect of trying to promote independence, self-sufficiency, the ability of the client to be in better control of himself or herself and his or her environment; and whether they constitute an enhancement of the range of responses the client is capable of making. Of these criteria the most important is that decisions should be clear, unambiguous and open to inspection and criticism, if necessary, by an ethics committee of the type pioneered by clinical psychologists. All the rest flow from these and are dependent upon them.

DECIDING WHO IS LIKELY TO BENEFIT FROM BEHAVIOURAL PROCEDURES

If the advocates of therapeutic and clinical approaches in social work are guilty of anything, then it is of giving insufficient thought to their choice of targets. The tendency of social workers, despite their radical language, to respond unthinkingly and uncritically to someone else's administrative contingencies remains a cause for concern. The reflex action of attempting to change the person who happens to get referred – as if referral were always a rational and representative process – is still in place. In this way, children with educational problems, persistent truants, hospital patients, debtors and the physically disabled have all been the individual recipients of therapeutic social work services, when in many cases the solution to their problems lay elsewhere –

with the school, the hospital, the social security office, the access and dignity-denying built environment or whatever. These are all contingencies and social workers worthy of the name must try to adapt these to the needs of individuals as well as individuals to their circumstances.

The criticism that behaviour modification is usually undertaken with the poor and the weak – people in reality suffering at the hands of others – is only partly justified. In fact it is a criticism of clinical social work as a whole rather than of any specific methods employed. The clinical model has tended to suggest that whoever comes forward should be helped, regardless of class, race, creed and so forth, and it has thought of itself as democratic in this respect. A genuinely democratic approach would place much greater emphasis on deciding with the client what is the just, the appropriate, and the propitious point for intervention. In its concentration on environmental factors (usually the behaviour of other people), behaviour modification already does this, and this approach actively counteracts the tendency to see the problem as belonging entirely to the person complaining of it.

FEELINGS ABOUT THE IMPOSITION OF TECHNIQUES

There is a certain arrogance about intervening in the life of another person, never better expounded than by Barbara Wootton (1959), who argued that if social casework could *really* do the things claimed for it in various textbooks then such casework skills were perhaps wasted on the poor and troubled, and should, for the good of us all, be applied immediately to politicians and world leaders for the prevention of war, famine and pestilence.

But then social work has always been well aware of this sort of thing, arguably too well aware of it and the literature positively oozes with cautionary phrases about 'starting where the client is', noting carefully his or her version of events, never offering advice except as a last resort however much clients clamoured for it (Hollis 1964). As discussed in Chapter 1, this over-reaction and hedging round what social workers are supposed actually to do about someone's problem can leave us with the impression that social work is meant to serve the same function as a warm bath – good for all sorts of aches and pains, so long as they amount to nothing very serious or specific – otherwise refer to a specialist. To social workers raised in this way, behavioural approaches can seem a bit brash and 'pushy'. However, if this book has a central theme, then it is to advocate a soft-hearted but not necessarily soft-headed approach to helping.

CONCLUSIONS

There are good technical as well as ethical reasons for condemning less and understanding more (to reverse our present leaders' reflexive phrase). Learning theory teaches us that decisions about good and bad behaviour, and about

blame, culpability and the prospects of reform need to be taken in full understanding that the environment – both yesterday's and today's – plays a key part
in determining behaviour and consequences. There is nothing in the nature of
the procedures discussed in this book to suggest that they need be applied in
an excessively clinical or mechanical way. Indeed, the principles themselves
suggest that this would be self-defeating. Cognitive-behavioural approaches
do suggest specific remedies for specifically defined problems, but *how* these
remedies are applied is also very important. Social workers, with their traditional (but by no means unique) concern for the individual, are
temperamentally well equipped to apply these techniques in a sensitive and
humane fashion. The introduction of a cognitive element should help this
process along by placing the individual interpretations of provocative stimuli
at the centre of discussions about what can be done therapeutically to remedy
matters.

Knowledge of basic research and of the procedures themselves has been
available for some time, but has produced only a very patchy response from
the profession. Other preoccupations aside, one reason for this may be that the
effective use of cognitive-behavioural techniques effectively requires a detailed
and a specific knowledge of the various procedures – ideally of the underlying
theory and the procedures together. This discipline cannot be approached in
the same way as so much else in social work – as general, background or
contextual knowledge – where the method of application is left almost entirely
to the worker. Social workers are not always well equipped by training in all
settings where these methods have a place. Indeed, in certain cases – e.g.
depression with an appreciable risk of self-harm – knowing the limits of one's
own skills, the scope of treatments and when to refer on is the most important
ethical consideration. However, if these techniques are to amount to anything
more than just another interesting sideline, then a reappraisal of the rather
'woolly' therapeutic stance developed in social work over the last fifty-odd
years will be necessary. Indeed, certain (I suspect, empire-building) psychologists who have just discovered counselling are beginning to question whether
social workers are well-trained enough to use these techniques at all, unless
closely supervised (by them). This in ignorance of the substantial and long-
standing behavioural social work literature (Thomas 1974; Gambrill 1977;
Hudson and Macdonald 1985; Scott 1989) and of the fact that we were
occupied with developing therapeutic approaches (Richmond 1917; Lehrman
1949) while they were busy thinking about better intelligence tests, based on
rather flawed data.

There is work here for us all, and given basic professional competence,
clients will benefit more from interdisciplinary co-operation than from demarcation disputes.

Using the language of this book, there has always been too little positive
reinforcement for this kind of considered and informed intervention. Indeed
we are now more likely to see a shift towards negative reinforcement – supplied

by our critics. It is important that we do not respond to this merely by jumping on to what, for the uninitiated, has the appearance of being a new bandwagon. Instead we should set about fostering a greater respect for *empiricism* in social work. We can do this first by adopting an active and critical approach to the research literature relevant to our field, and second by evaluating our own work in an exemplary way. Such is the longer but safer route to public confidence and professional self-respect.

APPENDIX 1

CHECKING BASELINE/OUTCOME DIFFERENCES BY SIMPLE STATISTICAL MEASUREMENT (AFTER BLOOM)*

Bloom (1975) has produced an admirably clear, step-by-step guide for the evaluation of marginal results from single case designs. A version of this is reproduced below, together with a case example (Figure A.1), and the appropriate statistical table for calculating results (Table A.1).

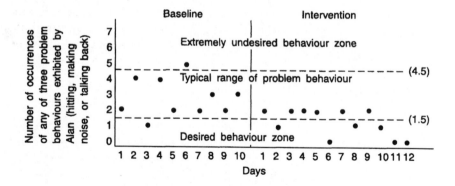

Figure A.1 Problem behaviours (Alan)
Source: Adapted from Bloom (1975). Reproduced by permission of the author and publisher.

(a) Count the *number of time units* on the horizontal line of the baseline period. (This is ten in Alan's case.) Do *not* count the number of individual acts (two the first day, four the next . . .).

(b) Next identify the typical range of problem events. 'Typical range' refers to a statistical pattern like the middle two-thirds of a normal curve. To find the middle two-thirds, divide the number of time units by three and

* Appendix 1 is reproduced from Sheldon (1982).

multiply the result by two. (For Alan, this would be 10 divided by 3, which is 3.3; and then 3.3 times 2, which is 6.6.)

(c) Draw lines enclosing the nearest approximation to this middle range of problem behaviours. The nearest whole number to 6.6 is 7, but as is often the case there is no way to enclose seven events representing a typical middle range in Alan's case. We must leave at least one event above and below the typical range in order to calculate the proportions needed.

(d) The middle range of problem behaviours is represented by the nearest approximation to two-thirds of the stable baseline distribution of problem occurrences; this is what the teacher expects as typical problem behaviour from Alan. The desired behaviour zone includes at least one event from the pre-intervention period and represents the zone in which the goals of intervention appear. In Alan's case, this zone includes one and zero occurrences. Even if the teacher's goal is to have zero occurrences of problem behaviour, we must include the entire zone in our calculations because we must start from where the client is in evaluation as well as in practice. The extremely undesired behaviour zone includes those behaviours worse than typical. Because it is possible that the intervention may be harmful, we must be able to indicate when matters have become significantly worse. When there is a choice in approximating the middle range of behaviours, as in Alan's case where we might include either the six occurrences of 2s and 3s or the eight occurrences of 2s, 3s, and 4s – both being one unit away from the approximate middle range of seven occurrences – we must let the nature of the problem determine our choice.

Comparison of pre-intervention and intervention period events

Now the question arises: how statistically likely is a set of events that occurred during the intervention period to have occurred by chance alone? This question is one form of the statistician's null hypothesis, comparing what might have happened by chance with an alternative hypothesis, that is, that the worker's intervention affected the events in a planned way. (This is a one-directional hypothesis, assuming a positive outcome; we must be prepared to test for a negative outcome, using a two-directional test, as will be discussed below.) The question is answered by the following procedure.

(a) On how many occasions during the pre-intervention period was the client's behaviour in the desired zone? For Alan it was 1 time out of 10, or a proportion of 0.10 which is the number of desired instances divided by the total number of occurrences during the pre-intervention period.) Look at Table A.1 and locate the left-hand column labelled *Proportion*, which stands for the proportion of observations of the type considered during the preintervention period. The proportion is listed in steps of 0.05, with several common fractions also included for convenience.

(b) How many time units are in the intervention under consideration? Locate *Number*, which stands for the total number of observational units during the intervention period. The numbers run by 2s up to 20 and 4s up to 100. Figure A.1 shows twelve time units in the intervention period with Alan. Note that the intervention period begins at day 1, not at day 11 continuing from the pre-intervention period.

(c) Enter the body of Table A.1 at the intersection of the proportion of occurrences during pre-intervention and the total number of time units in the intervention period. (In Alan's case these numbers are 0.10 and 12, respectively, and the cell entry is 4.) The table shows the number of occurrences of a specific type – in this case, the number of desired occurrences of fewer-than-typical acting-out behaviours, during the intervention period, that are necessary to represent a significant increase at the 0.05 level over the proportion of such occurrences during the pre-intervention period. Actually the cell entry means 4 or more – 5, 6, 7, 8, 9, 10, 11, or 12 – any one of which would be a significant increase beyond the 0.05 level of significance. Figure A.1 reports six out of twelve occurrences of acting-out behaviours were below Alan's typical pattern and thus the pattern of events showed a statistically significant improvement.

Evaluation of results

The intervention plan in this example was designed to reduce acting-out behaviours by systematic use of positive reinforcements. This pattern of reduced acting-out behaviours did occur after the initiation of the intervention plan, and, by using the statistical procedure in connection with Table A.1, we are able to say that such an event could have occurred by chance less than five times in one hundred. Evaluation of results involves an *inference* that, within the context of the client–worker situation and the conceptualized network of events that constitute the individualized plan of intervention, the occurrence of the desired pattern of events leads to support for the *hypothesis* that the worker's efforts were the likely *cause*. There is no necessary connection between a statistically significant event and causation, but it is by inference, within the context of a theory, that we can entertain such a hypothesis. We continue to use this causal inference in the development of other hypotheses to be tested in practice.

Table A.1 Showing the number of observations of a specified type (for example, a desired behaviour) during the intervention period that is necessary to represent a significant increase at the 0.05 level over the proportion during the pre-intervention period[1]

Proportion	Number 4	6	8	10	12	14	16	18	20	24	28	32	36	40	44	48	52	56	60	64	68	72	76	80	84	88	92	96	100
0.05	2	2	3	3	3	3	3	4	4	4	4	5	5	5	6	6	6	7	7	7	8	8	8	8	9	9	9	10	10
0.10	3	3	3	4	4	4	5	5	5	6	7	7	8	8	9	9	10	10	11	12	12	13	13	14	14	15	15	16	16
1/8	3	3	4	4	5	5	5	6	6	7	8	8	9	10	10	11	12	12	13	14	14	15	15	16	17	17	18	19	19
0.15	3	3	4	4	5	5	6	6	7	8	8	9	10	11	12	12	13	14	15	15	16	17	18	18	19	20	21	21	22
1/6	3	4	4	5	5	6	6	7	7	8	9	10	11	12	13	13	14	15	16	17	18	18	19	20	21	22	22	23	24
0.20	3	4	5	5	6	6	7	8	8	9	10	11	12	13	14	15	16	17	18	19	20	21	22	23	24	25	26	27	28
0.25	4	4	5	6	7	7	8	9	9	11	12	13	14	16	17	18	19	20	22	23	24	25	26	27	29	30	31	32	33
0.30	4	5	6	6	7	8	9	10	10	12	13	15	16	18	19	21	22	24	25	26	28	29	30	32	33	35	36	37	39
1/3	4	5	6	7	8	9	9	10	11	13	15	16	18	19	21	22	24	26	27	29	30	32	33	35	36	38	39	41	42
0.35	4	5	6	7	8	9	10	11	12	14	15	17	18	20	22	23	25	27	28	30	31	33	35	36	38	39	41	42	44
3/8	4	5	7	7	8	9	10	11	12	14	16	18	19	21	23	25	26	28	30	31	33	35	36	38	40	42	43	45	47
0.40	4	5	6	8	9	10	11	12	13	15	16	18	20	22	24	26	28	29	31	33	35	37	38	40	42	44	46	47	49
0.45	4	6	7	9	9	10	11	13	14	16	18	20	22	24	26	28	30	32	34	36	38	40	42	44	46	48	50	52	54
0.50		6	7	9	10	11	12	13	15	17	19	22	24	26	28	31	33	35	37	40	42	44	46	48	51	53	55	57	59
0.55		6	8	9	10	12	13	14	16	18	21	23	26	28	31	33	35	38	40	43	45	48	50	52	55	57	59	62	64
0.60		6	8	9	11	12	14	15	17	19	22	25	27	30	33	35	38	41	43	46	48	51	54	56	59	61	64	66	69
5/8			8	10	11	13	14	16	17	20	23	25	28	31	34	36	39	42	45	47	50	53	55	58	61	63	66	69	71
0.65			8	10	11	13	14	16	17	20	23	26	29	32	35	38	40	43	46	49	52	54	57	60	63	65	68	71	74
2/3			8	10	12	13	15	16	18	21	24	27	30	32	35	38	41	44	47	50	53	55	58	61	64	67	70	72	75
0.70				10	12	13	15	17	18	21	24	28	31	34	37	40	43	46	49	52	55	58	61	64	67	70	73	75	78
0.75					12	14	17	17	19	22	26	29	32	35	39	42	45	48	51	55	58	61	64	67	70	74	77	80	83
0.80						14	16	18	20	23	27	30	34	37	40	44	47	51	54	57	61	64	67	71	74	77	81	84	87
5/6							18	18	20	24	27	31	34	38	42	45	49	52	56	59	63	66	69	73	76	80	83	87	90
0.85									20	24	28	31	34	38	42	46	49	53	56	60	63	67	70	74	78	81	85	88	92
7/8										24	28	32	36	39	43	47	50	54	57	61	65	68	72	76	79	83	86	90	94
0.90												32	36	40	44	47	51	54	58	62	66	69	73	77	80	84	88	91	95
0.95																	52	56	60	64	69	72	76	79	83	87	91	95	99

[1] Tables of the Cumulative Binomial Probability Distribution – By the staff of the Harvard Computational Laboratory, Harvard University Press, 1955. Tables constructed under the direction of Dr James Norton, Jr, Indiana University – Purdue University at Indianapolis, 1973. Reprinted by permission of Harvard University Press.

APPENDIX 2

SOCIAL SITUATIONS QUESTIONNAIRE*

This questionnaire is concerned with how people get on in social situations, that is, situations involving being with other people, talking to them, etc.

How difficult?

The first page deals with how much difficulty, if any, you have in these situations. Having difficulty means that the situation makes you feel ANXIOUS or UNCOMFORTABLE, either because you don't know what to do, or because you feel frightened, embarrassed or self-conscious.

1   Across the top of p. 1 you will see five different choices of difficulty, each with a number underneath (e.g. 'no difficulty' = 0).
2   Down the left-hand side of the page are listed twenty-nine situations you might encounter which some people have said they find difficult. If some of these situations are ones in which you have never found yourself, please imagine how you would feel if you did.
3   Down the right-hand side of the page are two columns which refer to two different points in time. They are headed (a) the present time; (b) this time a year ago.

For each situation, and for each point in time, select the choice or difficulty which most clearly fits how you feel, and write the number of your choice in the appropriate column.

Examples:

		Present time	Year ago
A	Going to a public meeting	3	1
B	Going to the cinema	0	0

---

* Reproduced by kind permission of Dr Peter Trower.

256

Example A means that someone had great difficulty (3) at the present time, and slight difficulty (1) a year ago. Example B means that someone had no difficulty (0) at either of these points in time.

Please note: Choice 'avoidance if possible' should only be used if you find the situation so difficult that you would avoid it whenever you could. It should NOT be used for situations you avoid because they are not to your taste – e.g. not going to concerts because you dislike music.

How often?

The second page deals with how often you have found yourself in each of the twenty-two situations listed on the left-hand side of the page. The procedure is exactly the same as that for p. 1.

1   Across the top of p. 2 are seven different 'how often' choices, each with a number underneath it (e.g. 'at least once a week' = 2).
2   Down the right-hand side of the page are two columns referring to two three-month periods; (a) the last three months; and (b) the same three months a year ago,

For each situation, and for each three-month period, select a 'how often' choice and write the number in the appropriate column.

Please note: Choice 'never' (7) means that you have never in your life been in that particular situation. It should therefore be used in both columns.

Date: .... Sex: ....

Name: ....

No difficulty	Slight difficulty	Moderate difficulty	Great difficulty	Avoidance if possible
0	1	2	3	4

		At the present time	This time a year ago
1	Walking down the street	___	___
2	Going into shops	___	___
3	Going on public transport	___	___
4	Going into pubs	___	___
5	Going to parties	___	___
6	Mixing with people at work	___	___
7	Mixing with friends of your own age	___	___

8	Going out with someone you are sexually attracted to	___	___
9	Being with a group of the same sex roughly the same age as you	___	___
10	Being with a group containing both men and women of roughly the same age as you	___	___
11	Being with a group of the opposite sex of roughly the same age as you	___	___
12	Entertaining people in your home, lodgings, etc.	___	___
13	Going to dances, dance halls or discotheques	___	___
14	Being with older people	___	___
15	Being with younger people	___	___
16	Going into a room full of people	___	___
17	Meeting strangers	___	___
18	Being with people you don't know very well	___	___
19	Being with friends	___	___
20	Approaching others – making the first move in starting up a friendship	___	___
21	Making ordinary decisions affecting others (e.g. what to do together in the evening)	___	___
22	Being with only one person rather than a group	___	___
23	Getting to know people in depth	___	___
24	Taking the initiative in keeping a conversation going	___	___
25	Looking at people directly in the eyes	___	___
26	Disagreeing with what other people are saying and putting forward your own views	___	___
27	People standing or sitting very close to you	___	___
28	Talking about yourself and your feelings in a conversation	___	___
29	People looking at you	___	___

Every day or almost every day	At least once a week	At least once a fortnight	At least once a month	Once or twice in three months	Not at all in three months	Never
1	2	3	4	5	6	7

		Last three months	Three-month period a year ago
1	Walking down the street	___	___
2	Going into shops	___	___
3	Going on public transport	___	___
4	Going into pubs	___	___
5	Going to parties	___	___
6	Mixing with people at work	___	___
7	Mixing with friends of your own age	___	___
8	Going out with someone you are sexually attracted to	___	___
9	Being with a group of the same sex roughly the same age as you	___	___

10	Being with a group containing both men and women of roughly the same age as you	____	____
11	Being with a group of the opposite sex of roughly the same age as you	____	____
12	Entertaining people in your home, lodgings, etc.	____	____
13	Going to restaurants or cafes	____	____
14	Going to dances, dance halls or discotheques	____	____
15	Being with older people	____	____
16	Being with younger people	____	____
17	Going into a room full of people	____	____
18	Meeting strangers	____	____
19	Being with people you don't know very well	____	____
20	Being with friends	____	____
21	Approaching others – making the first move in starting up a friendship	____	____
22	Making ordinary decisions affecting others (e.g. what to do together in the evening)	____	____

Comments: If you wish to add any comments about your ratings of difficulty or frequency, please do so below and continue overleaf if necessary.

NOTES

CHAPTER 1

1 The Central Council for Education and Training in Social Work – a quasi-governmental body in charge of validating and monitoring social work courses in Britain.
2 There is a tendency in social work writing to use inverted commas, not to indicate special usage, but to show background uneasiness with a given concept – without having to take the trouble to propose a better one, e.g. 'science', 'mental illness'.
3 For more extensive reviews see Bergin and Garfield 1986, ch. 10; Rachman and Wilson 1980; and the *Journal of Behavioural and Cognitive Psychotherapy*, 1993, Supplement 1.
4 In Britain there has been a continuing debate on the need for an independent General Social Work or Social Services Council to govern and develop standards in the profession.

CHAPTER 2

1 By 'for now' I do not mean to imply that an indeterminate time should be granted whatever the absence of proposition-supporting effects, as do psychoanalysts when faced with an absence of symptom substitution.
2 The elements of cultural transmission which are also selected by consequences (see Dawkins 1976, ch. 11).

CHAPTER 3

1 The increasing use of rapid exposure techniques (see Chapter 7), in preference to slower desensitization approaches, enables us to side-step some of the implications of this research, but it is cautionary nonetheless.

CHAPTER 6

1 This example is dedicated to 'Tailgunner Parkinson', a noted British columnist who got into trouble as a probation officer for telling the truth, i.e. that many of his best successes had consisted of turning clients guilty of aggravated burglary into mere shoplifters.

REFERENCES

Alberti, R. E. and Emmons, M. L. (1970) *Your Perfect Right*, California: Impact.

Alexander, J. F., Hotzworth-Munroe, A. and Jameson, P. (1994) 'The process and outcome of marital and family therapy: Research review and evaluation', in Bergin, A. E. and Garfield, S. L. (eds), *Handbook of Psychotherapy and Behaviour Change*, Chichester: Wiley.

Allport, G. W. (1935) *Personality: A Psychological Interpretation*, New York: Holt.

Auden, W. H. (1976) *Collected Poems*, London: Faber & Faber.

Auden, W. H. (1977) *The English Auden: Poems, Essays and Dramatic Writings 1923–1939*, Mendelson, E. (ed.), London: Faber & Faber.

Ayllon, T. and Azrin, N. H. (1964) 'Reinforcement and instructions with mental patients', *Journal of the Experimental Analysis of Behavior* 7: 327–51.

Ayllon, T. and Azrin, N. H. (1965) 'The measurement and reinforcement of behavior of psychotics', *Journal of the Experimental Analysis of Behavior* 8: 357–83.

Ayllon, T. and Michael, J. (1959) 'The psychiatric nurse as behavioral engineer', *Journal of the Experimental Analysis of Behavior* 2: 323–4.

Ayllon, T. and Michael, J. (1968) *The Token Economy: A Motivational System for Therapy and Rehabilitation*, New York: Appleton–Century Crofts.

BABCP (1993) British Association for Behavioural and Cognitive Psychotherapies, *Supplement 1*.

Bandura, A. (1965) 'Influence of models' reinforcement contingencies on the acquisition of imitative responses', *Journal of Personality and Social Psychology* 1: 589–95.

Bandura, A. (1969) *Principles of Behavior Modification*, New York: Holt, Rinehart & Winston.

Bandura, A. (1977) *Social Learning Theory*, Englewood Cliffs, NJ: Prentice-Hall.

Bandura, A. (1978) 'Perceived self-efficacy', *Advances in Behavior Research and Therapy* 1(4): 3–22.

Bandura, A. and Rosenthal, T. L. (1966) 'Vicarious classical conditioning as a function of arousal level', *Journal of Personality and Social Psychology* 3: 7–19.

Barlow, D. H., Leitenberg, H. and Agras, W. H. (1969) 'The experimental control of sexual deviation through manipulation of a noxious scene in covert sensitization', *Journal of Abnormal Psychology* 74: 596–601.

Bateman, H. M. (1977) in Jensen, J. (ed.), *The Man Who . . . and Other Drawings*, London: Eyre Methuen.

Bateson, G., Jackson, D. D., Hale, J. and Weakland, J. H. (1956) 'Toward a theory of schizophrenia', *Behavioral Sciences* 1: 251–64.

BBC Horizon Publications (1993) '*Wot U looking at?*', London: BBC Broadcasting Support Services (Text adapted from programme transmitted 24 May 1993).

REFERENCES

Beck, A. T. (1970) 'Cognitive therapy: Nature and relationship to behavior therapy', *Behavior Therapy* 1: 184–200.

Beck, A. T. (1976) *Cognitive Therapy and the Emotional Disorders*, New York: International Universities Press.

Beck, A. T. and Emery, G. (1985) *Anxiety Disorder and Phobias: A Cognitive Perspective*, New York: Basic Books.

Beck, A. T., Hollon, S. D., Young, J. E., Bedrosian, R. C. and Badenz, D. (1985) 'Treatment of depression with cognitive therapy and amitryptine', *Archives of General Psychiatry* 42: 142–8.

Beck, A. T., Sokol, L., Clark, D. A., Berchick, B. and Wright, F. (1992) 'Focused cognitive therapy of panic disorder: A cross-over design and one-year follow-up', *American Journal of Psychiatry* 147: 778–83.

Bem, D. J. (1967) 'Self perception: an alternative interpretation of cognitive dissonance phenomena', *Psychological Review* 74: 183–200.

Bentler, L. E., Machado, P. P. P., and Neufeldt, S. A. (1994) 'Therapist variables', in Bergin, A. E. and Garfield, S. L. (eds), *Handbook of Psychotherapy and Behaviour Change*, Chichester: Wiley.

Bentley, K. J. (1990) 'Evaluation of family-based intervention with schizophrenia using single-system research', *British Journal of Social Work* 20: 101–6.

Berger, M. (1985) 'Temperament and individual differences', in Rutter, M. and Hersov, L. (eds) *Child and Adolescent Psychiatry: Modern Approaches*, London: Blackwell Scientific Publications.

Bergin, A. E. and Garfield, S. L. (1986, 1994) *Handbook of Psychotherapy and Behaviour Change*, Chichester: Wiley, (3rd and 4th edns).

Berleman, W. C., Seaburg, J. R. and Steinburn, T. W. (1972) 'The delinquency prevention experiment of the Seattle Atlantic Center: A final evaluation', *Social Service Review* 46: 323–46.

Birchwood, M., Hallet, S. and Preston, M. (1988) *Schizophrenia: An Integrated Approach to Research and Treatment*, Harlow: Longman.

Blackburn, I. M., Bishop, S., Glen, I., Whalley, L. J. and Christie, J. E. (1981) 'The efficacy of cognitive therapy in depression', *British Journal of Psychiatry* 137: 181–9.

Blackburn, I. M., Ennson, K. M. and Bishop, S. (1986) 'A two-year naturalistic follow-up of depressed outpatients treated with cognitive therapy, pharmacotherapy and a combination of both', *Journal of Affective Disorders* 10: 67–75.

Blakemore, C. (1977) *Mechanics of the Mind*, Cambridge: Cambridge University Press.

Blanchard, E. B. (1994) 'Behavioural medicine and health psychology', in Bergin, A. E. and Garfield, S. L. (eds), *Handbook of Psychotherapy and Behaviour Change*, Chichester: Wiley.

Bloom, M. (1975) *The Paradox of Helping*, New York: Wiley.

Boden, M. (1981) *Artificial Intelligence and Natural Man*, Brighton: Harvester Press.

Bootzin, R. R. (1977) 'Effects of self-control procedures for insomnia', in Stuart, R. B. (ed.) *Behavioral Self-Control*, New York: Brunner/Mazel.

Boswell, J. (1740) *Life of Johnson*, Oxford: Oxford University Press, 1980.

Brown, G. D. and Tyler, V. O. (1968) 'Time out from reinforcement: A technique for dethroning the "Duke" of an institutionalized delinquent group', *Journal of Child Psychology and Psychiatry* 9: 1–14.

Brown, G. W. and Birley, J. (1968) 'Crises and life changes and the onset of schizophrenia', *Journal of Health and Social Behaviour*, 9: 269–312.

Brown, G. W., Birley, J. L. T. and Wing, J. K. (1972) 'The influence of family life on the course of schizophrenic disorders: A replication', *British Journal of Psychiatry* 121: 241–58.

Brown, R. (1969) *Social Psychology*, New York: Free Press.

Bucher, B. and Lovaas, O. I. (1968) 'Use of aversive stimulation in behavior modification', in Jones, M. R. (ed.), *Miami Symposium on the Prediction of Behavior: Aversive Stimulation*, Miami: University of Miami Press.

Butler-Sloss Report (1988) *Report of the Inquiry into Child Abuse in Cleveland*, London: HMSO.

Cannon, W. B. (1927) 'The James–Lange theory of emotions: An analytical examination and an alternative theory', *American Journal of Psychology* 39: 100–5.

Carkhuff, R. (1968) *Helping and Human Relations*, New York: Holt, Rinehart & Winston, vol. 1, Appendix B.

Carroll, L. (1872) *Alice's Adventures in Wonderland, Through the Looking Glass, The Hunting of the Snark*, London: Bodley Head, 1974.

Central Council for Education and Training in Social Work (1989) 'Requirements and regulations for the Diploma in Social Work', Paper 30, London: CCETSW.

Chadwick, P. D. and Lowe, C. F. (1990) 'Measurement and modification of delusional beliefs', *Journal of Consulting and Clinical Psychology* 58: 225–32.

Children Act (1989) London: HMSO.

Claridge, G. (1985) *Origins of Mental Illness*, Oxford: Basil Blackwell.

Clyde, J. J. (1992) *Report of the Inquiry into the Removal of Children from Orkney in February 1991*, Edinburgh: HMSO.

Cohen, A. (1964) *Attitude Change and Social Influence*, New York: Basic Books.

Conan Doyle, A. (1928) *Sherlock Holmes: Short Stories*, London: John Murray (1976).

Cooke, G. (1968) 'Evaluation of the efficacy of the components of reciprocal inhibition psychotherapy', *Journal of Abnormal Psychology* 73: 44–51.

Cotter, L. M. (1967) 'Operant conditioning in a Vietnamese mental hospital', *American Journal of Psychiatry* 124(1): 23–8.

Daily Mirror (1978) 'Let Her Stay Out 'Til Dawn!' 21 October 1978 (Front page story recounting critical reactions on the use of a contract with a wayward adolescent girl).

Dalrymple, J. (1994) 'Devil's Island: What really happened on the Orkneys', *Sunday Times* 27 February 1994.

Davey, G. (ed.) (1981) *Applications of Conditioning Theory*, London: Methuen.

Davis, B. (1992) *Care Management, Equity and Efficiency: The International Experience*, University of Kent: Personal Social Services Research Unit.

Dawkins, R. (1976) *The Selfish Gene*, Oxford: Oxford University Press.

Dawkins, R. (1982) *The Extended Phenotype*, Oxford: Oxford University Press.

Dennett, D. C. (1991) *Consciousness Explained*, London: Allen Lane.

Descartes, R. (1664) *Traité de l'homme, plus Translation and Commentary*, Holt, T. S. trans. Cambridge: Cambridge University Press, 1972.

Deschner, J. P. (1984) *The Hitting Habit*, New York: Free Press.

Dixon, N. (1976) *On the Psychology of Military Incompetence*, London: Jonathan Cape.

Dixon, N. (1981) *Preconscious Processing*, Chichester: Wiley.

Dobson, K. S. (1989) 'A meta-analysis of the efficacy of cognitive therapy for depression', *Journal of Consulting and Clinical Psychology* 57: 414–19.

Donaldson, M. (1978) *Children's Minds*, London: Fontana Press.

DSM III[R] (1987) *Diagnostic and Statistical Manual of Mental Disorders III: Revised Edition*, Washington, DC: American Psychiatric Association.

Dunn, J. (1980) 'Individual differences in temperament', in Rutter, M. (ed.), *Scientific Foundations of Developmental Psychology*, London: Heinemann.

Edelman, G. (1987) *Neural Darwinism*, New York: Basic Books.

Ellis, A. (1977) 'Rational Emotive Therapy: Research data that supports the clinical and personality hypotheses of RET', *Journal of Counselling Psychology* 1: 221–48.

Ellis, A. (1979) 'The basic clinical theory of Rational Emotive Therapy', in Grieger, R. and Boyd, J. (eds), *Clinical Applications of Rational Emotive Therapy*, New York: Van Nostrand Reinhold.

Emmelkamp, P. M. G. and Mersch, P. P. (1982) 'Cognitive therapy and exposure *in vivo* in the treatment of agoraphobia: Short-term and delayed effects', *Cognitive Research and Therapy* 16: 77–90.

Eysenck, H. J. (1964) *Crime and Personality*, London: Routledge & Kegan Paul.

Eysenck, H. J. (1965) *Fact and Fiction in Psychology*, Harmondsworth: Penguin.

Eysenck, H. J. (1978) 'Expectations as control elements in behavioural change', *Advances in Behaviour Research and Therapy* 1(4): 7–15.

Eysenck, M. W. and Keane, M. T. (1990) *Cognitive Psychology: A Student's Handbook*, London: Lawrence Erlbaum Associates.

Farber, I. E., Harlow, H. F. and West, L. J. (1966) 'Brainwashing, conditioning and DDD (debility, dependency, and dread)', in Ulrich, R., Stachnic, T. and Mabry, J. (eds), *Control of Human Behavior*, Glenview, IL: Scott Foresman, vol. 1.

Ferster, C. B. and Skinner, B. F. (1957) *Schedules of Reinforcement*, New York: Appleton–Century Crofts.

Festinger, L. (1957) *A Theory of Cognitive Dissonance*, Evanston, IL: Row Peterson.

Fischer, J. (1973) 'Is casework effective?: A review', *Social Work* 1: 107–10.

Fischer, J. (1976) *The Effectiveness of Social Casework*, Springfield, IL: Charles C. Thomas.

Folkard, M. S. (1980) 'Second thoughts about IMPACT', in Goldberg, E. M. and Connolly, N. (eds) (1981), *Evaluative Research in Social Care*, London: Heinemann.

Folkard, M. S., Fowles, A. J., McWilliams, B. C., McWilliams, W., Smith, D. D., Smith, D. E. and Walmsley, G. R. (1974) *IMPACT, Home Office Research Studies I*, London: HMSO, no. 24.

Folkard, M. S., Smith, D. D. and Smith, D. E. (1976) *IMPACT, Home Office Research Studies II*, London: HMSO, no. 36.

Folstein, S. and Rutter, M. (1977) 'Infantile autism: A genetic study of 21 twin pairs', *Journal of Child and Adolescent Psychiatry* 18: 297–321.

Foucault, M. (1965) *Madness and Civilization*, New York: Pantheon.

Galassi, M. D. and Galassi, J. P. (1977) *Assert Yourself!*, New York: Human Sciences Press.

Gambrill, E. (1977) *Behavior Modification: A Handbook of Assessment, Intervention and Evaluation*, San Francisco, CA: Jossey-Bass.

Gambrill, E. (1981) 'The use of behavioral practices in cases of child abuse and neglect', *International Journal of Behavioral Social Work* 1 (1): 640.

Garcia, J. and Koelling, R. A. (1966) 'The relation of cue to consequence in avoidance learning', in *Psychonomic Science* 4: 123–4.

Garfield, S. L. (1986) 'Research on client variables in psychotherapy', in Bergin, A. E. and Garfield, S. L. (eds), *Handbook of Psychotherapy and Behaviour Change*, Chichester: Wiley.

Garner, D. M. and Bemis, K. M. (1982) 'A cognitive-behavioral approach to anorexia nervosa', *Cognitive Therapy and Research* 6: 123–50.

Gendreau, P. and Ross, R. R. (1987) 'Revivication of rehabilitation: Evidence from the 1980s', *Justice Quarterly* 4(3): 349–407.

Gibbons, J. S., Butler, J., Urwin, P. and Gibbons, J. L. (1978) 'Evaluation of a social work service for self-poisoning patients', *British Journal of Psychiatry* 133: 111–18.

Gillies, D. (1993) *Philosophy of Science in the Twentieth Century: Four Central Themes*, Oxford: Basil Blackwell.

Gleick, J. (1988) *Chaos: Making a New Science*, London: Heinemann.

Goffman, I. (1968) *Asylums: Essays on the Social Situation of Mental Patients and Other Inmates*, Harmondsworth: Penguin Books.

Goldberg, D. and Huxley, P. (1992) *Common Mental Disorders: A Bio-Social Model*, London: Routledge.

Goldberg, E. M. (1970) *Helping the Aged*, London: George Allen & Unwin.

REFERENCES

Goldberg, E. M. and Connolly, J. (eds) (1981) *Evaluative Research in Social Care*, London: Heinemann.

Goldsmith, H. H. (1983) 'Genetic influences on personality from infancy to adulthood', *Child Development* 54: 331–55.

Goldsmith, H. H. and Gottesman, I. I. (1981) 'Origins of variation in behavioral style: A longitudinal study of temperament in young twins', *Child Development* 52: 91–103.

Gottesman, I. I. (1991) *Schizophrenia Genesis: The Origins of Madness*, New York: Freeman.

Gottesman, I. I. and Shields, J. (1982) *Schizophrenia: The Epigenetic Puzzle*, Cambridge: Cambridge University Press.

Gould, S. J. (1981) *The Mismeasure of Man*, London: Penguin.

Gray, J. A. (1975) *Elements of a Two Process Theory of Learning*, London: Academic Press.

Greenberg, L. S. and Dompiere, L. M. (1986) 'Specific effects of a Gestalt two-chair dialogue on intrapsychic conflict in counseling', *Journal of Counseling Psychology* 28: 288–94.

Greenland, C. (1985) *Preventing C.A.N. Deaths*, London: Tavistock.

Gregory, R. L. (1970) *The Intelligent Eye*, London: Weidenfeld & Nicolson.

Grossberg, J. M. (1964) 'Behavior therapy: A review', *Psychological Bulletin* 62: 121–34.

Hall, J. and Baker, R. (1973) 'Token economy systems: Breakdown and control', *Behavior Research and Therapy* 1 (3): 2–36.

Harris, P. (1972) 'Perception and cognition in infancy', in Connolly, K. (ed.), *Psychological Survey No. 2*, London: George Allen & Unwin.

Hays, V. and Waddell, K. J. (1976) 'A self-reinforcing procedure for thought-stopping', *Behaviour Therapy* 1: 12–24.

Heatherington, E. M. and Parke, R. D. (1986) *Child Psychology*, London: McGraw Hill International, 3rd edn.

Hebb, D. O. (1972) *Textbook of Psychology*, Philadelphia: Samdus, 3rd edn.

Heider, F. (1958) *The Psychology of Interpersonal Relations*, New York: Wiley.

Heine, R. W. (1953) 'A comparison of patient reports on psycho-analytic, non-directive and Adlerian therapists', *American Journal of Psychotherapy* 7: 111–28.

Herbert, M. (1978) *Conduct Disorders of Childhood and Adolescence: A Behavioural Approach to Assessment and Treatment*, Chichester: Wiley.

Heron, W. (1957) 'The pathology of boredom', in Coopersmith, S. (ed.) (1964), *Frontiers of Psychological Research*, San Francisco, CA: W. H. L. Freeman.

Hersen, M. and Bellack, R. (1981) *Behavioural Assessment*, Oxford: Pergamon.

Hilgard, E. R. (1948) *Theories of Learning*, New York: Appleton–Century Crofts.

Hilgard, E. R., Atkinson, R. C. and Atkinson, R. L. (1979) *An Introduction to Psychology*, New York: Harcourt Brace Jovanovich, 7th edn.

Hillner, K. P. (1979) *Conditioning in Contemporary Perspective*, New York: Springer.

Hollis, F. (1964) *Casework: A Psychosocial Therapy*, New York: Random House.

Hollon, S. D. and Beck, A. T. (1994) 'Cognitive and cognitive-behavioural therapies', in Bergin, A. E. and Garfield, S. L. (eds), *Handbook of Psychotherapy and Behaviour Change*, Chichester: Wiley.

Hollon, S. D., Shelton, R. C. and Loosen, P. T. (1991) 'Cognitive therapy and pharmacotherapy for depression', *Journal of Consulting and Clinical Psychology* 59: 88–99.

Homme, L. E. (1965) 'Perspectives in psychology 24: Control of coverants, the operants of the mind', *Psychological Record* 15: 501–11.

Howard, H. I., Kopta, S. M., Krause, M. S. and Orlinski, D. E. (1986) 'The dose–effect relationship in psychotherapy', *American Psychologist* 41: 159–64.

Hudson, B. L. and Macdonald, G. (1985) *Behavioural Social Work: An Introduction*, Basingstoke: Macmillan.

Isaacs, W., Thomas, J. and Goldiamond, I. (1966) 'Application of operant conditioning to reinstate verbal behavior in psychotics', in Ulrich, R., Stachnic, T. and Mabry, J. (eds), *Control of Human Behavior*, Glenview, IL: Scott Foresman, vol. 1.

Jackson, B. (1972) 'Treatment of depression by self-reinforcement', *Behaviour Therapy* 3: 1–14.

Jacobson, N. S. and Margolin, G. (1979) *Marital Therapy: Strategies Based on Social Learning and Behavior Exchange Principles*, New York: Brunner/Mazel.

James, W. (1890) *The Principles of Psychology*, New York: Dorer.

Jehu, D. (1967) *Learning Theory and Social Work*, London: Routledge & Kegan Paul.

Jehu, D. (1989) *Beyond Sexual Abuse: Therapy with Women who were Childhood Victims*, Chichester: Wiley.

Jones, J. A., Neuman, R. and Shyne, A. W. (1976) 'A second chance for families: Evaluation of a program to reduce foster care', New York: Child Welfare League of America.

Jones, W. C. and Borgatta, E. F. (1972) 'Methodology of evaluation', in Mullen, E. J. and Dumpson, J. R. (eds), *Evaluation of Social Intervention*, San Francisco, CA: Jossey-Bass.

Kanfer, F. H. (1965) 'Vicarious human reinforcement: A glimpse into the black box', in Krasner, L. and Ullman, L. P. (eds), *Research in Behavior Modification*, New York: Holt, Rinehart & Winston.

Kazdin, A. E. and Smith, G. A. (1979) 'Covert conditioning: A review and evaluation', *Advances in Behavior Research and Therapy* 2(2): 12–21.

Kazdin, A. E., Siegel, T. and Bass, D. (1992) 'Cognitive problem-solving skills training and parent management training in the treatment of anti-social behavior in children', *Journal of Consulting and Clinical Psychology* 60: 733–47.

Kazdin, A. E., Bass, D., Siegel, T. and Thomas, C. (1989) 'Cognitive-behavioral therapy and relationship therapy in the treatment of children referred for anti-social behavior', *Journal of Consulting and Clinical Psychology* 57: 522–35.

Kelly, G. A. (1955) *The Theory of Personal Constructs*, New York: Norton, vols 1 and 2.

Klein, M. (1975) *The Psycho-Analysis of Children*, London: Hogarth Press/Institute of Psycho-Analysis, rev. edn.

Krasner, L. (1968) 'Assessment of token economy programmes in psychiatric hospitals', in Porter, R. (ed.), *CIBA Symposium on the Role of Learning in Psychotherapy*, London: Churchill Livingstone.

Kuhn, T. S. (1970) *The Structure of Scientific Revolutions*, Chicago, IL: University of Chicago Press, 2nd edn.

Laing, R. D. (1960) *The Divided Self*, Harmondsworth: Penguin.

Laws, D. R. and O'Neill, J. A. (1981) 'Variations on masturbatory conditioning', *Behavioural Psychotherapy* 9(2): 33–41.

Lazarus, A. A. (1968) 'Behavior therapy in groups', in Gazda, G. M. (ed.), *Basic Approaches to Group Psychotherapy and Group Counseling*, Springfield, IL: Charles C. Thomas.

Lazarus, R. S. (1982) 'Thoughts on the relations between emotion and cognition', *American Psychologist* 37: 1019–24.

Le Grand, J. and Bartlett, N. (1993) *Quasi-Markets and Social Policy*, London: Macmillan.

Lehrman, L. J. (1949) 'Success and failure of treatment of children in child guidance clinics of the Jewish Board of Guardians', *Research Monographs* 1.

Levy, A. and Kahan, B. (1991) *The Pindown Experience and the Protection of Children: The Report of the Staffordshire Child Care Inquiry*, Staffordshire County Council.

REFERENCES

Lewinsohn, P. M., Steinmetz, J. L., Larson, D. W. and Franklin, J. L. (1981) 'Depression-related cognitions: Antecedent or consequence?', *Journal of Abnormal Psychology* 90: 213–19.

Linehan, K. S. and Rosenthal, T. L. (1979) 'Current behavioral approaches to marital and family therapy', *Advances in Behavior Research and Therapy* 3: 216–48.

Lovaas, O. I. (1967) 'A programme for the establishment of speech in psychotic children', in Wing, J. K. (ed.), *Early Childhood Autism*, Oxford: Pergamon.

Lovaas, O. I. (1987) 'Behavioral treatment and normal educational/intellectual functioning in young autistic children', *Journal of Consulting and Clinical Psychology* 55: 3–9.

Ludgate, J. W. (1994) 'Cognitive-behavioural therapy and depressive relapse: Justified optimism or unwarranted complacency?', *Behavioural and Cognitive Psychotherapy* 22: 1–11.

Luria, A. (1961) *The Role of Speech in the Regulation of Normal and Abnormal Behaviour*, New York: Liveright.

Macdonald, G. M. (1990) 'Allocating blame in Social Work', *British Journal of Social Work* 20: 525–46.

Macdonald, G. M. and Sheldon, B. (1992) 'Contemporary studies of the effectiveness of Social Work', *British Journal of Social Work* 22(6): 615–43.

Macdonald, G. M. and Sheldon, B. (forthcoming) 'An evaluation of services for psychiatric patients in the community', (Manuscript), more information from the authors at Royal Holloway, University of London.

McFall, R. M. and Lillesand, D. B. (1971) 'Behaviour rehearsal with modelling and coaching in assertive training', *Journal of Abnormal Psychology* 77: 21–34.

McFall, R. M. and Marston, A. R. (1970) 'An experimental investigation of behavioral rehearsal in assertive training', *Journal of Abnormal Psychology* 76: 33–41.

McGlynne, F. P. and Mapp, R. H. (1970) 'Systematic desensitization of snake avoidance following three types of suggestion', *Behavior Research and Therapy* 8: 16–31.

Maluccio, A. N. (1979) *Learning from Clients*, New York: The Free Press.

Maranon, G. (1924) 'Contribution a l'étude de l'action émotive de l'adrenolin', *Revue française d'endocrin* 21: 301–25.

Marks, I. M. (1971) 'Flooding versus desensitization in the treatment of phobic patients', *British Journal of Psychiatry* 118: 24–30.

Marks, I. M. (1975) 'Behavioural treatments of phobic and obsessive-compulsive disorders: A critical appraisal', in Hersen, R. *et al.* (eds), *Progress in Behaviour Therapy*, London: Academic Press.

Marks, I. M. (1978) 'Behavioural psychotherapy of neurotic disorders', in Bergin, A. E. and Garfield, S. L. (eds), *Handbook of Psychotherapy and Behaviour Change*, Chichester: Wiley.

Marks, I. M. (1987) *Fears, Phobias and Rituals*, Oxford: Oxford University Press.

Marzillier, J. S. (1980) 'Cognitive therapy and behavioural practice', *Behaviour Research and Therapy* 18 (4): 17–28.

Masserman, J. H. (1943) *Behaviour and Neurosis*, Chicago, IL: University of Chicago Press.

Mayer, J. E. and Timms, N. (1970) *The Client Speaks*, London: Routledge & Kegan Paul.

Meichenbaum D. (1974) *Cognitive Behaviour Modification*, Morristown, NJ: General Learning Press.

Meichenbaum, D. (1977) *Cognitive Behavior Modification: An Integrative Approach*, New York: Plenum.

Meyer, H., Borgatta, E. and Jones, W. (1965) *Girls at Vocational High*, New York: Russell Sage Foundation.

Milgram, S. (1974) *Obedience to Authority*, London: Tavistock.

REFERENCES

Mill, J. S. (1859) *On Liberty*, London: Dent, 1971.

Miller, W. B. (1962) 'The impact of a total community delinquency control project', *Social Problems* Fall: 168–91.

Milne, A. A. (1928) *The House at Pooh Corner*, London: Eyre Methuen, 1978.

Miron, N. B. (1966) 'Behaviour shaping and group nursing with severely retarded patients', in Fischer, J. and Harris, R. E. (eds), *Reinforcement Therapy in Psychological Treatment: A Symposium*, Research Monograph No. 8, California: Department of Mental Hygiene.

Mitchell, J. E., Pyle, R. L., Eckert, E. D., Hatsukami, D., Pomeroy, L. and Zimmerman, R. (1990) 'A comparison study of anti-depressants and structured group therapy in the treatment of bulimia nervosa', *Archives of General Psychiatry* 47: 149–57.

Mullen, E. J. and Dumpson, J. R. (eds) (1972) *The Evaluation of Social Intervention*, San Francisco, CA: Jossey-Bass.

National Health Service and Community Care Act (1990) London: HMSO.

NSPCC/DoH (1990) *Child Protection Adviser's Resource Pack*, Paley, J. (ed.), Section R, London: NSPCC/DoH.

Olds, J. (1956) 'Pleasure center in the brain', *Scientific American* 195: 105–16.

Olds, J. (1977) *Drives and Reinforcements: Behavioral Studies of Hypothalamic Functions*, New York: Raven Press.

Orne, M. (1965) 'Psychological factors maximizing resistance to stress with special reference to hypnosis', in Kranser, S. (ed.), *The Quest for Self Control*, New York: Free Press.

Ost, L. G. (1987) 'Applied relaxation: Description of coping techniques and review of controlled studies', *Behavior Research and Therapy* 25: 397–410.

Pavlov, I. P. (1897) *Lectures on Conditioned Reflexes*, Gannt, W. H. (trans.) 1928, New York: International.

Pavlov, I. P. (1927) *Conditioned Reflexes*, Anrep, G. V. (trans), London: Oxford University Press.

Piaget, J. (1958) *The Child's Construction of Reality*, London: Routledge & Kegan Paul.

Popper, K. (1963) *Conjectures and Refutations*, London: Routledge & Kegan Paul.

Popper, K. (1982) *The Open Universe: An Argument for Indeterminism*, London: Hutchinson.

Popper, K. R. and Eccles, J. C. (1977) *The Self and its Brain*, New York: Springer International.

Powers, E. and Witmer, H. (1951) *An Experiment in the Prevention of Delinquency – the Cambridge–Somerville Youth Study*, New York: Columbia University Press.

Premack, D. (1959) 'Towards empirical behavior laws; 1. Positive reinforcement', *Psychological Review* 66: 11–17.

Rachman, S. J. and Hodgson, R. (1980) *Obsessions and Compulsions*, Englewood Cliffs NJ: Prentice-Hall.

Rachman, S. J. and Wilson, G. T. (1980) *The Effects of Psychological Therapy*, Oxford: Pergamon Press.

Rajecki, D. W. (1982) *Attitudes: Theories and Advances*, Sunderland, MA: Sinauer Associates.

Rathus, S. A. (1970) 'A thirty-item schedule for assessing assertive behavior', in Thomas, E. J. (ed.), *Behavior Modification Procedure*, Chicago, IL: Aldine.

Rees, S. (1991) *Achieving Power: Practice and Policy in Social Welfare*, Sydney: Allen & Unwin.

Reid, W. J. (1978) *The Task-Centred System*, New York: Columbia University Press.

Reid, W. J. and Hanrahan, P. (1980) 'The effectiveness of social work: Recent evidence', in Goldberg, E. M. and Connolly, N. (eds), *Evaluative Research in Social Care*, London: Heinemann Educational Books.

REFERENCES

Reid, W. J. and Shyne, A. (1968) *Brief and Extended Casework*, New York: Columbia University Press.

Reiner, B. S. and Kaufman, M. D. (1969) *Character Disorders in the Parents of Delinquents*, New York: Family Service Association of America.

Richmond, M. E. (1917) *Social Diagnosis*, New York: Russell Sage Foundation.

Risley, T. R. (1977) 'The social context of self-control', in Stuart, R. B. (ed.), *Behavioral Self-Control*, New York: Brunner/Mazel.

Rogers, C. R. (1951) *Client-Centred Therapy: Its Current Practice, Implications and Theory*, Boston, MA: Houghton Mifflin.

Rogers, C. and Skinner, B. F. (1956) 'Some issues concerning the control of human behavior', *Science* vol. 124, no. 3231 (30 November 1956).

Rose, G. and Marshall, T. M. (1975) *Counselling and School Social Work: An Experimental Study*, New York: Wiley.

Ross, M. and Scott, M. (1985) 'An evaluation of the effectiveness of individual and group psychotherapy in the treatment of depressed patients in an inner city health centre', *Journal of the Royal College of General Practitioners* 35: 239–42.

Russell, E. W. (1974) 'The power of behaviour control: A critique of behaviour modification methods', *Journal of Clinical Psychology, Special Monograph Supplement.*

Ryle, G. (1949) *The Concept of Mind*, London: Hutchinson.

Ryle, G. (1979) *On Thinking*, London: Basil Blackwell.

Sacks, O. (1985) *The Man who Mistook His Wife for a Hat and Other Clinical Tales*, New York: Summit.

Salkovskis, P. M. (1989) 'Somatic disorders', in Hawton, K., Salkovskis, P. M., Kirk, J. W. and Clark, D. M. (eds), *Cognitive-Behavioural Approaches to Adult Psychological Disorder: A Practical Guide*, Oxford: Oxford University Press.

Salkovskis, P. M. and Warwick, H. M. C. (1986) 'Morbid preoccupations, health anxiety and reassurance: A cognitive-behavioural approach to hypochondriasis', *Behaviour Research and Therapy* 24: 597–602.

Salkovskis, P. M. and Westbrook, D. (1987) 'Obsessive-compulsive disorder: Clinical strategies for improving behavioural treatments', in Dent, H. R. (ed.), *Clinical Psychology: Research and Developments*, London: Croom Helm.

Scarr, S. and McCartney, K. (1983) 'How people make their own environments: A theory of genotype–environment effects', *Child Development* 4: 424–35.

Schacter, S. (1964) 'The interaction of cognitive and physiological determinants of emotional state', in Berkowitz, L. (ed.), *Advances in Experimental Social Psychology*, New York: Academic Press.

Schacter, S. (1965) 'A cognitive-physiological view of emotion', in Kleinberg, O. and Christie, R. (eds), *Perspectives in Social Psychology*, New York: Holt, Rinehart & Winston.

Schacter, S. and Singer, J. E. (1962) 'Cognitive, social and physiological determinants of emotional states', *Psychological Review* 69: 378–99.

Schlick, M. (1936) *Philosophical Papers*, Reidal, 1979, vol. 2.

Schmidt, J. P. and Patterson, T. E. (1979) 'Issues in the implementation of assertion training in applied settings', *Journal of Behaviour Therapy and Experimental Psychiatry* 10(1): 25–36.

Scott, M. (1989) *A Cognitive-Behavioural Approach to Clients' Problems*, London: Tavistock.

Seebohm Report (1968) (CMND 3703) *Report of the Committee on Local Authority and Allied Personal Social Services*, London: HMSO.

Seligman, M. E. P. (1971) 'Phobias and preparedness', *Behavior Therapy* 2: 1–22.

Seligman, M. E. P. (1975) *Helplessness*, San Francisco, CA: Freeman.

Shaw, M. (1974) *Social Work in Prison*, London: HMSO (Home Office Research Unit).

269

NAME INDEX

Adler, Alfred 36
Alberti, R.E. 210
Alexander, J.F., *et al.* 179
Allport, Gordon 155–6
Archimedes 8
Atkinson, Richard C. 46, 53
Atkinson, R.L. 46
Auden, W.H. v, 87, 238
Ayllon, T. 175
Azrin, N.H. 175

Bacon, Francis 128
Baker, R. 175–6, 238–9
Bandura, Albert 25–6, 44, 45, 82, 83, 84,
  85, 86, 94–6, 114, 126, 136, 194, 218,
  227, 233–4
Bard 102
Bartlett, N. 28
Bateman, H.M. 71
Bateson, Gregory, *et al.* 5
Beck, A.T. 22, 44, 151, 219, 220, 221,
  223; *et al.* 22, 218, 219, 220
Bellack, R. 164
Bem, D.J. 11, 112, 155
Bemis, K.M. 10
Bentley, K.J. 18
Berger, M. 46
Bergin, A.E. xii, 16, 24, 25, 28, 95, 227,
  260n
Berleman, W.C., *et al.* 13
Birchwood, M., *et al.* 5, 174
Birley, J. 5
Blackburn, I.M., *et al.* 22
Blakemore, C. 35, 93
Blanchard, E.B. 22
Bloom, M. 252
Boden, M. 38, 90
Bootzin, R.R. 212

Borgatta, E.F. 14
Boswell, James 41
Bottomley, Virginia 238
Brown, G.D. 171
Brown, G.W. 5; *et al.* 5
Brown, R. 10
Bucher, B. 240
Burt, Sir Cyril 46
Butler-Sloss Report 8

Cannon, W.B. 102
Carkhuff, R. 25, 26
Carroll, Lewis 2, 8, 9
Claridge, G. 59, 109, 157
Clyde, James J. 8
Cohen, A. 28, 202, 203
Conan Doyle, Sir Arthur 91
Connolly, K. 100
Cooke, G. 227
Cotter, L.M. 238–9

Dalrymple, J. 118
Davey, G. 54–5
Davis, B. 28
Dawkins, Richard 42–3
Dennett, D.C. 37–8, 44, 45, 57, 85, 90
Descartes, René 33
Deschner, J.P. 84
Dixon, N. 8, 38, 151
Dobson, K.S. 22
Dompiere, L.M. 27
Donaldson, M. 10, 49
Dumpson, J.R. 12, 13
Dunn, J. 51

Eccles, J.C. 35–6
Edelman, G. 38
Ellis, Albert 220, 222

272

SUBJECT INDEX